Sermons with
startling titles

Sermons with *startling titles*

IAN R. K. PAISLEY

AMBASSADOR

Belfast Northern Ireland **Greenville** South Carolina

Sermons with Startling Titles

Copyright © 1999 Ian R. K. Paisley

All rights reserved
No part of this book may be reproduced, stored in a retrieval system,
or transmitted in any form or by any means - electronic, mechanical,
photocopy, recording or otherwise - without written permission of the
publisher, except for brief quotations in printed reviews.

ISBN 1 84030 048 5

Ambassador Publications
a division of
Ambassador Productions Ltd.
Providence House
16 Hillview Avenue,
Belfast, BT5 6JR
Northern Ireland

Emerald House
1 Chick Springs Road, Suite 203
Greenville,
South Carolina 29609, USA
www.emeraldhouse.com

Foreword

SERMONS WITH STARTLING TITLES! The dictionary definition of the word *startling* is 'rousing, sudden, surprise, alarm or the like'.

These subject titles have all those ingredients. They are rousing, surprising and alarming.

The gospel of Christ is *arousing* for it deals with the greatest arousing of all, the bringing to life of the dead souls of men.

The gospel of Christ is *surprising* for it makes the greatest offer of pardon to the worst possible violators of God's holy laws.

The gospel of Christ is *alarming* because it pulls aside the curtain between time and eternity and reveals the reality of the lost soul's hell.

When the gospel of Christ is preached as it ought to be preached it arouses the intense fury of hell, the opposition of all false gospels and gospellers and the antagonism of conceited sinners.

The gospel requires no polish of man or decorations of oratorical skill. It must **not** be preached in words of man's wisdom but rather in the power of the Holy Ghost sent down from heaven.

These sermons have no literary polish nor do they require any, but God has used them to change men and women and boys and girls, to renew broken homes, and rescue derelicts of society and make them children of God.

May God renew their strength as they are issued in this book form. Yours to serve in the startling gospel.

Ian R. K. Paisley
Ephesians 6 vs 19-20

Preacher, Martyrs Memorial Church
356-376 Ravenhill Road, Belfast, BT6 8GJ

March 1999

Ian R. K. Paisley

List of *contents*

1 **The biggest liar** *in Belfast* 9
2 **A night of blood** *in the ballroom* 19
3 **Dead men's** *bones* 27
4 **The greatest crime** *in Christ's church* 33
5 **The octogenarian's** *prayer* 45
6 **The devil in a** *pigskin swimsuit* 51
7 **The talkback** *which ended all talkbacks* 65
8 **The house appointed** *for all living* 75
9 **Unholy water or** *the tears of Esau* 83
10 **Snow! snow!** *snow!* 89

11 Bad women and *jolly good fellows* 95

12 The break up *of a funeral* 105

13 The man who kissed the door of heaven *but went to hell* 115

14 The pigs that got *the permanent wave* 123

15 Quenching the *firebrands of hell* 135

16 Four black *Roman nones* 147

17 The gospel antidote *to L.S.D.* 161

18 It is only *a matter of dress* 173

19 Moon *madness* 181

20 How Pilate *lost his soul* 189

1 The biggest liar *in Belfast*

AS HAS BEEN ANNOUNCED I want to speak on the subject - *The Biggest Liar In Belfast*. Who is he? Some people have come to their own conclusions. I don't want to make any comments upon what some people said to me during the week. Some people have the biggest liar identified. They have him named and they also have his pedigree and his future all sealed up.

The Bible has much to say about liars and about lying.

The first mention of lying is found in the third book of the Bible, the book of Leviticus. There the sin of lying is exposed and underlined.

When we come to the last book of the Bible we discover that lying is the last sin that God mentions in His book. If you turn over to Revelation 22:15 you will discover there that having mentioned dogs and sorcerers and whoremongers and murderers and idolaters the last sin recorded in the Book, Revelation 22:15 is *"whosoever loveth and maketh a lie"*. So we have underlined in the Word of God the terrible nature of the sin of lying and the dark debauched character of the liar.

Now, of course, in the Bible there are different penmen and some of the great penmen of Scripture have various characteristics. In this first epistle we have presented as its penman the apostle John. The characteristic of the apostle John was love. He is known as the apostle of love. Yet it is in his epistle that we have exposed the biggest lie that man or woman can tell and we have identified the biggest liar in God's eyes.

THE FIRST REFERENCE IN JOHN'S EPISTLE

Now you just open your Bible at I John and you will find that there are five references in the book to liars. The first one you will find in I John 1:10 *"If we say that we have not sinned, we make him a liar, and his word is not in us."* Hear it - if there is not an acknowledgement before God in the depths of your heart that you are a sinner, a guilty sinner, a hell-deserving, ill-deserving and undeserving sinner then God indicts you as being a liar.

Turn over a little further in the epistle. Turn to the second chapter at verse four. *"He that saith, I know him, and keepeth not his commandments, is a liar, and the truth is not in him.".* So if a person says I know God and he breaks the ten commandments God says he is a liar. So those very eminent ecclesiastics and councillors who are all against the Lord's Day and the keeping of it holy and then they tell you what great Christians they are and how they worship God, God has something to say to them. He says if a man does not keep God's commandments he is a liar. That means the whole ten commandments. It does not mean you break one. They are all on the same level.

I was talking this week to a student from one of the universities. She is studying journalism. She said to me, "Well, don't you think it is a terrible thing that the Ballymena Town Council would not let people swim on a Sunday? After all, everybody should have the right to do what they like." I said, "Is that right. Now would you like me to get your handbag and take all your money out of it. I want to do it. I feel like doing it. I like your money. I will just take it." "Oh no," she said. Well I said, "The same commandments which say' thou shalt not steal' also says 'thou shalt keep holy God's Day'." You are not to desecrate the Lord's Day. Remember the Sabbath day to keep it holy.

The Lord's Day does not belong to the British Government. It does not belong to any town council. It does not belong to the Alliance Party although you would think it did! The Lord's Day belongs to the Lord. Keep your hands off God's day. That is why we contend for God's day and we are not against people if they want to go swimming elsewhere but we are not going to encourage them to do it. If they vote to do so be it but not with our vote.

Then those Marxists of the Ballymena Trade Union Council call themselves Labourites. They forfeited their deposit at the last election. It is a pity it had not been £150 instead of £25. They came in and said there are so many unemployed in Ballymena, it is a terrible thing to take this amenity from them for the only day they can use it is the Lord's Day.

Now if you are unemployed could you not do it on Monday, or Tuesday, or Wednesday, or Thursday, or Friday, or Saturday? Oh no, the only day an unemployed person can swim in a pool is Sunday. The Alliance councillor said they made a wonderful speech. She must have sawdust between her ears and no brain capacity herself at all. Let me make it clear to you. If you disobey God's commandments God says you are a liar.

When this Province was keeping holy God's day God was blessing this Province. A lot of our problems stem from the desecration of God's day. It is not a strange thing when you are in a Jewish country, like Israel, and they close down on the Sabbath nobody makes any complaints. Oh no, it is the done thing. If you are in an Arab country and they close down for a holy day no one makes any complaint. You don't hear these wonderful Sabbath desecrators saying "Israel is an intolerant country. You should be allowed to do what you like on the seventh day of the week." Oh no. Don't you notice Mr Began when he goes to do his business, he does not do any business on the Sabbath day. He waits until the Sabbath is over. Then we have the Housing Executive headed up with Tommy Seymour of Larne and he wants the people now to discuss the business of the Housing Executive on the Lord's Day. Thank God for the Rev William McCrea and the other councillors who said no, sir.

Keep the commandments. You are a liar if you do not keep God's commandments. I did not say it. That is not some bigoted extremist fundamentalist. That is what God says about you friend. Maybe there is someone here tonight. You thought I was going to talk about Mr Roy Mason didn't you? You thought I was going to talk about somebody who wasn't here. I am talking about you, sir. You are the biggest liar in this city in God's eyes if you are desecrating God's day. It is what God says. He is a liar, says He. If you love a person you will keep their commandments. You love your wives, you fellows. You do what she tells you, yes very obediently. Yes you smile as if you don't but you do. Yes, I know you do. I have a fellow feeling for you.

I was telling my wife the other night if I could only get her to obey me the way I obey her it would be a very happy home. You hear that bachelor laughing there! He is still in single bliss.

Let me tell you friend the Bible says if I say I have no sin I am a liar. Some of you people have not confessed your sin. You have never acknowledge you are a poor, lost, guilty, hell-deserving sinner. You do not like that language. You come on the Lord's Day and you look very well. You sit up in the pew and you think butter would not melt in your mouth. You think you are about to sprout wings from your shoulder blades and you are going to fly away to God's heaven. You never acknowledged you were a sinner.

When I was a boy preacher, (that is a lot of years ago), of course I was asked to hold a mission in the Isle of Man in a couple of Methodist Churches in Port Erin and Port St Mary. The Methodist minister there was a fundamentalist preacher and he invited me and then the conference changed him and put him away and they put a modernist, a cigarette smoking fellow in charge. There was I in at the deep end. When I had the prayer meeting he walked up and down outside smoking. I said I have got the fire, your parson only has the smoke. I told the people that. Well I preached the Gospel and we had a revolution in those churches. People started to be saved. One of the first persons to be saved was the Sunday School Superintendent. Man that caused a stir. As I was making the appeal and sinners were getting saved one of the circuit stewards walked down the aisle and he said "I don't know what you are doing." I said, "Don't you? You ain't seen anything yet, go back to your seat and you will see something." We saw people saved by God's sovereign and wonderful grace.

Now let me tell you something. When I told those people the first night that they were lost sinners if you had seen their faces! Man I tell you if their eyes could have fired the darts that were in them at my soul I would have been dead. They did not like it. Sinners don't like to be told they are sinners.

I was preaching some years ago in Jarvis Street Baptist Church in Toronto. When I gave the invitation a man came down the aisle and he said "Do you know who I am?" I said, "No, I only came here to preach and I will be leaving in about fourteen days I don't know many people in Toronto." He said "I am the minister of a local Presbyterian church. I never knew before I was a sinner and needed to get saved and I am getting saved today." Thank God he got saved.

He nearly had a riot in his church the next Sunday for the next Sunday he gave his testimony. It was bad enough saying he was saved but when he said he was saved through Ian Paisley, man I tell you that really put the wigs on the green all right. Let me tell you friend, you have got to acknowledge you are a sinner or you are a liar. That is what God says. Keep the commandments. You are a liar if you don't keep them and yet say you love God.

JOHN'S SECOND REFERENCE TO THE LIAR

Let us come on down chapter two to verse 22, *"Who is a liar but he that denieth that Jesus is the Christ?"* You could rightly hang the word liar over the majority of Protestant pulpits in this land tonight because the vast majority of preachers in Belfast, in Northern Ireland, in the United Kingdom, in Europe, throughout the world, and I am talking about Protestant preachers, they don't believe that Jesus is the Christ.

We have the curse of modernism so-called and they have gone through Heaven and they have taken the gold out of Heaven. They have gone through Hell and they have taken the fire out of Hell. They have gone through the Bible and they have taken the infallibility out of the Bible. They have gone through the Cross and they have taken the atonement out of the Cross. They have gone through the Blood and they have taken the power out of the Blood. They have gone through the miracles of Jesus and they have taken away the supernatural out of the miracles of Jesus. They have gone through Jesus and they have taken away His Godhead. They are not preaching that Jesus is the Christ, the Son of God. Unfortunately, in our land, good people, decent people, respectable people, honourable people, are bolstering up that false Protestant system which blights the souls of men and leads them down to the darkness of a lost sinner's hell.

Let me witness tonight dogmatically, unequivocally, that Jesus is the Christ - thou art the Christ, the Son of the Living God. Who is Jesus? Jesus is the Christ of God. Very God of very God and very Man of very Man. When you reject Christ you are rejecting God. When you reject the Lord Jesus you reject God Incarnate in the flesh. Let me tell you friend salvation is nothing to do with church, or creed, or sacrament, or ceremonial. It is to do with a personal relationship with Jesus Christ.

We had a distinguished American Senator in Ulster this week. Senator Eagleson. He was a running candidate for the Vice Presidential office in the United States, not with Carter, I understand, but with McGovern. He is a prominent Roman Catholic Senator. He asked to see me so I went down to the American Consulate to see him and he said some surprising things. He said, "Do you not think that the answer to this whole question, Dr Paisley, would be a great ecumenical movement which you could help to lead?" Man I really sat back and laughed at that. Yes. Great ecumenical movement which I could lead! I said, "Sir, do you know what ecumenism is? You know if your church is right I am totally wrong but if I am right your church is totally wrong. Ecumenism is to try and find the lowest common denominator and when you have taken away all your principles you have this unprincipled mongrel which you call ecumenism. It is mongrelism in religion." He said, "I don't look at it like that." I said, "Well, that is the way I look at it. Just before we finish on this subject I want to tell you that Christianity is the relationship of a person to Jesus Christ. The Bible tells me that Jesus said I am the way, the truth and the life, no man cometh unto the Father but by me. Senator, if you don't come to God by Jesus Christ you don't come at all. Let us get that straight."

That is what I mean when I say people need to be born again. That is what I am talking about. He did not want any further discussion on that particular aspect. He forgot about me leading an ecumencial movement after that.

Let me ask you a question, what is your relationship to Jesus Christ? I am not asking you about the church. I am not asking you about Protestantism. I am not asking you about Romanism. I am not asking you about your relationship to baptism or the Lord's Supper or to doctrine or creeds or confession, I am asking you about your relationship to Jesus Christ. If you really believe that Jesus Christ is God you would fall at His feet and worship Him. But you are a liar. Your actions deny that He is the Christ of God.

THE THIRD REFERENCE

Let us come a little bit farther then. Let us move to chapter four and verse 20 *"If a man say, I love God, and hateth his brother, he is a liar."* So if a person comes along and says I have love to God and yet that person has hatred towards his brother that person is a liar. No matter what he professes. Could I just, for a moment or two, define to you what Christian love is. I Corinthians chapter 13 'love rejoiceth not in iniquity but rejoiceth in the truth'. Some people have this strange idea that Christian love is prepared to overlook everything and not deal with righteousness or truth. Not so. When my family and my boys especially want to do something that they ought not to do I warn them. If they do it I lay on them and they know that. That is the way you do it. That is the way you bring up a family. Many a time my father laid on me and he used to say to me "This hurts me more than it hurts you." I did not believe him. I did not dare to say I did not believe him or he would have laid on more.

But I know now, as a father myself, that that is true and so does every parent. It hurts a parent to chastise their own flesh and blood but it has got to be done. That is not hatred friend, that is love. That is love. I would be hating my family if I let them go on. You hate your child parent if you do not chastise that child. Condoning evil is not love, it is hatred.

Of course people say Paisley is a hate monger. He hates everybody. The Bible says 'I have hated the enemies of God with a perfect hatred'. The Bible says there is a time to love and there is a time to hate and there are things that you should hate and there are things I hate. I hate liquor. I love drunkards that need to be saved. I hate gambling. I have seen so many homes wrecked with it but I love the poor man who is chained and tied with a gambling fever. I hate with all my heart the idolatry, the superstition, the priestcraft of Roman Catholicism but God knows my heart I love every Romanist. I never turn one from my door and I am glad they come to me and they say our priest won't help us but we know you help everybody. I have 25,000 of them in North Antrim and there is not one who has ever said, even my most bitter political foe, that Ian Paisley would do wrong by against of us. I love every Romanist and I love every Protestant. I want to see them saved, led to Christ but I hate the things that are darkening their lives, that are damning their souls and are taking them to hell.

So let us define what love is. You know the Lord Jesus defined it. He said which man really loved his neighbour. Do you remember when the man fell among thieves. What happened? The priest came by and he passed by on the other side. That is what the ecumenical church does to poor sinners they pass by on the other side. The Levite came and he looked at him and then he passed by. But, thank God, Jesus came. You see the Levite and the priest were going on the wrong way. They were going down but the Samaritan, as he journeyed, was coming up hill. It is only a person who is going up hill who can help a man who is going down hill and has fallen among thieves and has been robbed. What did he do? He lifted him up. He wiped away the stains of the dust, cleansed his wounds, poured in oil and wine. He took him to the hotel. He paid the money for his keep. Who was the man that loved him?

The people had passed by on the other side. I want to ask every Christian a personal question in this meeting. How many people in Belfast are saying about the Christians of this land, 'no man cared for my soul'. Do you really care for the souls of men. Are there ungodly people saying about the believer in Belfast 'no man cares for my soul'. Do you care enough to love them out of their sins into the arms of God.

THE LAST REFERENCE

Then we come to the last one and you will find in chapter five and verse 10 *"he that believeth on the Son of God hath the witness in himself: he that believeth not God hath made him a liar; because he believeth not the record of his Son."* I was greatly struck with the fact that Jesus Christ picked out one sin. He made that sin the chiefest of sins and He said when He, the Spirit of God, is come He will convict the world of sin. What sin? Because they believe not in Me. So the greatest of all sins is unbelief in the Son of God. That makes the man in God's eyes the biggest liar in the city. He believes not the record that God has given of His Son. There are many in this meeting and I want to say it most solemnly and that is the indictment God makes against you. I hope you will face it friend.

I was thinking why men don't believe in Jesus Christ.

Reason number one - **they don't believe in Jesus Christ because they are not prepared to think about it.**

Men don't want to think about Christ or think about eternity. They treat salvation as a trifle to be shrugged off. They treat the Son of God as someone for instant dismissal not worthy of consideration. Do you know why you are not saved, sir? You have never faced it. You shun it. You dodge it. You try to escape it. You are scared of it. You will not face up to the question - what shall I do then with Jesus which is called Christ?

Secondly, **men don't believe in Jesus Christ because of the demands He makes.**

You cannot have your sin and have the Saviour. You cannot have the world and have the Son of God. You cannot go on with your iniquity and have Jesus Christ as well. Old John Bunyan was right when he said, 'Sin and Jesus don't walk together on the road to heaven'. Neither they do, so there must be a true repentance and abhorrence for sin and a turning to Jesus Christ.

Thirdly, **men don't take Christ as their Saviour because of their pride.**

You are not prepared to face what your friends would say. Did you hear about him? He went to Paisley's church on Sunday night and he got saved. Hear about it? Think of it! Think of him even going to that place, that was bad enough, but then to get saved.

You know we were visiting around these doors some months ago when our brother Zimmerman was preaching and a woman said to one of our workers, "I would not go into that place, I am just a stone's throw from it. I would not be caught dead in it."

That night she was here and that night she got saved. I tell you it shook her and it shook her friends and the next day she said "I went to Paisley's and I got saved. I am converted to God. I am changed, old things have passed away, all things have become new."

Friend you need to be saved tonight. It is your pride that keeps you isn't it? You are not prepared to face the men at work tomorrow. You are not prepared to face your family. You are not prepared to face your neighbours so you dismiss Him and God says 'You are making Me a liar'.

I go up to heaven. I stand in the door of the city of the great King. I approach an immaculate angel and I say to the angel, "What shall be done to a man who makes God out to be a liar and rejects the testimony that God has given to all his family?" That holy angel points to the myriads of celestial beings around the throne and they are all crying - *Holy, Holy, Holy, Lord God Almighty.*

Yet you on earth, by refusing to believe the record God has given of His Son, are making God a liar. That angel says to me, 'If sinless beings must forever cry Holy, Holy, Holy, before the throne of God you ask me, what will be done with a sinful man who tries to make God a liar?' The angel then opens the book of God and reads the sentence - **he that believeth not shall be damned**. That is what the book says. He that believeth not shall be damned. No church synod can change that. No waters of baptism can change that. No parson or priest or pope or cardinal or bishop or moderator can change that. If you do not believe you are damned, you are lost.

May God help you to face up to it. You have committed the biggest lie that a human being could commit by your rejection of Jesus Christ. Turn to the Lord Jesus, confess your sin and be saved by God's matchless grace.

AMEN AND AMEN!

2 A night of blood *in the ballroom*

I WANT YOU TO look with me at Mark chapter six. I am going to speak of a night of blood in the ballroom.

There are certain sins which go together.

Drunkenness, for example, leads to vile language. Drunkenness often times leads to violence. Drunkenness often times leads to bloodshed and murder. Drunkenness often times leads to looseness and lewdness and impurity and uncleanness. So the sin of drunkenness never goes on its road alone.

That is also true of sins associated with the dance.

If you take the Word of God and you study the history of mixed dancing as recorded and condemned in the Bible you will find that the dance hall has associated with it a whole conglomeration of iniquity. We are going to see that, as we come to a study of this subject.

One of the associations of the modern dance is drunkenness. Drinking and dancing are tied together. Another association of the modern dance is the various sins of uncleanness and out of it comes looseness of association, lewdness of expression, infidelity in the marriage bond, immorality, adultery, fornication, sodomy and all the rest of the sins that are classified in God's Holy Word as uncleanness.

Suggestiveness is part of the lure of the modern dance. Uncleanness is the result of the modern dance. The break up of homes, the break up of families, the pollution of young lives, the start down the road to the black hell of immorality, is all part of the set up of the modern dance.

It seems to me that there is laxity among God's people in regard to the seriousness of the challenge of the modern dance today. It used to be that God's people were alerted to the potential and also to the potency for sin of the modern dance but not so today.

I have a copy of the Carrickfergus Advertiser and East Antrim Gazette in my hand and it says "Joymount Barn Dance". "A barn dance organised by Joymount Presbyterian Church Young Women's Group will be held in the Carlisle Hall in Carrickfergus on Monday night, February 6th, proceeds from the dance, which starts at 8.00pm, are in aid of the Joymount Presbyterian Church and missionary Miss R.V. who is a nurse serving in Africa."

So there you are. The church today thinks that the way to raise money for its activity, both missionary and otherwise, is to organise a barn dance. It used to be that the trustees of many churches prohibited dancing in the activities of the church. Today however we can say "I look for the church and I find it in the world, I look for the world and I find it in the church."

Now having prefaced my subject with those remarks on the present-day situation let us look at this passage of Scripture. Out into the pages of this word from God there stands King Herod.

HEROD THE KING

Herod the King. He is one of the most despicable, one of the most tragic, one of the most sickly characters in all the Bible.

The first thing that we notice about him is this that he is a man typified and characterised by fickleness.

He has no stability of character. He has no strength of purpose. He has no resistance to the lures of temptations and the fascination of this world's sin.

Let me tell you something, when the Bible portrays a sinner the Word of God is very careful to tell you everything good about him.

So if you look with me at verse 20 you will find the good things about Herod. Men, when they condemn their fellows, forget about the good points and they major in the bad points. The Bible does not do that. The Bible when it draws the character of the sinner and paints the character of a man who has gone down to hell, still portrays and chronicles all his good points.

I was reading in my Bible through this week the story of the sad break up of the family of Jacob with sin. Jacob had a daughter called Dinah and instead of staying with her mother she went into the world to see the way the daughters of the land behaved themselves. The daughters of the land in which she sojourned with her father Jacob were evil. It was not very long until Dinah lost her virtue. She lost her purity, she lost her modesty, through the machinations of a man called Shechem. Yet when the Bible writes up the character of that man it says that he was more honourable than his brethren. It still gives him credit for what he was.

In II Kings chapter five you have the story of Naaman the leper and it tells you he was an honourable man and a great man and a mighty man but he was a leper. The Bible plays fair.

Sinner, when you stand at God's judgment bar you are going to get a fair hearing.

Herod got a fair write up in the Word of God. What does it say about him? *"For Herod feared John, knowing that he was a just man and an holy, and observed him; and when he heard him, he did many things, and heard him gladly."* That is what the Bible tells us about Herod.

We have some points in his favour.

Number one, he recognised the holiness and the justice of John. He recognised that John was God's man. He recognised holiness, truthfulness, integrity when he saw it. He had no holiness himself. He had no justice himself. He had no integrity himself but he recognised it in the man of God. Point number one in his favour.

Point number two, he feared God's man.

He had a sense of fear when he heard God's man preach. One day he was out in his chariot. He saw an immense crowd. He called the charioteer to halt the horses. 'What is this crowd?' he said, 'A prophet is preaching sire.' 'Who is this prophet?' 'John the Baptist.'

Herod sat in his chariot that day and he heard the man of God preach. He was stirred in his heart. Then John saw the king and that fearless preacher pointed his finger of accusation and he said "King Herod, you are living in sin. You have taken your brother Philip's wife Herodias." I see the frown cover the face of the king and he says to the charioteer "Go on, drive on the horses." He returns in anger to his palace.

That did not keep him from going back again and he went back on many occasions to hear John preach and I want you to notice something.

The third thing about him, he heard him gladly.

He took a delight in hearing God's faithful man. He attended the services of the prophet of God and the preaching had an effect upon him but alas sin was too strong for him. Herodias, the adulteress said "You have got to stop John preaching. I want you to kill him." Herod said, "No, he is not going to be killed." She nagged away at him until he gave commandment to put John in prison. No longer the fearless prophet of God stood and denounced the sins of his day. He was silent in the prison cell.

Herodias had not given up her hatred or her spite against the man of God. You will notice what the Bible says in verse 21 *"And when a convenient day was come"*. A day that Herodias planned for. A day when that evil, filthy woman said' I will get my own back on God's man'. You will notice the subtle way in which it was done.

First of all there was a supper and the food and the drink were there and toast after toast was drunk in that feast with Herod the king and his courtiers and the great chieftains of the Galilean kingdom. All the evil of a Roman festivity was carried out that day. Herodias said 'Before night comes I will have the head of John the Baptist.' Then after the drinking and the feasting Herodias' daughter came in to dance.

In the oriental dance when a woman danced she danced a dance of lewdness, undressing herself as the dance proceeded and so there was not only drink but there was the filth of the dance. There was Herod prepared carefully by Herodias for the last act in the damnation of his soul, the killing of God's man.

After the dance there was the filthy language he swore. He opened his mouth, he took God's holy name in vain. I want you to notice the downgrade in this thing. It started with the drink. It went on to the dance and then to came to the oath. Here is a man the worse of drink., his passions aroused by the suggestiveness of the dance and he takes God's holy name in vain. He swears to Salome, Herodias daughter, 'I will give you to up to half of the kingdom.' I hear the cheers and jeers of the great men of that kingdom as they see the king prostrate himself before this half-dressed woman who was dancing.

What does she do? She heads for her mother. The mother says, "Ask for the head of John the Baptist". She says, "Be quick about it". You will notice what the Holy Spirit says in verse 25 *"She came in straightway with haste"*. 'Before his passion cools, before he sobers up, go in and tell him to kill John and take off his head and bring it drenched with blood on a charger and present it to me on the floor of the dance hall.'

It was a night of blood and it was a night of damnation for king Herod.

The king was sorry.

I want to tell you something, sin will make you sorry in time but sin will make you eternally sorry in the lake of fire for evermore.

I wonder how many sorry souls there are in hell? Souls that are sorry they ever rejected Christ. Sorry that they ever gave themselves to sin. Sorry that they ever pursued a life of iniquity. It will be too late to be sorrowful in hell, friend.

Do you remember the man called Esau?

He found no place for repentance though he sought it earnestly with tears. The sobs of Esau. There are sobs in hell. If I could open the door of the pit of destruction and if I could find among the tormented souls of men down there in the caverns of the damned the soul of Herod he is still sorry. Sorry for the mad fool he made of himself on that dance hall floor. Sorry for the fact that he put his hand to the murder weapon and sent his guard to take off the head of John the Baptist. He is sorry but it is too late to be sorry. He was sorry, yet for his oath's sake and for the people who sat with him, he did the deed of blood.

Company will take you to hell friend. He was afraid of the people who sat with him. There are men and women in this church and they are going to hell because of their companions. They are afraid to make the break. They are afraid to say yes to Christ because of the person with them. For their companion's sake they are prepared to walk over the blood of Christ again and do despite to the Spirit of grace.

He said, (read the margin), to one of the guards who was standing by. "Come forward", and you can hear the clank of that guard's armour as he steps forward to the king's throne. He says, "Go to the prison cell, pick out John the Baptist, cut off his head, put it on a charger and bring it to me."

The guard salutes and I hear the clank of the guard's metal armament as he goes down the pavement of the palace floor. It seems as if the echo of his footsteps come back and play the dirge of murder in the hearts of all who are present.

Then John the Baptist hears the guards coming along the stone flagged prison, Herod's prison in Jerusalem.

Suddenly the door is opened. The jailer said "Your death day has come." Without any prior notice he is made to lie down upon the floor. The guard draws his sword and in a moment or two that head is severed from the body. The special man, and there was no greater ever born of woman, humanly speaking, than John the Baptist, the forerunner of the Saviour, was done to death.

I see that guard and he produces this silver charger and he lifts up that grizzly and bleeding head and he sets it upon it. He puts his blood-stained sword into its scabbard and he starts marching up out of the prison across the pavement into the palace.

The music is stilled. Every voice is hushed as he enters the door and they see what he is carrying, a basin of blood, a charger of gore and the head of the preacher still bleeding in that charger. He presents it to Salome and she takes it and curtsies and gives it to her mother. It was a night of blood in the ball room.

You know what happened that night? Herod and Herodias sealed their doom for all eternity. Herod lost his soul at the dance. He lost his soul at the dance.

If you read the history of Herod you will find he went from bad to worse from that day.

Many years ago, I attended a Gospel meeting in Dunseverick Baptist Church. It is a little meeting house up on the North Antrim coast. My dear father was the preacher at that meeting.

It was the last meeting of a Gospel campaign that he conducted in that little meeting house. In that district there was a great man of God. His name was Charlie McCaw. He was well known to everyone. He had been a vile sinner whom God had graciously saved. I remember that when my father finished his message and was making the final appeal for souls that man got up and he said to my father "James, can I say a word." My father said, "Certainly." Charlie McCaw told this story. It has lived with me, I was only a little boy at the time but I have never forgotten it.

He said, "Friends in this countryside there was a young man and I knew him well. He attended Gospel services just like this. God had spoken to him and the Spirit of God had striven with his soul. But there was a dance coming on in the neighbourhood and this young man wanted to attend that dance so on the final night of the meetings he postponed getting right with God and he said he would get right with God after the dance. He wanted to go to the annual dance which was quite an affair in the society in that neighbourhood. But he took ill the following Monday. The service closed on the Sabbath. It was an illness unto death."

Charlie McCaw said, "When they approached his death bed he was whispering and he kept whispering one sentence. It was a strange sentence and they asked him why he kept repeating it. The sentence was 'Bury me at the gate, it was there that I made my decision.' They asked him what he meant. He said 'Well, when I came home from the service I stood at my garden gate and the forces of God and the forces of evil were striving for my soul and I chose the dance and the devil's way at that gate. I made a deliberate choice.' That was the last words that man whispered as he went out into eternity 'Bury me at the gate. It was there I made my decision.'"

You are going to make a choice tonight. A choice either for heaven or for hell.

A choice either for Christ or for the devil.

A choice either for light or for darkness.

What is your choice going to be?

O come, sinner come,
Accept the proffered grace,
For death, death may soon be calling you
Into her cold embrace.
The harvest will be ended,
The summer will be past,
Your lamentation then will be,
My soul is lost at last.

God save you from the hell in which Herod is damned.
AMEN AND AMEN!

3 Dead men's *bones*

THE BIBLE IS AN undefinable Book. In refererence to its great theme "the Salvation of man" it scans every subject, views every vista, teaches every truth, sentences every sin and condemns every crime. It is the Book of books which makes all the world a preacher and turns flowers, trees, hills, valleys, rivers and mountains into mighty pulpiteers proclaiming the message of the eternal God.

No wonder our Lord Jesus Christ told the beetle-browed, bleating mouthed, blackhearted Pharisees, the predecessors of our modern ecclesiastical biggies with their gaiters and grandeur, their aprons and arrogance, that if His disciples did not honour Him as God Incarnate **the very stones would cry out.**

We are going to listen now, not to stones crying out, but to dead men's bones crying out the unveiled evangel of heaven.

Our first scripture is found in the nineteenth chapter of the book of Numbers at the verse sixteen. It is one of the precepts of the mosaic economy.

"And whosoever touchest one that is slain with a sword in the open fields, or a dead body or **a bone of a man**, or a grave, shall be unclean seven days".

This Dead Man's Bones speak of:-
THE RUINATION OF SIN

Here we learn the lesson of sin's defilement. Sin is a filthy thing and it has contaminated the whole race.

You can start life with all respectability, all religion, all finery, all outward swank, all pomp, all pride and all vain show but when sin has finished with you it will leave you sullied, soiled and scarred.

"Sin, when it is finished, bringeth forth death." There is no incident that more forcefully illustrates this than that connected with the painting of Leonardo De Vinci's great masterpiece 'The Last Supper'". Long and in vain had the artist sought for a model for his Christ. "I must find a young man of pure life," he declared, "before I can get that look on the face I want." At length his attention was called to a young man who sang in the choir of one of the old churches of Rome, Pietro Bandinelli by name. He was not only a young man of beautiful countenance but his life was as beautiful as his face. The moment he looked on this pure, sweet countenance the artist cried out in joy, "At last I have found the face I wanted." So Pietro Bandinelli sat as the model for his picture of Christ.

Years passed on and still the great painting "The Last Supper" was not finished. The eleven faithful apostles had all been sketched on the canvas and the artist was hunting for a model for his Judas.

"I must find a man whose face has hardened and distorted," he said, "a debased man, his face stamped with the ravages only wicked living and a wicked heart can show." Thus he wandered long in search of his Judas, until one day in the streets of Rome he came upon a wretched creature, a beggar in rags, with a face of such hard villainous stamp that even the artist was repulsed. But he knew that at last he had found his Judas. So it came about that the beggar with the repulsive countenance sat as the model of Judas. As he was dismissing him De Vinci said, "I have not yet asked your name but I will now." "Pietro Bandinelli" replied the man, looking at him unflinchingly, "I also sat for you as the model for your Christ."

Astonished, overwhelmed by the startling declaration, De Vinci would not at first believe it, but proof was at hand, and he had finally to admit that Pietro Bandinelli, he whose fair, sweet face had been the inspiration for his great masterpeice the face of Christ, had now become so disfigured by the sins of a lifetime that no trace was left of that marvellous beauty which before had been the admiration of men.

Yes if sin finds you pure it will leave you putrid. If it finds you holy it will leave you hideous. If it finds you lovely it will leave you lustful. If it finds you clean it will leave you corrupt and if it finds you righteous it will leave you reprobate. Sin is both a desolation and an abomination. Shun sin today or sin will leave you shunned by God for all eternity.

Our second scripture is found in the second book of Kings chapter thirteen and at the verses twenty and twenty one.

"And Elisha died and they buried him. And the bands of the Moabites invaded the land at the coming in of the year. And it came to pass, as they were burying a man, that, behold, they spied a band of men; and they cast the man into the sepulchre of Elisha: and when the man was let down and touched **the bones of Elisha**, he revived and stood up on his feet."

This Dead Man's Bones speak of
THE RESTORATION OF LIFE

Our scripture tells out its own truth. The dead man left death behind him in the grave of Elisha. Now Elisha is a type of Christ and in our Saviour's tomb we can leave our death behind forever and rise with Him to walk in newness of life. The empty Tomb spells restoration of life to all who believe on Jesus.

This precious truth is sweetly expounded by Bunyan in his immortal dream. Describing Christian's visit to the Cross he writes, "Up the way of salvation did burdened Christian run but not without great difficulty because of the load on his back. He ran thus until he came to a place somewhere ascending and upon that place stood a cross and a little below at the bottom, a sepulchre. So I saw in my dream that just as Christian came up to the Cross his burden loosed from off his shoulders and fell from off his back and began to tumble and continue to do so till it came to the sepulchre where it fell in and **I SAW IT NO MORE.**"

Then Christian exclaimed,
"Blest Cross! Blest Sepulchre!
Blest rather be
The man that there was put to shame for me."

A visit to yonder cross sinner will bring the same happy results to your soul.

"Escape for thy life; look not behind thee, niether stay thou in all the plain; escape to the mountain, lest thou be consumed." (Genesis 19:17).

Our third scripture is found in the eleventh chapter of Hebrews at the verse twenty-two. "By faith Joseph, when he died, made mention of the departing of the children of Israel; and gave commandment **concerning his bones.**"

This Dead Man's Bones speak of
THE REALISATION OF FAITH

This is one of the brightest illustrations and examples of saving faith in the Bible. The three ingredients of faith are here aptly expounded:

1. Accepting the Promise

Joseph accepted the promise of God made to his great-grandfather Abraham. This is the first exercise of faith, accepting the testimony which God has given of His Son.

2. Acting on its Reality

Joseph acted on the reality of the promise and refused to be buried in Egypt. Saving faith acts on the reality of the promise and enters into the covenant blessing, refusing all the Egyptian suggestions of worldly doubt.

3. Anticipating its Hope

Joseph saw beyond the tombs and anticipated the exodus of Israel. Saving faith sees beyond this scene of time and knows that the world cannot eternally claim one particle of the redeemed one's body. God has given commandment concerning the bones of His people. Hallelujah!

Ours is the confidence of Job. "For I know that my redeemer liveth, and that he shall stand at the latter day upon the earth; and though after my skin worms destroy this body yet in my flesh shall I see God" (Job 19:25-26).

Thus is faith realised and perfected, by accepting the promise, acting on its reality and anticipating its hope.

Ask God for this priceless gift today.

Our final scripture is found in the eighth chapter of the prophecy of Jeremiah, verses one, two and three.

"At that time saith the Lord, they shall bring out **the bones of the Kings of Judah** and the bones of his princes, and the bones of the priests, and the bones of the prophets, and the bones of the inhabitants of Jerusalem, out of their graves: and they shall spread them before the sun, and the moon and all the host of heaven, whom they have loved and whom they have served and after whom they have walked and whom they have sought and whom they have worshipped; they shall not be gathered, nor be buried: they shall be for dung upon the face of the earth. And death shall be chosen rather than life by all the residue of them that remain of this evil family, which remain in all places whither I have driven them, saith the Lord of hosts."

These Dead Men's Bones speak of
THE RETRIBUTION OF JUDGMENT

The stench of these unburied bones tells out the solemn message of Judgment. These sinners were indicted on a charge of five counts -

1. Holding fast to deceit (verse 5)
2. Refusing to return (verse 5)
3. Repenting not (verse 6)
4. Rejecting the Word of the Lord (verse 9)
5. Provoking the Lord (verse 19)

and swift judgment overtook them in their crimes. Are we ready for the judgment? That is the vital question.

A Hungarian king, finding himself on a certain day depressed and unhappy, sent for his brother, a good natured but rather indifferent prince. To him the king said: "I am a great sinner and fear to meet God." The prince only laughed at him and treated the matter as a joke, just as you may be doing now. This answer did not relieve the king's unhappiness. Now at that time it was a custom in Hungary that if a trumpet was sounded by the servant of the King outside a man's door it was the signal that that man was doomed to die and was about to be led out to be executed.

That night the king sent his servant to blow the fatal blast outside the door of the careless prince. The prince, awakening from sleep, realised the dread import of the blast. He was dragged, pale and trembling, before his brother the King. He pleaded on bended knee for his life, imploring to know how he had offended the King's majesty.

"My brother," answered the King. "If the sight of a human executioner is so terrible to you, shall not I, having grievously offended God, fear to be brought before the judgment seat of Christ?"

In what frame will the trumpet blast summon us to the last great assize. Will that summons find us prepared to meet our God? Now is the time to settle this all important matter. Remember, "It is a fearful thing to fall into the hands of the living God."

AMEN AND AMEN!

4 The greatest crime
in Christ's church

WE ARE TURNING to the 51st Psalm this morning and I want to preach upon the greatest crime of Christ's church. We are reading Psalm 51. I want to draw your attention to verse 14 *"Deliver me from blood guiltiness, O God, thou God of my salvation: and my tongue shall sing aloud of thy righteousness."*

David was a guilty man.

He had devised evil in his heart. By the power that was his, as the king of Israel, he had brought his wicked plans and wicked devices to pass. Then after his adultery and his murder of Uriah for about a year he thought that all was well, that he had carefully covered his sin and no one knew about it.

Then there came a prophet from the Lord. Nathan pointed his finger of accusation and he said concerning David "Thou art the man" and stern conviction came upon David.

Great distress of soul and trouble of heart became his and then he poured out his confession. He poured out his confesion before God and laid bare the crookedness, the perverseness and the iniquity of his heart.

In Psalm 51 we have the Psalm of David in penitence.

Bowed at the cross!

Broken in spirit!

Overcome with grief!

Repenting with the repentance not to be repented of!

You will notice that David was absolutely honest in his confession. He did not try to minimise the sin that he had committed. He did not try to call his sin by any delicate name. He stands before God and he says, "There is blood upon my soul."

It was not the actual sword of David which slew Uriah. It was the sword of the enemies of Israel that slew Uriah in the battle but David had planned it and it was just as much his sword as it would have been his sword if he had brutally been an assassin and murdered Uriah when he came to his royal palace to bring his message from Joab.

Because of his sin of blood guiltiness, he declared "The blood of Uriah is upon me".

I am a murderer. I have committed murder. I have committed the greatest of all crimes and I have used the position that God has given me to do this wicked thing and to carry out this act of gross iniquity.

I want you to notice something else. I want you to notice the awfulness of this crime. This was a crime that could not be cleansed with the sacrificial hyssop. This is a crime that only God could deal with in His mercy. This was a crime that brought the man after God's own heart down into the very depths of despair and down into the very depths of heart-wrung repentance before God.

THE CRIME GREATER THAN DAVID'S

Now David destroyed the life of Uriah the Hittite but in the church of Jesus Christ, every one of us is guilty of a far worse sin than the sin of the killing of the body. The church of Jesus Christ today is guilty of the murder of precious souls. The body is only an outward thing. It is only, at best, a piece of clay. It is doomed already for the Divine sentence has been passed upon it - dust thou art and unto dust thou shalt return.

What shall I say of the immortal souls of men that are built to enjoy the bliss and the glory and the eternal happiness of heaven. What would be the crime of a person who deliberately and with malice aforethought sends that soul that should be travelling to heaven down to the darkness, down to the degradation, down to the debauchery and down to the damnation of hell itself. The church of Jesus Christ is guilty of the blood of souls. Let us make no mistake about it.

There is not a man in this meeting, there is not a woman in this meeting, there is not a person from the minister to every member of the congregation that has not been guilty of this crime of the murder of precious souls. Blood guiltiness is upon the skirts of this church. Blood guiltiness is upon the skirts of every individual in this meeting.

I am talking about soul murder. I am talking about the damnation of eternal fire. I am talking about those that will be forever lost because you and I have not been on fire for God, have not been overflowing in love for them, have not been living for them, witnessing for them, praying for them and winning them to Jesus Christ.

We have a most solemn subject for discussion and I trust that as this has burned into the preacher's heart that God will burn it into the souls of everyone that listens to its message.

I want to deal with four things.

I want, first of all, **to investigate this crime of blood guiltiness**.

Secondly, **I want to interrogate the criminal**, the person who is guilty of this crime.

Thirdly, **I want to designate the confession**. The Psalmist here is upon his knees. He has a broken heart. He has a contrite spirit and amid his tears he cries "Deliver me from blood guiltiness oh God of my salvation." **I want to designate that confession**. See exactly what it means and its nature.

Then, fourthly, **I want to anticipate the conclusion**. There is a glorious conclusion out of the darkness. There is a light that shineth in this text and what does it finish with? It finished with this - my tongue shall sing aloud of thy righteousness.

INVESTIGATE THE CRIME

So we are going to investigate the crime of blood guiltiness.

You say "Preacher how am I guilty of the blood of souls? How can you say that I am guilty of soul murder. How can you arraign me and charge me with such a crime?"

Every person in this meeting, every father and mother in this meeting that has neglected the family altar and the parental duties of the father and mother is guilty of blood guiltiness. Let us get it straight. When God gives us children they are not only a blessing but a solemn and awful responsibility. Their lives for the years when they can be trained are under our care and under our jurisdiction. We can train them for heaven or we can train them for hell. We can sow seeds upon their hearts that will enable them to grow up in the fear, nurture and admonition of the Lord, or we can be careless in our habits, we can be careless in our spiritual life and void of our prayers of concern and love.

So children destined for heaven can be led astray into the paths of unrighteousness and into the ways of worldliness.

In the Puritanical era the family altar was in every home. In the days of the Puritans the family was the nucleus of the Christian church. But alas parents have given up parental control and today children forsake the God of their father and of their mother and run wild in the ways of unrighteousness and in the path of wickedness.

My dear father, my dear mother, you are guilty of blood guiltiness if you have failed to have the family altar, if you have failed to chastise your children, if you have failed to correct them in the ways of error, if you have failed to train their hearts for Jesus Christ.

This subject of parental control and parental correction is one that is taboo in this age. Children are supposed to express themselves in whatever way they like. The Bible says, 'Train up a child in the way he shall go and when he is old he will not depart therefrom.' My Christian parents, you have a solemn and a serious responsibility.

At the bar of judgment will our offspring charge us with blood guiltiness? Will they say I was not trained in this way, I was not brought up to fear God. My father never prayed for me. My mother never wrestled alone with God for my salvation and I am here the child of Christian parents unprayed for, uncorrected, unloved and doomed forever to the damnation of hell.

Yes, parents are guilty. When a parent buys for the family a television set and allows their children to watch every iniquitous programme that is put over that set and never once has a family altar and never once calls the family to prayer that parent is guilty of the blood of their family. Let us be very honest about it. I find today that Christian parents want to shelve their responsibilities. I find today that Christian parents want to say, "Oh well, it is the age, we cannot help it, the children will go this way." No sir, the children will go the way you direct them to go and you have a responsibility.

Do you remember Eli? He was the priest of God but he corrected not his sons. They were evil men. God said, "I will do something in the house of Israel that will make every ear tingle because Eli trained not his sons in the ways of the Lord." Do you remember Samuel? He had two sons and he did not bring them up properly either, and the sons of Samuel were just as wicked as the sons of Eli. They took bribes and they indulged in iniquitous practices and God set aside the house of Samuel forever. Christian parents, the blood of your family will be required at your hands.

Then there are those in this service and they are guilty of the blood of souls because they have neglected the souls of men seeking Jesus Christ. Neglect of souls! The great crime of Christ's church. Do you think it helps a man who is anxious to be saved if he sees a believer hastening from the House of God with the spirit of levity and fun upon his lips. Do you think it helps him?

Here is a man convicted of his sin in the solemn Gospel service and he is going out through these doors with people who profess to know Christ and they are in the spirit of lightness. They are in the spirit of flippancy. They are in the spirit of unconcern.

Do you think it helps that man under conviction of sin to come to Christ, do you? My friend we must acknowledge our guiltiness before God. Let no man stand up this day and say I am not guilty. You are guilty and so is the preacher, every one of us. We have all the blood of souls upon us, every one of us.

Failing to warn the unconcerned, failing to blow the blast of warning, how many times have you failed my brother, my sister, to warn men to flee from the wrath to come? How many of your unsaved companions have you ever spoken to concerning Jesus Christ?

I was talking to a prominent newspaper reporter this week, from one of the big English daily papers. He rang me up about something and I said to him, "Now I want to talk to you, you have talked to me." He said, "What do you want to talk about?" I said, "I want to talk about where you are going to spend eternity and I want to ask you a question. You have interviewed many Protestant ministers." He said, "I have interviewed hundreds of them in my career." I said, "Did any one of them talk to you about eternity?" He said, "No, sir. Never did one person ever talk to me about where I would be in eternity." I said, "Well, you will not say that about me." So I talked to him about where he would be in eternity.

Think of it. Is there any hope for a man like that? A former Romanist who for 17 years had given up going to the mass. He did not believe in it. He had interviewed minister after minister, some of them professing evangelicals and not one of them had a word for his soul. God help us! No wonder the church of Jesus Christ is in the state it is in. My friend, if you fail to warn the unconcerned their blood God will require at your hand. Yes.

Is God saying to you, "See those members of Ravenhill, I have blessed them ten thousand times over. I have given them everything they have asked me for and yet they have no concern for a city that is going to hell. They have no real concern for dying men and women."

Is that what God is saying this morning? Is God bringing this sin of blood guiltiness home to your heart?

What about the Christian parents who are exposing their family to dangers? I have talked to parents and the only thing that they seem to be interested in is the worldly advancement of their family. They will put their young son to a business with the vilest associations and they say there are good prospects for him there. The boy learns to gamble and he learns to drink strong drink and he learns to curse in the business that his father chose for him. I am telling you there is a day when God will require it at your hand. Make no mistake about it.

There are some people who expose their families to an educational system that, will only bring them to despair. I think of young families who have been blasted because of the ambition of their parents. I am thinking of one family now. The father used to come to the prayer meeting, he never missed it. Then he started to slack off and I went to see him. I said, "You have been an absentee from the prayer meeting, what is wrong with you?" He said, "My boy is going forward in the educational field and I have to spend every night with him. He is swatting for a very important examination and I am spending every night to help him on." I put my hand on his shoulder and I said, "I want to tell you, you are doing the best thing to damn your son. Your prayers are more important than his education. If you neglect the prayer meeting for the education of your son God will blast both you and him." He was very angry but he is no longer a member of this church and God passed him by as well as his son. To see his son hanging on to the end of a drinking glass and associating with the world and the devil who is responsible? The father who failed God, that is who is responsible.

You say "Preacher those are strong things to say." I know, but God help this preacher if he is not faithful to your soul. God Almighty help Ian Paisley to be faithful in this evil day. It is all right to preach smooth things, to preach peace when there is not peace but, my friend, we expose people to danger by our actions.

There are of course things that I could do that would not hurt me. I am strong enough in the Christian faith. I could do those things but I refrain from doing them for the simple reason that I would hurt some weaker brother. If by hurting some weaker brother I caused him, for whom Christ has died, to perish, what a crime would be mine. There are things, Christian men and women, that are lawful but they are not expedient. No sir. In God's name don't do them. Because if you do them you are bringing disaster not to yourself but some other weaker person in the Christian faith.

What shall I now say this morning about our unholy silence. I was thinking many of us are silent when we should speak out.

How many of us have heard the Lord's name taken in vain and we have not rebuked those who took it in vain, we have just remained silent? How many of us have been in company, not of our own choosing, and something has been said that is dishonouring to the Lord. It has dishonoured the Book, dishonoured Jesus Christ, and instead of standing up and saying, "I am a Christian, I will not have that talk in my presence", we have shut our mouths.

We have remained silent, and my friend, the blood of those sinners is upon us. We did not warn them of their crimes. We did not warn them of the blasphemy of their lips or the vileness of their talk.

Then there are Christians and they are harsh with new converts. They don't treat the new convert with the love that they ought to treat them. They treat the converts harshly and they rebuke them. Some of them say of new converts, "I wonder are they really saved?" Do you think that is going to help them? Do you think when a man has come to Christ if an old Christian says "I hope you are saved, I am not too sure about you", do you think that is going to help them on their way? Do you think that spirit is going to encourage them on the Christian path? Do you think that spirit is going to hasten their feet Zionward and heavenward and homeward and Godward?

Oh my friend we need to have a tenderness with the babes. When you are bringing up young children, when they fall you don't beat them, do you? You lift them up again. You help them. I have two boys trying to walk and they fall many times but they are not scolded when they fall. They are not whipped when they make a mistake. They are lifted up with father or mother's hands, with the hands of love. That is what you need to do with young babes in Christ. Souls that last week were on the road to hell and today they are saved , need the love of God's people. We need to love them. You need to realise that they have come out of darkness. You need to realise that they need the blessing of heaven. Oh we need tender love in our hearts for souls. We need to love them with a father's love. With the love of a shepherd. With the love of a mother.

Then of course there is the unhallowed lethargy of the people of God. Lightness among God's people. Carelessness among the people of God. How many a soul has been driven on to hell because of the careless talk of the saints of God? How many a soul has said, 'Well if that is your Christianity and if that is what you think of the reality of hell when you can go out after a solemn Gospel message to crack a joke and to act the fool then I don't believe in it.'

Spurgeon, in his autobiography tells of a young preacher. This young preacher preached a solemn message on hell and he walked home with a young man. All the way home he never spoke to that young man about his soul. When they came to part company the young man said, "Sir, I don't believe you are an honest man." The preacher said, "What?" The man said, "I don't believe you are an honest man for if what you had said was true and you believed it, all the way home you would have spoken to me about my danger of hell but never once did you open your mouth to warn me of the solemn subject you were talking about in the service."

What a rebuke! what an awful rebuke! Are there men and women in this service and they are saying to God Almighty - do you see those people in the Ulster Hall, they say they believe in hell but they never warned me of hell. I live beside them. They are my neighbours. We have talked about business. We have talked about the weather. We have talked about politics. We have talked about the world situation. We have talked about our families. We have talked about our health but never once did they talk to me about eternity.

The blood of your neighbours is upon you, friend. Blood guiltiness. Those who withheld to pray. This is where it gets us all. The absentees from the prayer meeting, the people who have lost the quiet time at home and no longer pray, are saturated with the blood of souls that they are damning.

Every prayerless Christian is guilty of soul murder. God says, 'Ask and it shall be given.' You have not asked. God says, 'Seek and ye shall find.' You have not sought. God says, 'Knock and it shall be opened'. But you have not knocked. The souls that you could win through your prayers are being lost. The souls that you could win to Christ by your prayers are being damned. How can you sit apathetic this morning? How can you be unconcerned this morning when the blood of immortal souls is upon you. Does God see our hearts crimson red with the blood of souls? Is that how God views us? Withholding our prayers.

I have heard church members, thank God not in this church, in other churches, saying what is the use of a day of prayer and fasting. What is the use of a week of prayer. What is the use of these prolonged prayings. I met a man one day and he belonged to a so-called evangelical church and he said to me "Paisley, if God wants to send revival He will not need your prayer meeting." I said, "I believe that too but I want to tell you friend that praying is the beginning of revival. When God puts in my heart to pray for revival I am sure it is going to come for that is the beginning." "Oh," he said, "God does not need your praying. You with your long prayer meetings, God does not need you." I said, "How is your church doing?" He said, "It is not doing very well." I said, "Be honest it is not doing at all." He said, "That is right. Attendance of 14 and 15 on Sunday morning. 14 or 15 on Sunday night. Never a soul saved for generations." I said, "I am going to tell you something, with your attitude your church will close." "Oh, not at all." he said. I said, "It will."

Friend it is now shut up and sold. I could take you to it. Closed.

If you have you got the attitude, friend, that prayer is not essential then you are finished. The most essential thing for the Christian is prayer. Let me make it plain. Prayer is the Christian's native breath. When a child is born what does it need? It needs oxygen in its lungs. When a man is saved what does he need? He needs the oxygen of prayer and if he has not got it he will die, he will perish. The proof that a man is saved is the proof of praying. You show me a man who says he is saved and if he is praying that is the greatest proof you can have. A praying man is the proof that he is a Christian man, that a work of grace has been done in his heart.

Are we withholding prayers? Yes every one of us, from the preacher to the humblest member of this congregation we are guilty. If we would only say, 'O we are guilty. We have not prayed as we ought. We have not prayed as we should. We have not prayed the way we would.'

Then what about the want of earnestness among the people of God. What about this concern that should baptise us. What about, my friend, this earnestness of heart. When I am coming to the house of God I should be earnest. I should be saying to my soul, 'O soul be stirred up.' You are about the business of eternity. There are men and women sitting around you in this service and if they are not saved they will perish. O God give me concern for them. Give me love for them. Give me tears for them. Can my very attitude on the seat convict them. Can the very way I sing a hymn and listen to the Word of God and pay attention to the preacher be a means of winning them to Christ. When the service is over help me to speak a word in season to weary hearts. Help me to be on the outlook for souls. Help me to be a man that seeks for others. To be ever on the quest for souls.

What shall I say this morning about the blood of the heathen that is upon the church of Jesus Christ? What about the 100,000 souls a say that are passing one by one away in Christless guilt and gloom? What about those lands across the sea? What about missionaries we have never named this week in prayer? We have never spent one second before God to pray for them.

What about the dark lands unreached? What about the tribes that have never heard the name of Jesus? What about the dialects that have not one verse of the Word of God? What about them?

There is a cry from the heathen world and it is going up against every Christian in this hall and the heathen are saying, 'Take away their privileges. Take away their blessing. Take away their happinesses. We are sitting in darkness and they have got the light and they would not bring it to us. We are sitting in paganism and they have got the liberating word of the Gospel and they would not make an effort to bring it to us.'

Do you remember the story of the old African, 80 years of age and the missionary was speaking to him about Jesus. The old African said "How long have you know this?" The missionary said, "Since the day of my birth." "Did your father know about Jesus?" "Yes." "How long did he know?" "From the day of his birth." "Did your grandfather know about Jesus." "Yes." "How long did he know?" "From the day of his birth." He went on into generation after generation and the old African said "Why, why have you been so long bringing us the message?"

I would like to ask you young men and women in this meeting why are you so long responding to the call of God. Why are you so long sitting at home while the world calls for you to go and preach to them the message of the Gospel? Why are you so long at home while the world perishes? Why? The blood of souls is upon you.

You say you are waiting for a call. Are you? Did God call you to stay at home?" I am waiting for something to move me. I am waiting for some vision". Are you? Friend you will wait a terribly long time. The command has been given.

Go, and except you can give me reasons before God that God will accept why you cannot go, then you ought to be upon your way.

The blood of souls. It is not only the blood of my neighbours which is upon me. It is not only the blood of my family that is upon me. It is not only the blood of my street or my city but it is the blood of the world that I have failed to bring God's message to this generation. I will be answering for it. Deliver me from blood guiltiness thou God of my salvation. My we would need delivered.

What of you in this meeting, who are not saved? You are guilty of the blood of Jesus Christ. You have crucified afresh to yourself the Lord of Glory and you have put Him to an open shame and that is the greatest crime that you could commit. I wonder how many in this service have to say, 'Lord it is true I am guilty, I am guilty'.

I am not going to argue with God. David did not argue. He did not call it by a nice name nor did he try to get away. He said he was guilty. How many of you people are guilty? How many people in this service are saying, 'Deliver me from blood guiltiness. Lord deliver me.' What does that mean? That you will go back to the same old way of living? Is that what that means? No sir, this means a complete absolute deliverance.

May the Lord give you today an absolute deliverance for His Name's Sake.

AMEN AND AMEN!

5 The octogenarian's *prayer*

I'M SURE IT WILL surprise you to know that Daniel was over eighty years of age when he prayed this remarkable prayer. *"O Lord, hear; O Lord, forgive; O Lord, hearken and do; defer not, for thine own sake, O my God for thy city and thy people are called by thy name."* Daniel 9:19

It is the prayer of an octogenarian.

In verse one we are told that he offered this prayer in the first year of Darius the king. Darius reigned for two years and was succeeded by Cyrus. Now in the first year of Cyrus, according to Ezra chapter one, the seventy years captivity of the Jews were completed. So in two years from the offering of this prayer Daniel himself would have completed seventy years in Babylon. He was therefore sixty-eight years in Babylon at this time. When carried into captivity Daniel must have been at least fourteen years old. Add to that the sixty-eight years of his captivity in Babylon and you will discover that he must have been eighty-two years of age at this time.

Not only was Daniel an octogenarian but he held the highest political appointment in the land. He was Prime Minister of the second world empire, the Medo-Persian empire. Mark, however, though he was old and had tremendous duties to discharge, he still took time to pray.

We have here an exhortation to us all. You old people, you are not past the time when you can intercede with your God. You busy people, you have still plenty of time to supplicate the throne of grace. You young people, if old Daniel could find time and energy to plead with God, you are without excuse.

We will consider together five striking characteristics of this prayer - its preparation, posture, petition, plea and prevalence.

I. THE PREPARATION OF DANIEL'S PRAYER

"In the first year of his reign I Daniel understood by books the number of the years, whereof the word of the Lord came to Jeremiah the prophet, that he would accomplish seventy years in the desolations of Jerusalem." **Daniel 9:2**

Daniel had been pondering an old manuscript of the prophet Jeremiah. As he read he discovered that the time to favour Zion yea, God's set time had come. Encouraged by the promise he went to God with God"s own words in his mouth. With the plea "Thou hast said" he gripped the horns of the altar. He presented the cheque of the promise and demanded that God would honour His signature. This is the right way to pray. The command of the prophet Hosea must be obeyed as we intercede. "Take with you words, and turn to the Lord: say unto him, Take away all iniquity, and receive us graciously: so will we render the calves of our lips." (Hosea 14:2). God's own words on the lips of His people in fervent intercession become effectual, mighty, overcoming prayers. We take time to prepare to speak to men, we must take time to prepare to speak to God.

It is simply neglect of the Bible which leads to neglect of prayer. Prayer not inspired by the Word of God is cold, lifeless and useless. So the cry of exhortation must not only be "To your knees" but "To your Bible."

When George Muller, the orphan's famous friend, was asked how he prayed in over one million pounds for the support of his orphanages, he replied "I get down on my knees and turn the passage of scripture into petitions which I present as my own prayers at the throne of grace." Such prayers never go unanswered. Is this how you pray? You need not wonder if your prayers are unanswered if they are not prompted by the Word of God. How much praying is there which is only sham. The mere wordiness of the carnal mind, the froth of religious hypocrisy, the joy of hell and the shame of heaven. Saint of God, get to the Word of God. Let your soul be saturated in the water of the Word. When you are absolutely soaked in the precepts and promises of the Holy Book wring yourself out in intercession. Then and only then will you learn the true meaning of prayer and experience such answers to your pleadings that the very magicians of this old Egypt of the world will be forced to admit "This is the finger of God."

This is God's way of preparation. May we without delay take this royal highway to successful praying.

II. THE POSTURE OF DANIEL'S PRAYER

"And I set my face unto the Lord God to seek by prayer and supplications, with fasting, and sackcloth, and ashes." **Daniel 9:3**

There is no room for pride in the audience room of the great King. The whole posture of Daniel is one of deepest humiliation.

FASTING

The rich feasting must be laid aside. Yes, even plainest food required for daily upkeep must be sacrificed. The company of man and man's doings must be forsaken, and the body, its needs and desires bent to the will of God. Ours is an age of feasting Christians. Fasting Christians are very rare. Because of this the material and physical dominate the spiritual instead of the spiritual dominating the physical and material. We live for the things which are seen instead of for the things which are unseen. Fasting stomachs mean full souls. Alas with us full stomachs mean famished souls. If we were really burdened concerning the desperate plight of our nation the love of food would not have such a grip upon us. We would leave the table for the toil of prayer and the feast for the holy fire of supplicattion.

SACKCLOTH

Behold old Daniel leaving aside his royal robes of state. See him arrayed in the hairy garment of sackcloth. He is both inwardly and outwardly humiliated. Pride is abased in the very garments which he wears.

There is no room for pride of soul or pride of body in the chamber of true prayer. The proud soul is far too tall to enter the small and narrow doorway of the prayer closet. Proud flesh must be brought low before effective prayer can be uttered.

ASHES

Behold the man of God in the dust. He is on his knees, his face is on the ground. He is covered with a garment of hair. Over the garment is sprinkled ashes. Could you have a better picture of death? Dust man is, and unto dust he must return. Dust to dust, ashes to ashes. Only the man that is spiritually in the grave, dead to himself, his desires, ambitions, passions, prosperity, reputation and position, can truly pray. Humble yourself, dear Christian. Make no excuses for your sins. Down with you in the dust. Let sackcloth be your garment and ashes your covering. Then with pride gone and self abased you will gain the ear of heaven.

III. THE PETITION OF DANIEL'S PRAYER

"O Lord, hear; O Lord, forgive; O Lord, hearken and do; defer not."
Daniel 9:19

There is repetition here but it is not vain repetition but the repetition of a soul on fire with awful earnestness.

THE EAR OF GOD - "O LORD, HEAR"

The most important thing to the praying heart is the ear of God. For God to hear is for God to answer. The gods of the heathen have ears to hear but they hear not. Our God is the hearer of prayer. Do you have His ear? Are you confident He bends low to hear your cry? Have you sweet tokens that your supplications have soared to the highest heaven and made heaven attentive to your requests. We must get the ear of God before we can have the answer of God.

THE PARDON OF GOD - "O LORD, FORGIVE"

The first petition must always be for pardon. We are sinful, we ever need cleansing. How fervent we must be to obtain this greatest of all petitions, the forgiveness of God.

> *On the wings of faith arising,*
> *Jesus crucified I see;*
> *While His love, my soul surprising,*
> *Cries, "I suffered all for thee!"*
> *Then beneath the cross adoring,*
> *Sin does like itself appear;*
> *When the wounds of Christ exploring,*
> *I can read my pardon there.*
> *Here I'd feast my eyes for ever:*
> *While this balm of life I prove,*
> *Every wound appears a river*
> *Flowing with eternal love.*

THE ACTION OF GOD - "O LORD, HEARKEN AND DO"

God must do it. The impotence of man finds its source of strength in the omnipotence of God. The cry is for a divine intervention in the affairs of time. Prayer seeks to bring God into the situation. Prayer cries for the baring of the glorious arm of Jehovah.

THE IMMEDIATE INTERVENTION OF GOD - "DEFER NOT"

The true man of prayer will not be put off. With Jacob he cries in brokenness, "I will not let thee go except thou bless me." Persistence is the chief characteristic of true overcoming intercession. No power in earth or hell will stop the insistent voice of the soul aflame in Holy Ghost petition.

IV. THE PLEA OF DANIEL'S PRAYER

"For thine own sake, O my God; for the city and thy people are called by thy name." **Daniel 9;19**

He does not plead anything in himself. He does not plead his own courage or faithfulness in previous days of trail. Who more than Daniel could have uttered such a plea? No. He brings the strongest possible plea, the character and name of Jehovah. "For thy name's sake," he says, "for thy city and thy people are called by thy name." This is the true plea. God must honour His own Word. He must display His truthfulness amongst the nations. His honour and glory must be vindicated. His law must be magnified and seen to be honourable.

Oh, that we learned this holy art, facing the Holy Three with their promises and precepts in humble but holy persistence, pleading with God for His glory and His glory alone.

V. THE PREVALENCE OF DANIEL'S PRAYER

"And whiles I was speaking, and praying, and confessing my sin and the sin of my people Israel, and presenting my supplication before the Lord my God for the holy mountain of my God; Yea, whiles I was speaking in prayer, even the man Gabriel, whom I had seen in the vision at the beginning, being caused to fly swiftly, touched me about the time of the evening oblation." **Daniel 9:20-21**

True prayer cannot fail, it must prevail. Notice the answer came whilst the prayer was still being uttered. What encouragement is here! God answers before we get to the Amen. Such is the answer to real praying. Further, the answer is swift. Angels fly swiftly to minister the answer to fervent intercession. Again the answer was linked to the oblation. Prayers prevail because of Calvary. The basis for blessing is ever the cross of Jesus.

Lastly, Daniel got more than he asked. God always answers in the manner "far more abundantly than we can even ask or think." He asked for the restoration of Jerusalem and God gave him the redemption of His people. He got the vision not merely of the city but the King. His eyes were opened and he saw no man save Jesus only. True prayer ever leads to Christ. What greater inspiration do we need to: PRAY! PRAY! PRAY!

AMEN AND AMEN!

6 The devil in a
pigskin swimsuit

I HAVE A GREAT STORY to tell you, the story of the miracle working power of the Lord Jesus Christ.

My text is Luke 8:32, *"They (the devils) besought him that he would suffer them to enter into the swine."*

It is a great thing when the body is healed, or when some burden is lifted. It is a great thing when some problem is solved, when light shines after a night of darkness. But the greatest miracle of all is the miracle of the transforming power of the gospel of Christ in the heart of sinners. There is no miracle like the new birth. There is no miracle like the conversion of the soul. There is no miracle like the salvation of the lost.

If you open your Bible at the fifth chapter of the gospel according to Mark, and then leaf over to the eighth chapter of Luke, and if you compare the two, they are the record that we call the gospel narrative of this great story I am going to try and tell you.

THE DEGRADATION OF SIN

The first thing I want you to notice is the degradation of sin. This man that was possessed of the devil or of devils, is a perfect type of the sinner. He is the perfect type, madam of you, if you have not got Jesus. He is the perfect type, sir of you, if you have not been born again.

You say, "How dare you,! preacher. Imagine telling me I am like a man possessed of devils, living in the tombs, naked, a madman." Yes, that is you tonight. And I am going to show you that you have every characteristic that this man had.

SIX CHARACTERISTICS

This man had six characteristics. The first thing you read about him in verse two, is his environment. That is a modern word, but it is a good word. What was his environment? He came from the tombs. Characteristic number one was his deadness. Where do you find deadness? You find it in the tomb. Where do you find the darkness of death, and the degradation of death, and the depravity of death, and the debauchery of death? You find it in the tomb. This man was characterised by deadness.

DEADNESS

That is the first characteristic of every sinner. They are dead in trespasses and in sins. Our environment is the tomb of sin. We are wrapped in the shroud of sin. We are in the coffin of sin and we are buried in the grave of sin, and only Christ Himself can call us forth. Only the resurrecting power of Christ can make dead men live. Hallelujah! Sinners that were dead in trespasses and sins began to live, thank God. What a thrill it is to get out of the tomb. Are you not glad you are out of the tomb? Hallelujah! Let me tell you friend it is a great thing to have done with the shroud. Many a man has got rid of the shroud. My, the old shroud of sin has been on you a long time sinner, is that not right? You never knew anything better. And you know you were so dead you enjoyed the grave. What a fool you were. You thought the tomb was a nice place, you thought the coffin was a nice place to be. Then something happened. Thank God, in the Ballymena Town Hall life happened to you. You left the dead house did you not?

I was telling the other night about a friend of mine, a Christian man,Pastor Hardy. He had a very strange experience. That wee man was in hospital once and the doctors pronounced him dead. So they took him and laid him out on the slab but he was not dead at all. They sent a man down to prepare him for burial. And the man went in with a mug of hot water and a wobbling brush to shave the corpse. And Pastor hardy said to me, "Ian, I prayed that I could let him know I was living. I was so weak I could not move and I said, 'Lord, help me to wink my eyes'." And the man got the brush in his hand and as he was about to apply the soap the corpse winked its eye. Man, he threw that wobbling brush in the air and he broke the mug and he ran out and said, "He's living." The doctor said, "You are a fool." He replied, "I am not." They sent for the nurses and the doctors and they discovered that he was living. They did not keep him in the dead house, they got him back to bed. He lived twenty-five years after that.

Let me tell you friend, you do not stay in the dead house when you get life. Thank God, people have got out of the dead house.

Man, you are quite content! You like the shroud do you not? You do not know any better, for you are dead, you are in the grave. You do not know any better, for you are in the tomb. Every sinner is characterised by deadness.

You say, "All right preacher, I will accept that. You said there are six characteristics?" Sure!

UNCLEANNESS

Have a look at it again. The second thing is uncleanness. He had an unclean spirit: Uncleanness.

That takes us to the Old Testament, where the first time the word "unclean" is mentioned. Violation of the law made a man unclean.

Do you remember the lepers? They cried out "Unclean, unclean, unclean." They were not allowed to come into the camp lest the uncleanness of their leprosy should contaminate the rest of the tribes of Israel.

Tonight God blows the trumpet before your soul sinner, and that trumpet says, "Unclean, unclean, unclean." You are an unclean soul and there is not a man or woman who has not the Blood of Christ on their hearts who can claim cleanness. It is only the Blood that makes sinners clean. If you have not touched the Blood, then you are characterised by uncleanness. Who can bring a clean thing out of an unclean? Not one. You came out of the bosom of an unclean race. Born in sin and shapen in iniquity. God does not see anything nice about you.

A man brought a friend into my meeting one night. He brought him into the room and said to me "Here is a person, and you know Mr Paisley he is a real good person, although he is not saved." I said, "Do not tell lies. There is nobody good except they know Jesus." There is nothing nice about you in God's eyes. You are unclean. You are not a good person at all.

You say, "I am religious," but that does not make you good. The Pope is religious and I do not believe he is good. I want to tell you this, do not say you are religious and because of that you are clean. You can have all the garments, you can have all the garnishing of the temple and still be unclean. Read one of the Old Testament prophets, "and I saw one of the high priests and he was clothed in filthy rags." You could be as high up the ecclesiastical ladder as you can get, but if you are not saved you are unclean.

Maybe you are getting the message. Maybe you are beginning to see that this poor devil-possessed man in the tomb, is just like you.

The first characteristic, deadness. The second characteristic, uncleanness.

LAWLESSNESS

Look at verses three and four! Lawlessness! They tried to fetter him. They tried to make him conform to the law. They tried to make him conform to law and order. He broke the chains, he smashed the fetters. He lived in a state of perpetual lawlessness. Sin is lawlessness, that is what the Bible says.

You see, you are not only characterised by deadness, you are not only characterised by uncleanness, but you are characterised by lawlessness. You are a law breaker.

You say, "I have not broken all the commandments." No need to, "He that is guilty in one point is guilty of them all." You only need to offend in one point to be a law breaker. I just need to break one law and that is it. I am a law breaker. There is not a man or woman here who has not broken some of the laws of God. In fact if you examined your heart and the spirituality of God's law, you would have to hang your head in shame and you would find it hard to discover one law you have not broken. But let me say even if you have kept every law you are characterised by lawlessness.

NAKEDNESS

The fourth characteristic is nakedness. Luke chapter eight and verse twenty-seven tells us he could not keep his clothes on, he was exposed.

Nothing can cover your sin, nothing can cover it.

You remember Adam tried to sew fig leaves together and make himself an apron to cover up his sin, but God saw his sin. You cannot hide your sin from God. Man, sin will out. I tell you at the end of the day all sin will be exposed. Maybe you think you have got it all nicely put away. Maybe you think, like Achan, you have buried it in the centre of your tent and no one will ever find it. You have it all covered up, and it is all forgotten, and it is locked in the cupboard of memory and you have thrown away the key. Do not believe it, God will discover to you your nakedness in the day of judgment. What a day that will be, when every sin that men have committed will rise up to confront them at the judgment bar of God.

Praise God, on that day none of my sins will be exposed. Thank God they are all gone in the Blood of Christ. Gone forever, that is what God can do for you.

Here was a man and his fourth characteristic was nakedness.

RESTLESSNESS

The fifth characteristic, look at verse five, "And always, night and day, he was in the mountains, and in the tombs, crying." Restlessness! There is no rest for the wicked, they are like the troubled sea that cannot rest. "There is no peace, saith my God, to the wicked."

You say, "I am not too bad. I have no trouble with my conscience." Your conscience will waken some day.

There was a man in this town of Ballymena, I knew him well. And when he was a young boy he committed a terrible crime. He had not a qualm of conscience, he had no disturbance. He lived until he was over fifty years of age and his conscience never disturbed him. He was well known and he was undisturbed. After he turned fifty his conscience awoke and my, what an awakening it was. I sat with that man down in 16 Waveney Road, in my father's home, and that man wept and sobbed and cried until his frame shook as if a great hand had him by the scruff of the neck and was shaking the heart out of him. He had an awakened conscience. He said, "O, that I had never committed that sin. What a fool I was in my boyhood to put my hand to such a crime. If I had only known now that I am fifty I would have hell on earth I would never have done it." And for weeks that man felt the pangs of hell in his soul and body. I did my best to comfort him with the comfort of the gospel but there seemed no light in the midst of his hell's midnight. And one day, thank God, the peace of God came and his great sin was covered in the Blood. He entered into peace with God through Jesus Christ. I shall remember that man until my dying day. What a thing it is when conscience wakes up.

Your conscience, sir, will wake up one day. If it does not wake in time, it certainly will wake up in God's eternity. Down in hell every sinner feels the pangs of an awakened conscience. It is the serpent that never dies, it is the worm that never dies, it is the fire that is never quenched.

This man, night and day, was filled with restlessness. (Mark five and verse five.) Perhaps you know a little about that. You have run, sinner, from one pleasure to another have you not? You have run from one house of sin to another house of sin. You have run to one iniquity after another. You have tried to get some rest. You have tried to get some peace, but peace will not come. Why? Because your are a sinner. There is no peace for sinners. There is no peace from sin for unrepentant sinners.

MADNESS

Look at verse five again. He was a madman. He cut himself with stones, for he was mad.

I want to tell you, every sinner who is going to hell is touched with the madness of the pit. It is only a madman who would go to hell. It is only a man out of his real senses and every sinner is possessed to a degree with the devil.

In a meeting one night I said that and a man said to me afterwards, "I do not believe you." I said, "You turn to Ephesians chapter two and it says of the believers, 'And you hath He quickened, who were dead in trespasses and sins; Wherein in time past ye walked according to the course of this world, according to the prince of the power of the air, the spirit that now worketh in the children of disobedience.'" So every sinner to a degree is possessed with the devil. That is why you are a fool, friend. Any man who rejects Christ is a fool. The man that goes to hell is a fool. The man who turns his back on Heaven is a fool. Madness! That is the characteristic of a sinner. I hope you are having a look at yourself man. You thought you were not a bad fellow. Maybe you thought you could stand muster. Oh, you have got all these characteristics, deadness, uncleanness, lawlessness, nakedness, restlessness, madness.

Tell me, who can do a job here? Man tried and man failed. Man tried to bind him with fetters, put the rule of law on him and failed completely. "Neither could any man tame him." No man can save the human soul. No power on earth can do anything for the sinner, but Jesus can do it.

THE DESTRUCTION OF SATAN

I want to talk about the destruction of Satan. You know how it came about? It came about with the appearance of Jesus. Jesus came on the job. It is a great thing when the Lord comes on the job, because something happens. The Lord has the first word. But I want you to notice that when Jesus came on the job, the sinner was automatically and magnetically drawn to Him. Oh, there is drawing power in Christ: "I, if I be lifted up from the earth, will draw all men unto me." Lord Jesus draw men to yourself tonight! Make that the prayer of our hearts, that out into this meeting may flow from the Cross of Christ the magnetism of Jesus drawing men to Christ. If you do not make contact with Christ you are lost.

Jesus had visited the country of the Gadarenes and if this man had never made contact with Jesus he would still have been a lost soul. But he was drawn mysteriously, supernaturally, wonderfully and, praise God, eternally to Jesus.

Is it not wonderful when the sinner meets with Christ the devil has got to go. He cannot abide in the heart when the Lord Jesus Christ is around.

I want you to look at this chapter, it is a series of prayers. Some prayers are not answered because they are not according to God's will. There is a prayer in verse ten, "And he besought him much that he would not send them away out of the country."

The old devil wants away from Jesus. He cannot stand up to the Lord's presence. My, when the Lord comes the devil has to go.

I used to tell them in church that every Sunday morning the devil gets up early and he sends off his devils to do his job. And he used to send a wee devil up the Ravenhill Road and he would say, "Now you look after Paisley's congregation. There are not many of them. They will not do any harm. They are nice, orthodox, fundamentalist people. Watch them, See that they do not do any harm." And one morning the fire of God fell on my church and that wee devil got the biggest hiding he ever got. Man, when he got back to his father the devil, he was almost torn asunder. The old devil said, "What happened you?" He replied, "Oh, I will not go back there again. Something has happened in that church." And man, something had happened! After two days and two nights of prayer, God baptised some of us with real power and things started to happen. Sinners started to get saved, God's people started to rejoice. I like to think when the devil is doing the job now, he has to send a whole battalion up the Ravenhill Road to keep a bit of order. And thank God they flee, Hallelujah! And they are back every Sunday saying, "It is no good devil. They are still getting saved there."

Man, I am sure the old devil sent a few wee consumptive devils to the Town Hall at the beginning of these meetings. And he said, "Now do not be worrying. It will be just another wee evangelistic campaign and nothing will happen." And some of the devils said, "I am not so sure. You know those people have been praying. Maybe something will happen." After the first day in this hall the devil got a good hiding. Sinners came down this aisle and people got saved, and you know what the devil is doing? He is counting up his family now. He says, "I have lost one hundred and thirty-nine children. I will have no children left if it keeps on like this."

Oh, when Jesus comes, the devil has to go. I have seen Jesus come to a home. I am thinking of a home now where a man was a tyrant, a drunkard, an immoral man, an evil-speaking man, a vile man. And when he went home, his wife hastily retreated to the bedroom and locked the door and huddled in a corner as he cursed in his cups and his blasphemy. One day, thank God, that man (they called him Jack) got gloriously saved. When he came home, and when his wife saw him coming she ran upstairs, as she always did, and got the wee ones into the bedroom and locked the door. He came up the stairs and he called her by her Christian name, (he had not called her that for many a day). He said, "You need not fear, you have got a new husband. I have found Jesus."

She did not believe him. And after a while she opened the door and that big man just stood there and wept. And he said, "I have been a bad husband to you. I have been a bad father to the children that God gave me. I have wrecked and I have cursed and I have almost destroyed you. But in coming days I will make it up tenfold." I was in that man's home not so long ago and, man, the wife is waiting for him now when he comes home. The children are happy to be in their dad's company. Why? Jesus has come! That is why.

Man, it is a great thing when the Lord comes. He destroys the devil.

PRAYERS

The Lord did not answer that first prayer. He did not send them out of the country. He was going to give them a swimsuit instead.

We come to verses twelve and thirteen, "And all the devils besought Him, saying, Send us into the swine, that we may enter into them. And forthwith Jesus gave them leave." He answered that prayer. Why? Because he wanted to put the unclean into the unclean. Light produces light, so the Lord answered that prayer. That was one of the devil's prayers the Lord answered. You did not know that the devil's prayers are answered. Yes! That is a prayer the devil uttered that God answered. It is a wonderful Book this Bible.

Look at verses seventeen and eighteen, there is another prayer: "And they began to pray Him to depart out of their coasts."

Do you not see, friend, when the Lord starts working the ungodly do not like it. They say, "Lord Jesus, go away." And the Lord goes away. It is a very dangerous thing to tell the Lord to go away.

I had a young woman listened to my preaching in the early days of my ministry, and she was under deep conviction of sin. And I remember as the people got saved, she used to weep and tremble. Then one Sunday evening she came back to the service and I noticed a tremendous change. She was no more concerned, frivolity and lightness had overtaken her. At the end of the service I called her into the prayer room and I said, "What has happened to you? Last Sunday you were concerned, you wept, you were moved, but you did not come. There is a great change." She said, "You are right. As I went home last Sunday night I knew I should have taken Christ as my Saviour. There was a voice speaking within me saying, 'Come to Jesus and forsake the world.' I went home, I could not eat any supper, I went to bed and pulled the blankets over my ears and tried to quench that voice, but it became louder and louder, 'Come to Jesus, forsake the world.' In the middle of the night I could stick it no longer and I got out of my bed and knelt down and I said, 'Holy Ghost leave me. Quit speaking to me. Do not speak again.' And suddenly the voice stopped. I have had peace ever since and I will never be back to church, for I realise tonight that this is no place for me. I am not a bit interested." ("They desired Him to depart out of their coasts.") That is nearly thirty years ago, and to this day that young woman has never felt a pang, as far as I know, about the things of God or eternity. Does she carry in her body a damned soul that has committed the unpardonable sin? I do not know, God only knows that.

To pray to God to leave you, man! He will answer it. He will leave you. And some of you have been mighty near to it these past nights. You have been saying "Lord, I am not coming. I am not coming down the aisle. I am not putting up my hand. I am not going to be saved." Take care, there may come a day that you will want to be saved and there will be no salvation for you. You say, "What are you talking about preacher?" I am talking about what God is talking about. He says, "Because I have called and ye have refused. I have stretched out my hand and no man regarded it. Some day ye shall call and I will refuse. I will laugh at your calamity and I will mock when your fear cometh." Listen, a mocking God in Heaven and a damned soul in hell. Is there anything more tragic than that? Take care it is not you friend, take care it is not you!

Here is another prayer that was not answered. It is the same man, verses eighteen and nineteen, he says "Lord, I just want to be with you."

Now there are things that we want but the Lord will not give us. It was a proper prayer. It is a nice prayer to want to be with Jesus. You see that man had duties. And the duties were that he should go home and tell. And the Lord said, "No, you are not coming with me. You have a job to do, you have to go home."

Christmas Evans, the great Welsh preacher, pictures the day when that man came home. He had been driven from his home, his wife and family had asked the men in the village to put him out. He was mad, they asked them to drive him from the village. One day with stones and sticks the villagers took him and they hammered him and they beat him until they drove him to the tombs and the mountains. They warned him never to come near the place again. And one day on the outskirts of that village there arose a cry. Now, he walked as a man who had seen the angels of God. When he came to the home, he stopped and called his wife by her name, and he said, "Something has happened. I have met Jesus of Nazareth." That woman with trembling fingers undid the barricades of the door. She looked out at a new man in Christ.

Christmas Evans says: "What a happy day that was in Decapolis. He published the great things that the Lord had done for him."

"Oh, what a change since Jesus came into this town,
The devil has been wearing a frown,
Many hearts have been changed,
Many homes re-arranged,
Since Jesus came into our town."

I trust he will come into this Town Hall tonight. He will change a lot of things, He will change homes and change hearts.

DELIVERANCE

Let me show you the deliverance of the sinner. I have shown you the degradation of sin, the destruction of Satan, let me show you the deliverance of the sinner.

Three things, he is in his right place, sitting. The restlessness has gone. He has got peace at last, he is not running around the mountains now. He is sitting, peace has come.

I wish I could tell you what the peace of Jesus means to me. I have been in a few tight places in my day, I have been in jail twice. I am an unrepentant jailbird, I have no repentance. If I had to do the same thing at the General Assembly I would do it again. If I had to do the same thing in Armagh, I would do it again. Yes! I have no repentance. I am glad that I did it, I am not a Johnny-come-lately loyalist. I have been in this fight for a long time, indeed all my days. I laugh at some voices that are raised today. I wonder where they were when the first shot was fired. They were probably not out of their nappies, still sucking the bottle, and they did not get enough orange juice anyway! I have been around a few corners, and I want to tell you that the best thing you can have is the peace of Jesus. Rest from sin. Rest from fear of the past, and fear of the present and fear of the future. Blessed rest in Jesus. This man is sitting. He is not running around any more. Thank God, he is sitting down. The whole quest of restlessness is over, he is in the right place.

He is in the right apparel, he is now clothed. When the Lord meets you, He clothes you with a beautiful garment of righteousness. It covers all the uncleanness. How beautiful the saints appear to Jesus, for they are covered in His own garments. He has brought me to His own wardrobe, He has taken out His best suit and He has put it upon my poor, sin-scarred, sin-soiled, sin-stained body. I am covered, clothed in the righteousness of Christ, Hallelujah! What a clothing, to be clothed in the righteousness of Christ.

Look at the other thing, he is in his right mind. Yes! What does it say? It says that he is sitting and clothed and in his right mind. The madness has gone, he is no longer a fool. He is a wise man, he has seen the folly of his ways. He has said, "My old companions fare ye well, I will not go with you to hell, I mean with Jesus now to dwell, Won't you come?" He said farewell to the old way of doing things. He is a surprise to himself.

If I had told you a fortnight ago that you would be a changed man tonight and you would be at the prayer meetings at six in the morning to pray, you would have said, "Paisley, you are a madman." But you are a surprise to yourself. Man, there have been changed homes. One brother was praying the other night. He said, "Lord, I am floating." I said, "Float upward brother. Do not be floating down. Just float upward." Amen! He had felt the thrill. Oh, you laugh! But I could not explain to you the thrill of being saved. Man, what a thrill to be in your right mind, to be clothed, sitting at the feet of Jesus.

Tell me, is that where you are? Are you out in the mountains wild and bare tonight, away from the tender Shepherd's care?

Look at the demands of the Saviour. He said, "Go home and testify. Tell your friends. If ye believe in your heart and confess with your mouth, ye shall be saved."

The man went home, and oh the delights. I would love to have heard that man preach. Some day we will hear his testimony! It will be a great day when we meet him. I will say, "I preached about you friend, about the devil in a pigskin swimsuit." We will sit down with that old sinner who was once possessed with the devil, the preacher will sit down under the evergreen tree that grows in the midst of the paradise of God, and we will talk it o'er together by and by. What a place Heaven is. At times I am homesick for the Glory Land. When you are battling on here and the road to heaven is rough, and there are thorns and cutting stones by the way, it is not an easy road we are travelling to Heaven, and many are the thorns by the way. But some day the gates will open, and we will say good-bye to earth with its sins and we will say, "Welcome to Heaven." And God will say, "Welcome Home" and we will see Jesus. Man, what a shout I am going to give when I see Jesus!

If you are in Heaven it will be good that you will have celestial ears, for the drums would burst with the shout I am going to give when I see my lovely Christ. The One Who went up Calvary's Hill with a cross on His back and a pang in His soul. The One Who bore my burden on His own Body to the tree. I am going to clasp His feet and feel the imprint of the nails; and gaze upon that face until glory, glory, thrills my celestial glorified soul. We will bathe in the fulness of God. Man, what a day that will be. Eye hath not seen, ear hath not heard, neither hath it entered into the heart of man what God hath prepared for those that love Him. You my poor foolish sinner, are choosing darkness instead of that wonderful light. You are choosing the dungeon instead of the palace. Damnation instead of glorification of the saints.

> *"I am going Home to Glory soon,*
> *To see the City Bright,*
> *To walk the golden streets of heaven,*
> *And bask in God's own Light,*
> *But you my friend are out of Christ,*
> *You are held by many a snare,*
> *I cannot leave you lost and lone,*
> *I want you over there."*

I tell you, I want you over there. Come on friend, start for Heaven. Get saved tonight. Get God's peace. Then it will be brightness today, and greater brightness tomorrow and exceeding brightness for evermore.

AMEN AND AMEN!

7 The talkback
which ended all talkbacks

THE TWENTY-SECOND CHAPTER of Matthew's Gospel, the last verse of the chapter reads, *"And no man was able to answer Him a word, neither durst any man from that day forth ask him any more questions."* Here we have the Talkback that ended all talkbacks.

A TEST DAY IN OUR LORD'S MINISTRY

This chapter is one of the most interesting chapters in the history of our Lord's sojourn on earth, because it highlights one day in His public ministry.

It is interesting to note that when the Jews chose their Passover Lamb, for fourteen days, two periods of seven days each, the Lamb was under the closest possible scrutiny. It was examined to see if it had any flaw, any imperfection or any blemish, for it must, if it was to be fit for the Passover Sacrifice, be without blemish and without spot.

He, Who is the anti-type of all the typical Passover lambs in Jewish history, our Lord and Saviour Jesus Christ, is here approaching to His great act of reconciliation on the cross, and in this period before His Passion he is under the closest possible scrutiny.

In this chapter we have His critics examining Him, focusing their attention upon Him, seeking in every way possible to find some flaw in the perfection of His character, in the integrity of His Person and in the uprightness and righteousness of His speech.

In this day in Matthew's Gospel, chapter 22, there is a concentration - a conspiracy between the three groups that made up society in our Lord's day, to find some flaw, to penetrate the purity of Christ's armour.

THE THREE GROUPS

First the *Herodians*, the politicians of our Lord's Day, came with their question concerning the relationship between Church and State. The Lord answered them to their confusion of face and to the astonishment of the listening multitudes.

Second came the liberal theologians of the day - *the Sadducees* who denied the resurrection either of spirit or of body, and they put to Him a question - a theological question on the resurrection from the dead. Once again the Lord Jesus Christ showed from the Scriptures that God is not the God of the dead but of the living.

Notice He did not say *"I was the God of Abraham"* (Abraham having been long since dead when He spoke to Moses at the bush), *"I was the God of Isaac. I was the God of Jacob,"* but He said, *"I AM the God of Abraham, Isaac and Jacob."* The spirit of Abraham was not in the tomb, neither were the spirits of Isaac and of Jacob.

Thirdly there came the Pharisees, and they wanted Christ to pick out of the three hundred and sixty-five commandments of the Torah what was the principal commandment. Jesus Christ, not dealing with details but annunciating the principle said, *"Thou shalt love the Lord thy God with all thy heart, and with all thy strength and with all thy mind."* And that love must not only be manifested to God but it must have its counterpart in loving one's neighbour as one's self.

THE TURNING OF THE TABLES

Suddenly the tables were turned. Christ looked at His opposers and said, "hear me, I have a question to ask. What think ye of Christ, whose

Son is He?" And they immediately answered, "The Son of David." And He said, "How can that be? For do not your own Scriptures teach you that David said himself that the Lord said unto my Lord. If He is David's Lord how can He be David's Son?"

And, of course, these Pharisees, not knowing the mystery of the Person of the Messiah, that Messiah, when He came, would be both God and Man, the Word made flesh dwelling upon this earth, and they, rejecting Christ as God's Messiah, were put to silence. After that no other question was put to the Master, and he proceeded on His way to the Death of the Cross.

WHAT THINK YE OF CHRIST?

I want to ask that question of you. What think ye of Christ? Could I underscore for a moment that Christ is here speaking of the heart, *"As a man thinketh in his heart so is he."*

This is not an outward profession of what men think of Christ, this is the real thought of the innermost heart, the quick of the man's being, the depths of the human soul. Right down in the spring of your life what do you think of Jesus Christ? That is the most vital question that could be asked of you.

SOME OPINION

Everyone in this house tonight has some opinion of Jesus Christ. You have heard about Him. You have read about Him, His Life, His History, His Words, His Deeds, His Death and His Resurrection.

The facts of His sojourn on earth as recorded in the Gospels are well known to you, and somewhere in the depths of your heart you think something of Him. Upon that secret thought, upon that secret relationship between you and God Incarnate in the flesh, hangs your destiny and your Eternity.

If you have wrong thoughts about Christ and a wrong relationship with Him, if you are found in a state of rebellion against Him, then your life not only will be marred, but your eternity as well.

If you think rightly of Christ in keeping with the teaching of the Authoritative Word of God then you are building on a foundation that cannot be moved. "On Christ the solid Rock I stand, All other ground is sinking sand."

BASE YOUR VERDICT ON EVIDENCE

Now in coming to a right opinion concerning Christ, it is only right that you base your verdict upon evidence, upon knowledge, upon understanding. The evidence brought by witnesses to you. So tonight we will turn this house into a Court room. We will turn this pulpit into a witness box, and we will bring to the pulpit certain witnesses who shall witness to us as eyewitnesses of the Christ of God. Let us then hear the evidence. Let us weigh it. Let us test it. Let us find out the weight of that evidence, and then let us make that great verdict upon which our soul's eternity rests and hangs.

Now in every court case there are those who are called to witness from the camp of the enemy. Those who put forth their witness in opposition to the person on trial. Then in every case there are those called who put forth their evidence from the friendly camp, those who are convinced of the righteousness of the person on trial and the righteousness of his cause.

FIRST HOSTILE WITNESS

First of all we will call some witnesses from the enemy camp. First we invite to the witness box the *Pharisees* themselves.

Now, of course, they are prejudiced, they have already declared themselves in opposition to the Lord Jesus. They have made it clear times without number that they neither accept His Word nor His message nor His authority. They say He is linked with Beelzebub. His power is from Hell. His strength is satanic. His whole claims are bogus and He Himself is a fraud.

So there is no doubt that these witnesses are hostile witnesses motivated by their prejudices against the Son of God.

So when they enter the witness box we remind them of their prejudices. We remind them of their opposition and then we remind them of their final statement which they made under the shadow of the Cross. Before God took the curtains of darkness and wrapped them around the scene of the Blood-stained tree of Calvary, just before the light was extinguished and the darkness fell. We remind them of what they said: *"He saved others."* That is some statement, is it not, coming not from a friend, coming not from someone convinced of our Lord's authority, compassion and power, but from His sworn enemies? "He saved others." But let us finish it, " *Himself He cannot save."*

In that witness we have the very heart of the Gospel revelation. We come to the very core of the mystery of the Gospel of grace. If Jesus Christ saves Himself He cannot save others. If Jesus Christ saves us He cannot save Himself. The unsaved Saviour becomes the Saviour of sinners. If He be a saved Saviour He saves no one but Himself.

You see, the Cross is one of the mysteries of substitution. Someone must be found Pure enough and True enough and Powerful enough to take upon Himself our sins and in an act of reconciling Death to purge away their guilt by the shedding of His own life's Blood. "He was wounded," says the old prophet Isaiah, "for our transgressions. He was bruised for our iniquities, the chastisement of our peace was upon Him, and by His stripes we are healed."

SECOND HOSTILE WITNESS

Let us bring another enemy to the witness box, the man who betrayed Christ, *the Iscariot*, the Traitor, Judas of ill memory and shame.

Did he not plan and scheme to use his friendship and betray the Son of God with an act of affection - with a kiss?

Did he not seize willingly the blood money - the thirty pieces of silver - to do that terrible deed?

Now he stands in the witness box. What ill word will Judas speak of Jesus? What ill testimony will he give concerning the Christ of God?

As he stands here in his guilt and in his shame, the marks of his treason and the scars of his treachery upon his person, he exclaims, *"I have betrayed Innocent Blood."*

What? Judas, is Christ innocent? Is this Person, whom you betrayed for thirty pieces of silver, innocent? Did you actually use that kiss of affection to identify an Innocent Person to be handed over for the awful crucifying of the Cross?

"I have betrayed Innocent, Innocent, Innocent, Innocent Blood."

His testimony rings down through the Ages, the testimony of an enemy, a traitor, a man who received the blood money.

Before he goes out to commit suicide he leaves his last will and testimony - a testimony to the fact that the Blood of Christ is Innocent Blood.

THIRD HOSTILE WITNESS

Let us dismiss Judas and bring the Judge himself who sat on the judgment throne, who pronounced sentence upon Christ, who ordered Him to be scourged, crowned with thorns, tormented and then led out and upon that tree of death to hang stark naked in agony and shame, *Pilate* the appointee of the Imperial Caesar, Pilate the Governor of Judea, Pilate the representative of the Roman power. I say to Pilate, "Thou didst judge the Galilean. Thou didst sentence Him to die. Thou didst see to His scourging. With thine own hand thou didst write His accusation to be hung above His head upon that Cross."

"Yes I did but I must say that three times I reiterated my personal conviction, and three times I said to His accusers, *'I find no fault in Him.'*" No fault in the prisoner and yet you condemned Him: No fault in Christ, yet you ordered Him to be scourged. No fault in Jesus yet you allowed your soldiers to crown Him with thorns, to buffet Him, to spit upon Him, to mock Him, to make Him the object of shame and misery in that place called Gabbatha, and then thou didst order Him to die." *"I find no fault in Him at all,"* Pilate yet again exclaims.

FOURTH HOSTILE WITNESS

The last witness from the enemy's camp is the *soldier* who helped to do the dastardly deed, the man who stripped Christ of His garments, the man who took the hammer and pierced His hands with nails and His feet with spikes.

I hear the sound of the hammer swung low, they are nailing my Lord to the tree! What does this soldier say? "You did take His raiment. You did put Him down upon that tree. You did fasten His hands with the nails and His feet with the spikes. You lifted up that Cross. You knocked its butt into the hole in the ground and drove the stones to hold it firmly in place."

"Yes I did. After the light there was darkness, and after the darkness there was light, and in that second light the Christ did cry from His Cross one word, 'FINISHED'.

"As He uttered it the whole earth groaned, the rocks were rent, and as I stood, there was borne upon my soul this great conviction, and I uttered it, and I utter it again this night, *Surely this is the Son of God.* Surely this is the Son of God."

TWO FRIENDLY WITNESSES

Having heard these four witnesses from the enemy camp, let me briefly bring you two witnesses from the camp of His friends,

Let us call the apostle *Peter*, Peter the fisherman, Peter the follower, bold blustering Peter, and yet how sadly we must add, blaspheming Peter. With oaths and curses he denied his Lord in the hour of dark temptation.

He comes to the witness box in penitence because his life is now forever shadowed by his blasphemy. The sorrow of that dread hour when one servant girl caused him to publicly reject any knowledge of the Blessed Lord Jesus Christ *will always be with him.* In penitence and in pardon he stands and I say to him, "Peter, you once denied your Lord." "I did," he sobs. "But what think ye of Christ?"

Peter replies, *"Neither is there salvation in any other, for there is none other name under heaven, given among men, whereby we must be saved* - Thou art the Christ, the Son of the Living God."

To Peter's testimony we would add the testimony of *Thomas*. Thomas, the man who in harshness said, "Except I take my finger and poke it into the print in My Lord's hand. Except I take this fist and thrust it into the great gash in His side left by the spear, I will not believe." Thomas too is shadowed by those harsh words so easily spoken, but in his penitence and pardon he comes to bear witness to His Lord. "Thomas, what thinkest thou of Jesus Christ," he affirms, "My Lord and my God."

A GREAT CLOUD OF WITNESSES

Of course we could fill the witness box with men who step out of the pages of Old Testament history, of men who step out of contemporary society and they all could bear witness to the fact that Jesus Christ is the Son of God, the Saviour of the world.

They have met Him and He has met with them. They have received Him and they have been received by Him. In their heart there is this testimony - the testimony that Jesus Christ is their Lord and their personal Saviour. They know Whom they have believed, and like the crowds in Decapolis they have seen Him at work and cried out, "He has done all things well."

WHAT WILL YOUR VERDICT BE?

"What think ye of Christ?" This night before the Court room is closed, a verdict will be given.

Every man and every woman, every boy and every girl in this house will make a verdict.

What think ye of Christ? Whose Son is He? You will either confess Him as your Lord, receive Him as your Master and Saviour, cleanse your sins away in His most Precious Blood and leave this house of God in His company, or you will leave this house having passed a verdict of opposition, rejection, denial and blasphemy against Him, counting His Blood an unholy thing, treading on His Holy Body and doing despite to the Spirit of grace.

What will your verdict be? Upon that verdict rests, not only the life that now is, but the life that is hereafter. Upon this verdict will rest your future, your attitude to life, your attitude to your fellows, your attitude to relationships that are personal and public, your attitude to all things, and especially to the things that are unseen.

Remember the things that are seen are only temporal, but the things that are unseen are eternal.

I pray God this night that every man and woman who hears my voice, in the silence of their heart will bring in the right verdict and will kneel down with Thomas and say in penitence, "My Lord and my God." In that word of penitence there shall come from Him that word of pardon and life everlasting.

There is another verse. It is the question of Pilate, and you can ask yourself this question now, "What shall I do then with Jesus which is called Christ?" You will do something with Him this night. See that you do the right thing.

AMEN AND AMEN!

8 The house appointed *for all living*

MY TEXT IS Job 30:23, *"For I know that thou wilt bring me to death, and to the house appointed for all living."*

Something we all know but something we don't like to think or discourse upon - death. Old Job had been brought into the valley of death's shadows. His frail tabernacle was rudely shaken by the tempests of destruction. His soul melted in the fires of tremendous affliction. The chains of his sickness secured him firmly in their galling grasp. His bones and flesh, pierced with the keen edge of awful pain in the night season, forced him to exclaim, "My sinews take no rest." The bony fingers of death had him by the throat so that he declares "It bindeth me about as the collar of my coat."

As the frail tent of life's mortality seemed ready to collapse, the patriarch tested by bitter experience could say, "For I know that thou wilt bring me to death and to the house appointed for all living." He had learned this ancient lesson of truth in the school of his own experience, "Dust thou art and unto dust thou shalt return."

In order that we may all consider our latter end and be wise unto eternal salvation we will expound the solemn subject of death as set forth in Job's metaphor, "the house appointed for all living."

I. A HOUSE OF DARK SHADOWS

The house appointed for all living is first of all a house of dark shadows. O Death, thy dark shadow lies ever across mortals. At the commencement of life's journey, at the starting point of our pilgrimage, death is near. There is

DEATH'S DARK SHADOW AT OUR BIRTH

As soon as we begin to live we begin to die. Our mother went down into death in order to bring us forth. We were all begotten as it were on the doorstep of the house appointed for all living. Yes, we were not only born to live but were also born to die. How many birthdays have been deathdays! How many have gone straight from the cradle to the coffin!

There is

DEATH'S DARK SHADOW AS WE LIVE

We grow up amongst dying men and women. We mortals can never get away from the shadow of this house appointed for all living. In our days of joy its shadows subdue us. In our days of leisure death is not an absentee. We lift the paper. It has its death column. We go down the street. A funeral confronts us. Every city, every town, every village and every district have their graveyards. Death is never too far from any one of us. Yes, and at the end of this journey there is

DEATH'S DARK SHADOW AS WE DIE

The gloom is going to deepen. As we have had our sunrise and midday so we will have our sunset and midnight. When we approach to enter the great house appointed for all living the darker will be its shadows upon us. Perhaps for you the shadow has already deepened and alas, you know it not. Unprepared, unregenerate, unconverted soul, remember there is but a step between you and death and that death, eternal death - the death that never dies.

To you, dear, unsaved friend, there will be

DEATH'S DARK SHADOW FOR EVERMORE

Your death will but lead to the second death, damnation in the lake of fire. The dark shadow of physical dissolution will give place to the black shadow of eternal damnation. Before you, soul without hope in Christ, is nought but the blackness of darkness for ever. Verily, the house appointed for all living is a house of dark shadows.

II. A HOUSE OF DISTRESSING SEPARATIONS

Death is the great separator. It rends asunder the strongest links ever forged on earth. It respecteth not the marriage tie but with desecrating finger unlooses ruthlessly the marriage bonds. It heeds not the cries of children as it ushers their parents down its long dark corridors. It strikes at homes and leaves the family unit in ruins. Husbands must leave their wives at its dread command. Wives must forsake their husbands at its orders. Children must be rent asunder from the parents and parents from their children when death speaks. It is the great divider. It cleaves the soul from the body, the immortal from the mortal, the spiritual from the physical and the eternal from the earthly. O death, what rents thy cold fingers have made! What chasms thou hast dug! What bonds thou hast broken! What distresses thou hast caused! What breaks thou hast made! Thou sparest not, but cruelly divideth the mortal sons of Adam's accursed race! Ah, friend you will not leave your sins, but death will separate you from them. You will not forsake the world but death will force you from it. You will not separate from your vile companions but death will smash that cherished relationship. No human bond too strong but death can break it. No human union too close but death can smash it. No human relationship too sacred but death can destroy it. There is only one bond, not human but divine, which death can never destroy. That bond, that union, that relationship, is found in Christ and in Christ alone.

"Who shall separate us from the love of Christ? Shall tribulation, or distress, or persecution, or famine, nor nakedness, or peril or sword? As it is written, for thy sake we are killed all the day long: we are accounted as sheep for the slaughter. Nay in all these things we are more than conquerors through him that loved us. For I am persuaded, that neither death, nor life, nor angels, nor principalities, nor powers, nor things present, nor things to come, nor height, nor depth, nor any other creature, shall be able to separate us from the love of God, which is in Christ Jesus our Lord." Romans 8:35-39

Are you in Christ? Has everlasting love bound you to heaven eternally? By the new birth have you entered into this eternal relationship that naught can sever? If not, why not? Remember, the house appointed for all living is the house of distressing separations and the Divider Death is sole master there.

III. A HOUSE OF DEVASTATING STRENGTH

How strong is this house appointed for all living! Its massive walls have stood unshaken as centuries crumbled into oblivion. Its chains hold fast its occupants and its great iron gates open not to the commands of men. Man, proud man, sinful man, wilful man, talks of conquering space but he cannot conquer death. All are subject to its power. All must obey its awful sceptre. Queen Elizabeth the First of England shrieked as death approached her, "All my possessions for a moment of time." No time was granted her, for queens must die. The vile Voltaire who blasphemously named Christ "the wretch" said to his doctors, "I'll give you all I have if you save my life six months." His doctor said, "You can't live six hours." Soon death struck him, for infidels must die. Yes, and if you walk through any graveyard you will find quite short and narrow graves there, for children too must die.

O Death! Thou great invisible,
Pale monarch of the unending Past,
Who shall thy countless trophies tell,
Or when shall be the last!
By thee high thrones to earth are flung -
By thee the sword and sceptre rust -
By thee the beautiful and young
Lie mouldering in the dust.
Into thy cold and faded reign
All glorious things of earth depart;
The fairest forms are early slain,
And quenched the fiery heart.
But in yon world thou hast not been,

Where joy can fade, nor beauty fall:
O mightiest of the things unseen,
Save One that rulest all!

Oh, what power has death. With one fell stroke it can turn the healthy body into a corpse. With but one blow it can lay the mightiest low. How quickly it can turn the house of rejoicing into the house of mourning, the house of merriment into the house of bereavement. How swiftly it can transform the song into the sigh. How, frail man, can you battle with such a foe? With the old prophet let me ask of you the question, *"If thou hast run with the footmen, and they have wearied thee, then how canst thou contend with horses? and if in the land of peace, wherein thou trustedst, they wearied thee, then how will thou do in the swelling of Jordan"* Jeremiah 12:5

Only Christ is a match for the last great enemy, death. On the Cross Christ, Emmanuel, Victor of Calvary, destroyed him who has the power of death, that is to say the devil, and delivered them who through fear of death were all their lifetime subject to bondage.

Through Him and through Him alone you can be completely delivered from the devastating strength of death and be enabled to shout at the grinning monster, "O death where is thy sting?"

Only by being a partaker of eternal life can you escape the tremendous power of the king of terrors. Hear now, the sweet and glorious message of the gospel, "For God so loved the world, that He gave His only begotten Son, that whosoever believeth on Him should not perish but have everlasting life." John 3:16

IV. A HOUSE OF DESPAIRING SORROWS

The house appointed for all living, is, to those who contemplate its sombre structure, a house of despairing sorrows. Death is ever an enemy and even to those in Christ who have only to face the shadow and not the substance there must, because of the necessity of human circumstances, be sorrow.

THE SORROW OF DYING

The sorrow of those who die in Christ is the sorrow of saying farewell. It is only natural that we should long to remain with our families and our friends. With Paul we can say, "It is needful for me to abide in the flesh." Nevertheless, the Christian must say farewell. The house of despairing sorrows lies in his path to the land of no sorrow and care, and through its foreboding portals he must pass on his journey upward to glory. With young Hugh McKail the Scottish martyr we will have to say sorrowfully, "Farewell, father and mother, friends and relations; farewell the world and all delights; farewell meat and drink; farewell sun, moon and stars." We shall continue joyfully, however, with that same dear warrior. "Welcome, God and Father, welcome, sweet Jesus Christ, the Mediator of the new covenant; welcome, blessed Spirit of Grace and God of all consolation; welcome, glory, welcome, eternal life and welcome death."

What must be the sorrow of the soul who dies with no welcome on his lips? For him it is farewell forever. Separation for all eternity. An isolation which never ends.

THE SORROW OF THOSE LEFT BEHIND

This sorrow is very real. At the grave of His friend Lazarus our Lord Jesus wept. Yes, and at the open graves of our departed loved ones we stand with sad and weeping eyes. How we long for the touch of the vanished hand and the sound of the voice that is still. We sorrow not, as Christians, like those who have no hope but we do really sorrow.

THE SORROW OF THOSE WHO DIE WITHOUT HOPE

What shall we say of those whose sorrow in death is but the prelude to the sorrows of everlasting woe. Alas, my unsaved friend, real sorrow for you will only be beginning to begin when you enter the house appointed for all living, that house of despairing sorrows. What tongue could describe the sorrows of the damned in perdition? Eye hath not seen, ear hath not heard, neither hath it entered into the heart of man what God hath prepared in hell for those who have rejected His Son.

> *There is a place in a black and hollow vault,*
> *Where day is never seen; there shines no sun,*
> *But flaming horror of consuming fires;*
> *A lightless sulphur choked with smoky fogs*
> *Of an infected darkness; in this place*
> *Dwell many thousand thousand sundry sorts*
> *Of never dying deaths; there damned souls*
> *Roar without pity; there are gluttons fed*
> *With toads and adders; there is burning oil*
> *Poured down the drunkard's throat; the usurer*
> *Is forced to sup whole drafts of molten gold.*
> *There is the murderer forever stabbed,*
> *Yet can never die; there lies the wanton*
> *On racks of burning steel, while in his soul*
> *He feels the torment of his raging lust.*

What sorrow! Appetites for sin, but no way to satisfy them. Cravings for iniquities but no possibility of fulfilment. This is eternal sorrow indeed. Will this be your bitter portion forever?

V. A HOUSE OF DEADLY SUMMONS

Note well the divine instrumentality. It is God who brings men to death and to the house appointed for all living. That house is the house of deadly summons. Soon shall the Almighty direct His mighty angel to deliver his death warrant to your soul. Perhaps already the swift messenger has commenced his flight from the everlasting throne. Soon shall his sharp sword of justice drink your blood. Soon shall his arrows of retribution penetrate the armour of your life. Man, you are doomed, and soon, except you repent, you shall be damned.

I would use the burning language of Jonathan Edwards as I plead with you to turn to Christ: "O sinner! consider the fearful danger you are in: it is a great furnace of wrath, a wide and bottomless pit, full of the fire of wrath, that you are held over in the hand of that God, whose wrath is provoked and incensed as much against you, as against many of the damned in hell: you hang by a slender thread, with the flames of divine wrath flashing about it, and ready every moment to singe it, and burn it asunder; and you have no interest in any mediator, and nothing to lay hold of to save yourself, nothing to keep off the flames of wrath, nothing of your own, nothing that you ever have done, nothing that you can do, to induce God to spare you one moment."

> *How shocking must thy summons be, O Death!*
> *To him that is at ease in his possessions.*
> *Who, counting on long years of pleasure here,*
> *is quite unfurnished for that world to come!*
> *In that dread moment, how the frantic soul*
> *Raves round the walls of her clay tenement,*
> *Runs to each avenue, and shrieks for help,*
> *But shrieks in vain! How wistfully she looks*
> *On all she's leaving, now no longer hers!*
> *A little longer, yet a little longer,*
> *Oh, might she stay, to wash her stains,*
> *And fit her for her passage! Mournful sight!*
> *Her very eyes weep blood, and every groan*
> *She heaves is big with horror; but the foe,*
> *Like a staunch murderer, steady to his purpose,*
> *Pursues her close through every lane of life,*
> *Nor misses once the track, but presses on,*
> *Till, forced at last to the tremendous verge,*
> *At once she sinks to everlasting ruin.*

Before the awful warrant is executed flee to Christ. A week's, a day's, an hour's, nay verily a moment's delay could be fatal. Turn ye, oh, turn ye, for why will ye die? May God save you from an unready deathbed and from the worm that never dies and the fire that is never quenched.

9 Unholy water or
the tears of Esau

I WANT TO SPEAK tonight on a character that appears in the Old Testament record. I want to speak upon Esau. Esau's biography is summed up in two verses in the twelfth chapter of the New Testament epistle to the Hebrews. Hebrews chapter 12 and verse 16. *"Lest there be any fornicator, or profane person, as Esau, who for one morsel of meat sold his birthright. For ye know how that afterward, when he would have inherited the blessing, he was rejected, for he found no place of repentance, though he sought it carefully with tears."*

We have five great things, five very sad things, very solemn heartbreaking things about Esau. We have first of all, *His Sale* - "He sold his birthright." Then we have *His Sentence* - "He was rejected." Then we have *His Search* - "He found no place of repentance." *His Sobs* - "Though he sought it carefully with tears." *His Soul* - "He was a fornicator and a profane person."

I want to speak upon Esau's sale, his sentence, his search, his sobs and his soul.

ESAU'S SALE - "He sold his birthright"

Esau's sale, he sold his birthright. What a fool he was. One day for a morsel of meat he put to auction, and he sold the greatest thing that he had, his birthright, as the elder son of Isaac. Every man born into this world has got a glorious birthright. He has a right to listen to the glorious gospel of God's redemption, and he has a right to bow and acknowledge the claims of Jesus Christ, and receive the mercy, and receive the forgiveness of heaven's peace and pardon.

But, alas, today men sell their birthright, the right to hear, the right to accept, the right to experience, and the right to know God's glorious salvation. What are you selling your birthright for?

The Bible says that Esau sold it for one morsel of meat. Many a man is selling heaven for a glass of booze. Many a man is selling heaven for a dance, for an illicit relationship, for an act of lust - for something that's vile and hideous and hellish and damning. What are you selling your birthright for, sinner?

ESAU'S SENTENCE - "He was rejected"

The scripture goes on and it talks about his sentence. These words - they strike the death knell, don't they? He was rejected. The man without Christ, is a reject. Rejected by heaven. Rejected by God. Rejected for all eternity. Rejected in time. Rejected at death. Rejected at the judgment bar. Rejected from heaven and peace forever. Yes, you're a reject if you have rejected Jesus Christ. He was rejected.

Poor Esau, looking for acceptance, but there's no acceptance for him. Looking for a right of audience to the blessing, but there's no right of audience and no blessing for him. Looking for the father's smile, the father's benediction, the father's glory, the father's inheritance and the father's authority, but there are none of these for him.

There is no blessing. There is no audience for him. He was rejected.

My dear sinner friend this evening, what a day that will be when you will feel the full weight of this dread sentence. He was rejected. Why are poor souls yonder in the darkness of eternal despair? Why is hell inhabited with damned souls? Why are there shrieks and groans from the eternal incarceration of souls in the lost caverns of perdition? I will tell you why, it is because they were rejected.

Heaven's door is barred to them. God's palace has no place for them. God's heaven has no room for them. Why? Because they rejected Christ on earth. They spurned Him Who could have saved them. They rejected the One Who could have redeemed them. They turned their back on the only One Who could pardon. They refused to listen and heed the voice that alone could bring them from their awful lost condition, into a position of peace and plenty, and pardon. So they were rejected. How terrible to hear the sentence passed upon you. "You are rejected. Depart from me ye cursed, I never knew you." So much for the sentence.

ESAU'S SEARCH - "Found no place of repentance though he sought it carefully"

What about his search? He searched, he sought, and he cried and he struggled. He planned and he schemed, and he purposed to get back to the old position, but he couldn't reach it. Esau committed the unpardonable sin when he put his birthright up for auction. When he sold it for one morsel of meat. Then the sentence was passed irrevocably, never to be changed, or recalled, or rescinded. He had indeed committed the unpardonable sin.

Oh, he sought a way back, but every avenue was blocked up. He sought a way back, but every door was bolted and barred. He sought a way back, but every road was now impassable. Alas for his poor deceived, deluded, darkened, and already damned soul! There is no way back. No way in. No way up, but a way down, down, down to hell.

My friend, take care, lest the plight of Esau becomes your plight, and lest the condition of Esau becomes the eternal condition of your soul.

ESAU'S SOBS - "with tears"

He not only searched, but friend, he sobbed. Don't you hear the sobs of Esau? He puts his head in his hands and tears run down through his hands to the ground, and I see his figure shaking with the power of deep emotion stirred in its very depths, and he cries, "Father bless me, even me also".

But there is no blessing for him. The opportunity to be saved, to be blessed, has gone. He that is filthy, let him be filthy still. He that is unclean let him be unclean still. The saddest thing is to listen and behold the sobs of a soul for whom there is no mercy. There are tears in hell tonight, but they're unavailing tears. There are prayers in hell tonight, but those prayers are not heard. There are cries to heaven from hell tonight, but those cries are not listened to . God says, "Because I have called, and ye have refused; I have stretched out my hand, and no man regarded; but ye would none of my reproof: Then shall ye call upon me, but I will not answer. They shall seek me early, but they shall not find me. I also will laugh at your calamity; I will mock when your fear cometh."

A sobbing soul on earth or in hell, and a mocking God in the heavens. What a portrait of dark, indescribable tragedy is that. Is that your condition tonight? Oh, my friend, please God for you the time of grace is not concluded. Please God for you the door of mercy still stands ajar. Please God for you the nail pierced hand of Jesus still is outstretched. Please God for you the gracious Spirit is still working, striving in your heart. Please God for you this very night you can be saved from wrath to come, and escape forever the worm that never dies, and the fire that's never quenched. His sobs - the sobs of Esau.

Let those sobs shake your slumbering souls tonight. Let those sobs awaken you to the eternal realities, and the truth and verity of the gospel that I preach. Let those sobs tonight shake you to the very depths of your being. Let those sobs beckon you away from damnation and doom and death. Let those sobs stir you to flee to the cross and find you kneeling in time in penitence at the old tree of Calvary. God help you tonight. His sale - he sold his birthright for one morsel of meat. His sentence - he was rejected. His search - he found no place for repentance. His sobs - he sought it earnestly with tears.

ESAU'S SOUL - "A fornicator, a profane person"

What of his soul? He was a fornicator. He was a profane person. What does that mean? It means he treated holy things as if they were unholy. He treated sacred things shamefully. He put out his fingers and with hands of sacrilege he stained the holy things with the marks of his own unrighteousness. That's what you are doing. You are counting the Holy Blood that Jesus shed as something to be spurned. That is what you are doing. You are treating the Wonderful Saviour as someone to be passed by with a shrug of your shoulders. You are treating the message of salvation as something to be repudiated, and rejected, and sneered at, and made a joke of.

My friend, your soul is like the poor benighted, deceived, debauched, depraved soul of Esau - a profane person. It would be terrible, friend, if the state of your soul this evening became its eternal state, and you settle down eternally in the attitude that you now have to God, and to heaven, and to Christ, and to pardon and to peace. What a terrible thing if your present state is your eternal state, and your Christ rejection is not merely a thing of time, but a thing for all eternity.

May this tragic character from the Old Testament history book challenge you, and make the sale, and the sentence, and the search, and the sobs, and the soul of Esau be a warning to you. God save you from Esau's life, Esau's sin, Esau's sentence, Esau's sobs, and Esau's dark and damnable eternity. May God help you to come and be saved right now.

PRAYER

Heavenly Father, bless the preaching of the Word. Bless this solemn Word to the hearts of men, and grant that this night they will come to Christ. They will flee youthful lusts. They will haste to the cross, fall there and cry for pardon, and find peace through the blood of Calvary's Lamb. Hear us in heaven Thy dwelling place, and save the people for Christ's sake.

AMEN AND AMEN.

10 Snow! snow! *snow!*

THE BIBLE USES EVEN the figure of snow to teach us the tremendous truths of the glorious gospel of free grace.

"And Elisha said unto him, Whence comest thou, Gehazi? And he said unto him, Went not mine heart with thee, when the man turned again from his chariot to meet thee? Is it a time to receive money and to receive garments, and oliveyards, and sheep and oxen and menservants and maidservants? The leprosy therefore of Naaman shall cleave unto thy seed forever. And he went out from his presence **a leper as white as snow**" (I Kings 5:25-27).

Here snow suggests

THE INESCAPABLE CURSE

Behold Gehazi the covetor, the deceiver, the liar, staggering out from Elisha's presence a leper as white as snow. The curse, the inescapable curse, has fallen not only on him but upon his family. His leprous offspring in generations following must bear the curse. They cannot escape. The blood stream is forever polluted. The seed is perpetually leprous. The family is eternally accursed.

As with Gehazi's seed, so with us. Our father Adam was driven from paradise, cursed with a greater curse than that which fell upon Gehazi, the curse of sin, and we his offspring share that curse. The bloodstream of the race is forever polluted. The Adamic seed is perpetually leprous. Every generation must bear the inescapable curse. As sons of Adam we are accursed. The virus of sin's cancer has diseased every human heart. Apart from divine intervention we are totally and hopelessly corrupt.

"The whole head is sick and the whole heart is faint. From the sole of the foot even unto the head there is no soundness in it; but wounds, and bruises, and putrefying sores: they have not been closed, neither bound up, neither mollified with ointment" Isaiah 1:5-6.

Sam Jones, the famous American Methodist preacher from the south, illustrated in the following incident the solemn fact that the virus of sin is fatal;-

"I took up a newspaper some months ago and read that Senator Benjamin H Hill, our brilliant, brainy statesman of Georgia, had a little trouble on his tongue. They made light of it and said it was caused by a fractured tooth. A few days after that, in reading a daily paper, I saw that Senator Hill had been under the surgeon's knife, and they had removed one-third of his tongue, and the doctors had said to him: 'This wound will heal and you will be all right in a few days.' In a few weeks I saw again that Senator Hill was back under the surgeon's knife in Philadelphia, and the doctors had cut out the glands from his face and neck. The paper told how young Benjamin Hill had turned to the doctors and said: 'Will my father get well?' The surgeons replied guardedly: 'If we have extracted the last particle of this cancer from his system, he will certainly get well. But if there is the least particle of cancer left in his system it will appear in some other gland and this trouble will be renewed.' The next I heard of Senator Hill was that he was at some famous springs in the West. Some weeks afterwards I walked down to the depot in my home town, and when the passenger train rolled into the city, trembling under her air brakes, and stopped, I looked towards the window in the sleeping car and thought I saw the outline of Senator Hill's face. I walked down to the car, and he pushed his bony hand out of the window and took mine, and I looked into his face, and said to myself, 'O my Lord! is this all that is left of Senator Benjamin H Hill, one of the grandest men Georgia has ever produced?'

"A few days afterward I read in the Atlanta Constitution, 'The grandest procession that ever marched out of Atlanta marched out yesterday, and buried Senator Benjamin H Hill out of the sight of men forever.'

"I want to tell you, just as certain as the virus of cancer killed Senator Hill's body, just so certain does the virus of sin kill your soul at last."

Sinner, the inescapable curse of the race has fallen upon you. You are marked with the brandmark of sin.

Spiritually speaking, you go out from the presence of God a leper as white as snow.

"If I wash myself with **snow water**, and make my hands never so clean; Yet shalt thou plunge me in the ditch, and mine own clothes shall abhor me" Job 9:30-31.

Snow here suggests

THE INEFFECTIVE CURE

The trouble with men and women is not so much that they refuse to acknowledge their sin but that they refuse the only effective cure and choose the ineffective cures of their own devising. Having discovered their malady, they repudiate God's remedy and spend their all on many physicians and in the process grow worse. This is clearly stated in the text. The ancients thought that snow water had special cleansing qualities and that a garment washed in the same would be ever so clean.

How many of this generation are trying to wash away the stains of sin with man-manufactured snow water. Sinner, does this message find you a Pilate trying to wash out the damning stains by a washing of your own devising. Perhaps you are trying to cleanse your sins away in **the snow water of fine reasoning**.

You foolishly reason that as you have inherited sin you'll not be held responsible for its pollution. Such reasoning has in it the rebellion of the pit and will lead to righteous retribution. You'll not be damned for Adam's sins but you'll be damned for your own sins.

Have you never deliberately and wilfully chosen evil rather than good? You dare not answer Nay. Your mouth is stopped. You are guilty before God. Your own sins are enough to damn you ten fathoms deep in the brimstone of perdition. The snow water of fine reasoning cannot wash away your guilt.

Perhaps you are trying **the snow water of good resolution**. How foolish to think that cleansing can be achieved in such a manner. Even if it were possible for you from this day by a good resolution to keep God's law perfectly, how would your past guilt be atoned for? Your past sins alone are sufficient to banish you eternally from God's presence. Heaven is not attained by good resolutions. The snow water of good resolution cannot erase your humanly indelible stains.

Perhaps you are trying **the snow water of religion**. Many think that baptismal water can remove sin's guilt. Alas! The stains are too deep for water to cleanse. Baptism cannot save; hell is peopled with unregenerate baptised souls. Communion cannot convert; hell is full of unredeemed communicant sinners. Church membership cannot remove the curse; many church members can be counted amongst the damned in hell.

With Spurgeon we would thunder out:- "Vain is the baptism or the confirmation of your youth, faith in Jesus is the one thing needful; vain is the fact that you were born of Christian parents, ye must be born again; vain is your sitting as God's people sit, and standing as they stand, in the solemn service of the sanctuary, your heart must be changed; vain is your observance of the Lord's Day, and vain your Bible reading and your form of prayer night and morning, unless you are washed in Jesus' blood; vain are all things without living faith in the living Jesus. Though you had been descended from an unbroken line of saints, though you had no unconverted relative, your ancestry and lineage would not avail you; the sons of God are born, not of blood, nor of the will of man, nor of the will of the flesh, but of God."

Sacramental snow water has no sin-cleansing properties.

"Come now, and let us reason together, saith the Lord; though your sins be as scarlet they shall be as **white as snow**; though they be red like crimson, they shall be as wool" Isaiah 1:18.

Snow suggests

THE INFINITE CLEANSING

Sinner,

I know a fount where sins are washed away,
I know a place where night is turned to day.
Burdens are lifted, blind eyes made to see,
There's a wonder working power in the blood of Calvary.

A gospel preacher was called one evening to a slum area in the city in which he laboured. He made his way along the dismal narrow streets until at last down an alleyway he entered a cold, damp garret. Huddled on a bed of straw in a corner lay the form of a once beautiful young woman, but whose body was now blighted and diseased and dying as the result of a misspent life of immorality and sin.

The preacher, after listening to her story, opened his Bible and read to her several portions of Scripture, but none of them seemed to satisfy the deep longing of her heart. Then he turned to Isaiah 1:18 "... though your sins be as scarlet they shall be as white as snow ..." The young woman raised herself up and said: "Preacher, that verse describes me, I am a scarlet sinner. Put my finger on the word 'scarlet'". He placed her finger on the word and said to her: "Young woman, you are now at the first 's'. If you will now accept Jesus as your Saviour, place your finger on the second 's' snow." She hesitated a little as two forces within her strove for the mastery of her soul, then she moved her finger across the page to the word 'snow".

The battle was won! Her past life, in all its evil hideousness, had been purified in the sin-cleansing blood of the Lamb, and her sins, though scarlet, were now as white as snow. She sank back onto her bed of straw and in a few short minutes passed into the presence of the Friend of Sinners, cleansed by His precious blood.

Sinner, haste to the Cross, cleanse in the fountain. Cry out with David: "Wash me and I shall be whiter than snow". Only the blood, the precious

Blood, the pardoning Blood, the powerful Blood of Jesus can make atonement for the sinful soul.

"His head and His hairs were white like wool, **as white as snow**; and His eyes were as a flame of fire". Revelation 1:14

In this our final text, snow suggests

THE INCOMPARABLE CHRIST

Christ is the gospel and the gospel is Christ. He, a living Person, is the glorious glad-tidings. We preach Christ, Christ of pre-incarnate glory and of eternal Deity, Christ of the Virgin's womb and of Incarnation wonder, Christ of Galilee's preaching, Gethsemane's praying and Golgotha's passion. The Christ of Calvary. Christ of High-priestly intercession, the Christ of the soon-coming glory.

With Paul we can say: "Moreover, brethren, I declare unto you the gospel which I preached unto you, which also ye have received and wherein ye stand; by which also ye are saved, if ye keep in memory what I have preached unto you, unless ye have believed in vain. For I delivered unto you first of all that which I also received, how that Christ died for our sins according to the scriptures; and that he was buried, and that he rose again the third day according to the scriptures" I Corinthians 15:14.

Of this Christ we can say "His head and His hairs are white like wool, as white as snow".

Like John, fall at His feet, acknowledge His Sovereignty, appropriate His Sufferings and acquiesce in His Saviourhood. Then you will hear the sweet words "Fear not", and your soul will be lost in rapture, love and praise. Happy, thrice happy the soul who can sing:

On life's rough sea, how frail my barque,
But in the drear and densest dark
I have a safe and trusted ark,
O, praise the Lord, I've Jesus.

This Incomparable Christ invites you to Himself, and His gracious promise is "Him that cometh unto Me, I will in no wise cast out" John 6:37.

Hear His effectual call today and as He draws run after Him.

11 Bad women and *jolly good fellows*

WE ARE READING THE Word of God tonight from Luke 15

"Then drew near unto him all the publicans and sinners for to hear him. And the Pharisees and scribes murmured, saying, This man receiveth sinners, and eateth with them. And he spake this parable unto then, saying, What man of you, having an hundred sheep, if he lose one of them, doth not leave the ninety and nine in the wilderness and go after that which is lost, until he find it? And when he hath found it, he layeth it on his shoulders, rejoicing. And when he cometh home he calleth together his friends and neighbours, saying unto them, Rejoice with me; for I have found my sheep which was lost. I say unto you, that likewise joy shall be in heaven over one sinner that repenteth, more than over ninety and nine just persons, which need no repentance. Either what woman having ten pieces of silver, if she lose one piece, doth not light a candle, and sweep the house, and seek diligently till she find it? And when she hath found it, she calleth her friends and her neighbours together, saying, Rejoice with me; for I have found the piece which I had lost. Likewise, I say unto you, there is joy in the presence of the angels of God over one sinner that repenteth. And he said, A certain man had two sons: And the younger of them said to his father, Father, give me the portion of goods that falleth to me. And he divided unto them his living. And not many days after the younger son gathered all together, and took his journey into a far country, and there wasted his substance with riotous living. And when he had spent all, there arose a mighty famine in that land; and he began to be in want. And he went and joined himself to a citizen of that country; and he sent him into his fields to feed swine. And he would fain have filled his belly with the husks that the swine did eat: and no man gave unto him. And when he came to himself, he said, How many hired servants of my father's have bread enough and to spare, and I perish with hunger! I will arise and go to my father, and will say unto him, Father, I have sinned against heaven, and before thee, And am no more worthy to be called thy son: make me as one of thy hired servants. And he arose, and came to his father. But when he was yet a great way off, his father saw him, and had compassion, and ran, and fell on his neck, and kissed him. And the son said unto him, Father, I have sinned against heaven, and in thy sight, and am no more worthy to be called thy son. But the father said to his servants, Bring forth the best robe, and put it on him; and put a ring on his hand, and shoes on his feet; And bring hither the fatted calf, and kill it; and let us eat, and be merry: For this my son was dead, and is alive again; he was lost, and is found. And they began to be merry. Now his elder son was in the field: and as he came and drew nigh to the house, he heard musick and dancing. And he called one of the servants, and asked what these things meant. And he said unto him, Thy brother is come; and thy father hath killed the fatted calf, because he hath received him safe and sound. And he was angry, and would not go in: therefore came his father out, and intreated him. And he answering said to his father, Lo, these many years do I serve thee, neither transgressed I at any time thy commandment: and yet thou never gavest me a kid, that I might make merry with my friends: But as soon as this thy son was come, which hath devoured thy living with harlots, thou hast killed for him the fatted calf. And he said unto him, Son thou art ever with me, and all that I have is thine. It was meet that we should make merry, and be glad: for this thy brother was dead, and is alive again; and was lost, and is found."

I want to draw your attention to the verse 30. The thirtieth verse of the fifteenth chapter of Luke's Gospel "But as soon as this thy son was come, which hath devoured thy living with harlots, thou hast killed for him the fatted calf."

The title of my subject this evening is Bad Women And Jolly Good Fellows.

The Lord Jesus Christ, in this most important passage of Luke's Gospel, sets forth in parable form the way of salvation. He commences with a story of a lost sheep. He continues with the story of lost silver and he concludes with the story of the lost son. The whole purpose of these three parables is to set forth clearly and distinctly the way of salvation.

But there is a difference between the final parable and the first two. Because the action in the first two parables is the action of the owner or the action of the seeker. The shepherd goes seeking the lost sheep. The woman goes hunting in her home and searching for the lost piece of silver. So the message of the first two parables is the Godward aspect of salvation or Christ bringing back the sinner.

It is entirely different in the final parable. Here we have the manward aspect of salvation. It is not God bringing back the sinner, it is emphasising the sinner coming back to God. So in the first two we have the reaction of the shepherd and we have the reaction of the woman but in the last parable we have the reaction of the sinner himself. The sinner wakening up to his deeds. The sinner facing up to the future. The sinner saying I will arise and go to my father. The sinner making the long journey from the far country back to the father's house. And the sinner received in the father's embrace and receiving the father's kiss of reconciliation.

Now there are not two ways of salvation neither are there two gospels but these are two complementary aspects of the way people are saved. The Lord puts them so graciously and so clearly in these parables.

THE WATERSHED

I want to speak on the prodigal. If you look at verse 17 you will find the watershed. You will find the dividing ridge in this parable. Verse 17 *"And when he came to himself"*. I want to take that suggestive statement of Scripture - when he came to himself.

I want to talk about the prodigal **beside** *himself.* I want to show you his folly, his foolishness, his insanity and his madness. The prodigal beside himself.

Then I want to show you the prodigal **coming** *to himself.* Down at the swine trough he came to himself.

Then I want to finalise the prodigal **at** *himself.* When he really came to himself.

Let us look at the prodigal beside himself.

FIRST HE IS BESIDE HIMSELF

I want now to make a very strong statement. Every Christ rejecting sinner is a fool. Let me repeat that. Every Christ rejecting sinner is a fool. Of course Christ rejecters don't like that. The apostle Paul, in Ephesians 4:17 has this to say. *"This I say therefore, and testify in the Lord, that ye henceforth walk not as other Gentiles walk, in the vanity of their mind, Having the understanding darkened, being alienated from the life of God through the ignorance that is in them, because of the blindness of their heart."* So the understanding of the ungodly, unregenerate, unsaved man is blinded. Blinded by the deceptions of sin and by the deceptions of Satan.

I want to show you this young man's madness.
First of all, he was mad about *the assessment* of his own home.

He sat down one day and said I don't like this home. I don't like my father's restraints. I don't like the way this home is ordered. I don't like the law that my father makes me keep. Oh to get away from all these restraints. Oh to get away from the puritanical outlook of my father. Oh for a happy release from it all.

One day, in his folly, he went to his father and he said, "Father, what are you going to give me when you die? I don't want to wait until you die. I want it now." That is the arrogance of insanity, folly and vanity. The father said, "All right," and he called his two boys in and he divided unto them his living.

The young man was mad in the assessment of his home. He did not know where real happiness lay. He did not know that that home was the most happy place on earth for him, the safest place on earth for him, the most secure place on earth for him. No, he went away. His home was like a prison. My father is like a jailor. These laws of my father, they are like chains and I must get away.

Second, he was mad in his *caressment* of his goods.

Then you see his madness and his insanity when he took everything with him. Turn back and look at verse 13 *"Not many days after the younger son gathered all"* everything. You should never put everything in one bag. You should never stake everything in one throw. That is folly. But he gathered up everything. He took everything with him. What a fool he was. To intend never to come home again, never see the father's house, hear the father's voice, sit at the father's table, take of the father's food and the father's provision. He was a fool. He gathered all together.

Thirdly, he was mad in his *abusing* of his heritage.

Then I want you to notice he was a fool because he wasted it all. It says here in this verse that he wasted his substance with riotous living. He devoured his father's hard-earned cash with harlots. Oh when he got to the far country there were many jolly good fellows to welcome him there. What parties he had. What pleasures he had. What music he had. What jollification he had. As long as he had money to spend, there were plenty of the world's pleasures.

There are three things in this world.

There is the lust of the eye, that is immorality.

There is the lust of the flesh, that is sensuality.

There is pride of life, that is vanity.

These three things set about the destruction of this young man. Down there in the far country he learned the depths of sin and the night of sin's wasting.

You all have Bibles before you. I would like you to open those Bibles at Proverbs 7 because Proverbs 7 gives you a description of the way this young man was destroyed with the scarlet sin - bad women and jolly good fellows. There are plenty of them around where sin abounds. Solomon, in Proverbs 7:6 says, *"For at the window of my house I looked through my casement and beheld among the simple ones I discerned among the youth a young man void of understanding,"* Maybe the devil is telling you, young person tonight, to have your fill of sin and have your fling with lust. But you are a fool. The Bible says you are simple. You are void of understanding. The scarlet road blazes a trail to hell. That is what the Bible says.

What happened? *"Passing through the street near her corner; he went the way to her house."* Don't flirt with sins that challenge your virtue, your modesty and your purity. Don't flirt with them. They will be too strong for you. They will suck you down into the destructive vortex of their terrible current and the whirlpool of their destruction.

"In the twilight, in the evening, in the black and dark night:" It is a very dark night when the soul goes out to do the sin of lust and shame and virtue losing.

This is a solemn passage of God's Word. *"And behold, there met him a woman with the attire of an harlot, and subtil of heart."* The woman met the prodigal son in the far country. The jolly good fellows and the bad women met him. How many jolly good fellows and bad women have met poor souls as they have gone down sin's road, gone down the road to their soul's destruction. *"She is loud and stubborn; her feet abide not in her house: Now she is without, now in the streets, and lieth in wait at every corner. So she caught him, and kissed him, and with an impudent face said unto him, I have peace offerings with me; this day have I paid my vows."* Covering over their sin with their religion. *"Therefore came I forth to meet thee, diligently to seek thy face, and I have found thee. I have decked my bed with coverings of tapestry, with carved works, with fine linen of Egypt. I have perfumed my bed with myrrh, aloes, and cinnamon. Come, let us take our fill of love until the morning: let us solace ourselves with loves. For the goodman is not at home, he is gone on a long journey: He hath taken a bag of money with him and will come home at the day appointed. With her much fair speech she caused him to yield".* The poor prodigal in the far country. Attacked, his virtue attacked!

All that his father had schooled him in, attacked. *"With the flattering of her lips she forced him. He goeth after her straightway, as an ox goeth to the slaughter, or as a fool to the correction of the stocks; Till a dart strike through his liver; as a bird hasteth to the snare, and knoweth not that it is for his life. Hearken unto me now therefore, O ye children, and attend to the words of my mouth. Let not thine heart decline to her ways, go not astray in her paths. For she hath cast down many wounded: yea, many strong men have been slain by her. Her house is the way to hell."*

Hear this tonight! Her house is in the way to hell. In this permissive society it is scarcely possible that every person in this building is pure. Am I addressing someone caught up in the chains of scarlet sin and in the bondage of lust. Listen, *"Her house is the way to hell going down to the chambers of death."*

He devoured his substance with harlots. Poor, broken young man stained, scarred, smashed by the power of sin.

He was mad in the *judgment* of his companions.

But he discovered something. When the cash ran out his companions ran out. When finance ran out then all the feasting was finished. He discovered when he had no money those jolly good fellows would not even give him a loan. The Lord said, "No man gave unto him".

Oh he went round and he knocked on their doors and he said, "Do you remember the feast that I gave to you." They said, "Get away, we don't want you." "Remember the good times we had?" "Get away!" The jolly good fellows slammed their doors and the companions in sin rejected him and no man gave unto him. What did David say in the day of trouble? He said "No man cared for my soul."

The world will not care for you sir. The world will not care for you madam when the money runs out and the energies in life are gone and youth is blighted. Do you remember Lord Byron on his 30th birthday? He had enjoyed all the pleasures of Europe. He had committed every sin in the book and now at 30 years of age with a life blighted and blasted he took up his pen and he wrote those words, "My days are in the yellow leaf.

The flowers and fruits of life are gone.

The worm, the canker and the grief are mine alone."

SECONDLY, HE IS COMING TO HIMSELF

So he goes to get a job. Now Jews are not supposed to have anything to do with pork or with pigs. The old rascal that he went to said "I will humble you, you Jew. Go away into the field there to the herd of swine. Sit at the swine trough." He went to the place of legal uncleanness as far as the religious laws of Moses were concerned. See him there, he is at the swine trough. Have a look at it. He did not like the father's house. He thought he would break the restraints of home. He thought he would find happiness. What did he find? He found trouble and sorrow and ruination and damnation, that is what he found.

He is sitting at this swine trough. He is beside himself, now he is coming to himself. You know what happened to him. When his stomach was empty his brain became clear and when hunger and disappointment ravaged his soul he began to think. What did he think about? He thought about the future. Would to God sir I could make you think about the future. Would to God madam I could make you think about the future.

I was out at the La Mon restaurant after that terrible inferno had gutted it. I was sitting in the house with the proprietor, Mr Huddleson. As we sat there amongst the ruins I thought of those dear people who went out there to have a night of pleasure, recreation and enjoyment. Alas tragedy overtook them. They never thought, when they entered that restaurant, what their exit would be. The tragedy of our day is that people don't think.

But this man started to think. He started to think. What did he say? He said, look at the hired servants of my fathers with bread enough and to spare. Then he said, I perish. I am a perishing soul. Until you are able to know from your heart you are perishing in your sin there will be no salvation for you. He was coming to himself when he discovered he was perishing.

Do you know you are a perishing sinner? Do you know that God sent His Son, John 3:16 *"For God so loved the world that He gave His only begotten Son that whosoever believeth in Him should not perish."* There is hope for your soul if you know you are perishing. There is a word here and it is the greatest definition of grace in the Bible - **bread enough and to spare**. That is what the Gospel is, provision enough, an unlimited supply, the grace of God.

Then he said something more. He said I have sinned. I perish, I have sinned, and until you are prepared to say I have sinned there is no repentance or grace or salvation for you. You have got to take the sinner's place and acknowledge you are a lost, ruined, ill-deserving, undeserving hell-deserving sinner. I perish. I perish. I have sinned. I will arise and go and I will say. That is the way of salvation. The devil said to him you cannot go, look at your clothes. How can you go to your father's house in those rags.

There is a great painting in one of our art galleries of the prodigal leaving the swine trough to go back to his father's house. The man that painted that picture tells the story of how he got a suitable subject to be the prodigal. He said he went away down into the lower parts and hovels of London and he saw a man with a bag upon his back, his trousers tattered and his coat torn, his hair matted and with dirt and evil grimed into his body until he was the incarnate rejection of all humanity. He went to the man and asked him if he wanted to earn some money. The man said, "Yes." He said, "You come to my studio. Come as you are."

The next day the man turned up at the studio but the artist did not recognise him. He had washed his face. He had cleaned his body. He had combed his hair. He had put on a new suit of clothes and the artist said, "I don't want you. You have to come as you are or you are no good to me."

I want to tell you you have to come to Jesus just as you are. You can wash in the water of baptism, clean up your garments with the washing of religion.You can try and make yourself better, try and make yourself more presentable but God will not have you.

You have got to come as you are. You have to go with a torn coat. You have to go with the marks of grime and sin and the smell of the unclean upon you. He had to go in his uncleanness - just as I am, I come. If you are not prepared to come like that you cannot come at all and there is no reception for you at the father's house.

THIRDLY, HE CAME TO HIMSELF

He found it was a long way. When the sinner starts coming back to God he never realises how far he has strayed. As he is coming, wondering what a reception he will have and how he will make himself known. I will slip into the back garden and I will tell one of the servants and he will go and tell my father and my father will come out and I will tell my father I am sorry. I have sinned against heaven. I am a sinner. Make me a hired servant. Make me a skivvy in the kitchen. Ah, but the father was waiting for him. It is the greatest picture of grace in the Bible.

Five is the number of grace and the father did five things. Notice he **saw** him. He had **compassion**. He **ran**. He **fell on his neck**. He **kissed** him. That is the number of grace. That is the Gospel of Christ. The Father is waiting for you tonight.

*I have wandered far away from God
Now I'm coming home.*

The Father's waiting for you. Will you come? Will you come? He saw him. He ran. He had compassion. He fell on his neck. He kissed him. You know what the boy said? He said, "Father I have sinned against heaven and in thy sight and am no more worthy to be called thy son." He never got the rest of the prayer out.

The father would not listen to him. He said, "Bring the best robe and put it on him. Put shoes on his feet. Put a ring on his finger and kill the fatted calf. Set the table. Let us sit down to the feast." Oh there is always a feast when a sinner comes home. There is always rejoicing when a soul gets saved. There is always music and dancing in the father's house when a soul returns to God. Sinner friend, will you come? This message is for you. Come, there is welcome in the Father's house for you.

AMEN AND AMEN!

12 The break up *of a funeral*

A VERY GOOD FRIEND and neighbour of mine died during the past week, Pastor Robert Mercer, the minister of Euston Street Bible Pattern Fellowship Church. I have known Pastor Robert Mercer for many years. He was a great man in the Word and very strong in the principles of Biblical Protestantism. Many times I have sat with him in his home and he has sat with me in my home and we have together discussed the great things of the Lord.

Pastor Mercer passed on and, I might say, as a family my wife and myself deeply appreciated his friendship and his fellowship. Could I just say that during the time of my imprisonment twice every week that man of God called at our home and comforted my wife and prayed for her and for me. It is in a friendship like that that we can see the triumph of the grace of God.

Now, of course, I felt it was my duty to attend the funeral if I would be able and I was able to organise my schedule and be there. They invited me to go with them to the grave and to pay a tribute to my departed brother at the grave side. The grave was in the Belfast City Cemetery and it was near to the railings of the Falls Park.

Of course, as you know, in the Falls Park they have erected all these shelters and wooden huts which house the people who burned down their own houses during the troubles. Don't you think that Protestants burn them all down they burn them down themselves and they were overheard saying let us burn these houses for we will get better ones.

Well, when the funeral service commenced Pastor Tweed called on me to speak a few words. There was a crowd, first of all, of children and then of young thugs gathered at the railings. There was no commotion while I was speaking but immediately I finished and another dear brother opened the Word to preach the Gospel we were simply overwhelmed with the vilest language that I have ever heard. I hope never to hear such language again.

The Special Constabulary were relegated to the lowest hell. The people of the Shankill Road were called all the vile names of the day. As for myself and the Protestant people the language was just the off scouring of the pit. This was going on as a servant of God was trying to read the Scriptures and to say some words of comfort to those who had come to mourn the passing of this servant of God.

Then after the abuse came the stones and the glass breaking. One pastor, Pastor William Mullan of Melbourne Street Elim Hall was cut in the face with flying glass. Two pastors from England, Pastor Edgar and Pastor March were struck with stones. The windscreen of the mourners' car was absolutely shattered, the side window was broken as well and large pieces of concrete were hurled on to the grave and on to the mourners. The grave diggers had to leave the site and could not fill in the grave. They could not lay the flowers in order on the grave and the hearse was, of course, the target for stone throwing.

Mr Wilton, the funeral undertaker who directed the funeral said to me, "Ian, I think you should get into the hearse and we should remove it further down the cemetery grounds". This we did. It was bad while I was there but it was ten times worse when I left. They had to close the service altogether and they had to leave the grave side and there were continual attacks mounted on the mourners' cars. Pastor Ayling of the Ulster Temple was there and he came down to where I was sitting in the hearse further down in the grounds and he consented to get me away. He said, "I'm sure they will be gathering at the gates." I just got out in time because they did gather at the gates and were prepared for a further attack on the mourners as they were leaving the cemetery grounds. One group of mourners had to go to a second gate before they could get out of the graveyard and escape the murderous fury.

Now this was what took place on Friday. Let me tell you friend law and order in this city has broken down. There is no doubt about that. The authorities have not the power to stamp out this thing because the Church of Rome is riding her high horse at the present time and the Wilson Government is in collaboration with the Roman church and with the republican opposition. If you go up to Stormont and see the people who Mr Burrows, the United Kingdom representative, hob nobs with, when you see Wilson's representative keeping company with the enemies of our Province.

I got on to the Prime Minister's office. I could not get the Prime Minister. He was at the Balmoral Show. He would be better looking after the welfare of Ulster than spending his time at a show at such a crucial time in Ulster's experience.

I protested to the Minister of Home Affairs. I got the city commissioner and the city commissioner was appalled when I told him the story. He said, "I never thought I would live to see or hear such a story."

INEFFECTIVE LAW ENFORCEMENT

Now I understand that summonses are going to be issued on certain people. I want to say the summonsing of people in that area is far too ineffective. There should have been immediate arrests. I want to make that clear from this pulpit. I do not accept that this is a matter for summonses. I want to further say from this pulpit if this incident had happened the other way (but of course it would not have happened the other way) but if Protestants had stoned a Roman Catholic funeral you would have had a score of men in the lock-up tonight. You would not only have had them locked up but you would have had shrieks from every ecumenical pulpit in this city crying aloud and condemning such a dastardly attack.

I have not heard a squeak from one Roman Catholic priest in condemnation. I have not heard a squeak from Dr Eric Gallagher, who is so great at making statements. I have heard nothing from the ecumenical movement in condemnation because I want to tell you that the spirit that hurled the stones at that grave and the spirit that taught the young people who were there to hate Protestants is the spirit of Rome and the spirit of the ecumenical movement. It is the same Spirit that devised the inquisition. It is the same spirit that makes Rome drunk, according to this Bible, with the blood of the martyrs of Jesus. Make no mistake about it. This is the spirit of antichrist that we are battling against at the present time in this Province.

THE FUNERAL CHRIST BROKE UP

When standing there in the cemetery I was thinking of the day when the Lord broke up a funeral.

You know we believe, as Christians, in the resurrection. One day the city of Nain was going about its business as usual. The chariots were rolling along the streets and the hammers of industry could be heard with their solid din and ring. Work with its thousand fingers and its thousand feet and hands was all busy in this city. Then through the streets of that busy city came a lonely and tragic funeral procession. Walking behind the coffin was a mother, a widow, who had lost her only son, and industry stood still and the chariots stopped and the city of Nain came to a halt. Some trifler in the crowd said it was only a funeral but a close observer said it must be an important funeral for there was a great procession. Then from lip to lip was whispered the word it was the funeral of that widow's only son. It passed silently onwards down the streets of the city towards the gate. It passed through the gate.

Industry started its din once again and the chariots rolled through the streets once again and work, with its thousand hands and feet, commenced its business once more. Outside the city gate the Lord Jesus Christ was there and there never was a funeral ever got past the Lord Jesus. Do you know every time in Scripture when death and Jesus met, death gave place to Christ. Do you know that?

WHEN DEATH HAD DONE ITS WORK

Do you remember when He was face to face with death? Jairus' little daughter lies stretched on the bed and He takes her by the hand and says, 'Daughter arise'. Death cannot stand before the King of death. Do you remember when they rolled the stone from the tomb and Jesus was face to face with the corpse of Lazarus and Jesus Christ cried *"Lazarus come forth"*. Lazarus came forth.

An old Puritan writer commenting on that said it was a good thing that He said "Lazarus come forth", for if He had shouted "come forth" there would have been a general resurrection. For death can never stand before Jesus Christ.

NOTE THE FOLLOWING

There are some things about this funeral procession I want you to note. There are some things that make it even more sad than a mere funeral. This was the death of a young man. To the aged in Christ death is a beautiful thing.

THE AGED SAINT

I was speaking a few days ago to an aged saint. She was over 90 years of age and when she took my hand in her bony fingers she said "Ian, I am just waiting for the call. It will be coming any day. I have marched along life's pilgrimage and I am tired now. I am weary now and as far as I am concerned I have just a little way to go and then it will be glory for me."

You know death to the aged in Christ is blessed. It is a great thing when the weeping is over. It is a great thing when the weeping is past and the saint who has wrestled on towards heaven against storm and wind and tide goes in to see the King in His beauty, that is a great thing.

THE YOUNG MAN

Could I say this was not the death of an aged person. It was the death of a young man. He had just put on his armour. He was just going out into the battle of life. He was just getting ready for the great struggle of life, to run life's race and to win life's prize. Suddenly, in a moment, life was blasted. The future was laid low. All the hopes, all the ambitions of youth were suddenly and brutally shattered. The young man ceased to live. That was most certainly a day of deep and terrible sorrow. It was the death of a young man.

THE ONLY SON

The second thing I want you to note. He was an only son. You know you cannot spare any one of the flock. You fathers and mothers know if you were asked to make a choice what child you would have to say good-bye to, you could not make such a choice. Although different, all have their special niche in a father or mother's heart.

You could not make a choice. But this dear woman had only one son. One tender son she had and that one son fell ill and he died. There was no doubt great rejoicing at his birth. There was no doubt great expectation as he grew up and came to young manhood. No doubt he was his mother's pride and his mother's joy. Then suddenly and rudely death marched into the home and death drew its icy breath across the face of that young man and he lay down and died. He was a young man but he was not only a young man but he was an only son.

THE WIDOW'S SON

Then there is something else. He was a widow's son. I am sure there was great sorrow in that house when the father died. Can you remember when death came to your home and when the father of the home passed on? There must certainly have been sorrow when the father in that home died. I think I see that young man go to his mother and say "I will take my father's place as best I can. There are only two of us now and I will stand in the gap, mother, I will win the bread for you. I will keep the home together. I will do the job that father did so well and so ably before me".

THE LOVE OF JESUS

You know this young man must have been a young man of character because it says in verse 11 much people attended the funeral. That reflected on his character. Some young men forget their home. They forget the struggle of their parents. They forget those who wrought to give them their clothes and their food and their education in the early part of life but this young man did not forget. He was faithful to the home and to his mother. There was no doubt about that. We read here the sad and solemn words - the only son of his mother and she was a widow.

Something happened. The city went on with its work. Jesus Christ met that funeral procession. There are two things I want you to notice about Jesus Christ. First of all He was very sympathetic. You know that sorrow touched a sympathetic cord in the heart of Christ. Yes He was very sympathetic.

You know the Lord Jesus Christ was truly man. He was perfect man. He was the impeccable man. He knew how that mother felt. He knew the sorrow that tugged at her heart strings. He knew the bitterness and the loneliness that had come upon her. He had read her life's story in the mind of His omniscience and He understood it all.

There He stands, the great sympathetic Saviour and His first words are these "Weep not, Mother dry up your tears. I have got an answer to your problem. I have got the solution to your troubles. I can bring back the lost joy and the lost peace and the lost rejoicing. I have got an answer to your problem."

I am glad the Lord Jesus Christ feels for us. There is not a pain that rends the human heart but the Man of Sorrows has a part. There is not one affliction in life that Jesus Christ does not fully and completely and absolutely understand. Yes, He understands it all.

Is there someone here and you are carrying a burden that no one else knows about? Is there some mother here, some widow here, some father here, some brother in this great meeting and you have a burden that no one else knows anything about? You have passed into a valley and no one else knows that you have passed such a dark and sad valley.

I want to tell you Jesus knows and Jesus understands. He knows what you need. He understands what you need. He knows everything about you and, friend, He loves you just the same.

THE TOUCH OF JESUS

Oh that you might come to Christ and feel His touch and hear His voice saying, "Weep not". Is there some sin that has put a dark stain on your soul? Is there some habit that has tied you in its chains and those chains are unbreakable? Is there some companionship that has shattered your peace and led you down the road of evil and iniquity? Listen, let me tell you Jesus understands everything which concerns you. He said to the mother, "Weep not". He is a sympathetic man.

He is the Sovereign God and He took His stand beside that funeral and He put forth His hand and halted the procession. You know that was a wonderful thing. A young man carried out dead and he walked home with his mother. My, what a sensation in that city. The grave digger did not get his fee that day. I am sure the funeral undertaker had a bit of an argument and the widow said, you only did half the job, you never got there so you are only getting half pay for that job. Oh what a situation, Jesus stopped the procession and He went forward to the young man and took him by the hand and raised him up. The young man did speak and he looked round and there was the funeral with himself in the coffin.

Imagine viewing your own funeral. I would like to read my obituary notice, that is one thing I would like to read. I am sure it will be choice. That young man went home and read his own obituary notice in the press. Oh what a day that was. Jesus Christ the Sovereign God touched him.

I love that little verse tucked in there, did you notice it as I read it to you? Oh how very blessed is the language of the Spirit of God. Never miss anything of importance from the Spirit as He records it. What does it say - and Jesus delivered him to his mother. That was a blessed introduction was it not? Jesus took him in His hand from the coffin and he brought the mother in His other hand and said "Mother here is your son." My what an embrace there must have been on the road. The tears of sorrow became tears of joy and the young man and his mother returned to the city and great fear fell upon all men.

My I am sure there were a lot of callers that night at that home. People wanting to see him. All his companions came and they said "You are alive again, why?" "Because Jesus met me on the road."

LIFE FULL OF FUNERALS

Friend, I want to tell you that life's road is full of funerals and it is full of deaths. Life's road is clogged up with graves. The graves of ambition, the graves of achievement and the graves of our planning. All life is full of death and sorrows and burials. When Jesus comes death gives place to life. I want death to give place to life in your life. There are men here and they are buried in their sin. They are wrapped up in the shrouds of their own iniquities and their friends are mourning for them for they are going down, down, down deep to the lowest hell. Blessed be the name of the Lord Jesus, Christ can meet you tonight. He can meet you at the very point of your need. The procession downwards to the grave can be halted and the tears of loved ones who are weeping because of the sad fate of your soul can be dried away and praise God you can receive life from the hands of the One Who is the Resurrection and the Life.

Will you meet the Lord Jesus Christ? He is here. He is the sympathetic man. He is the Sovereign God and He wants to meet you.

IF CHIRST HAD NOT STOPPED THE FUNERAL

What if Jesus Christ had not met that procession? That procession would have gone on its weary way to the graveyard and the mother would have stood and wrung her hands and the tears would have run down her cheeks on to the tomb and they would have laid her son away in the tomb and rolled the stone to its door and the mother would have turned her back on the earthly remains of her son and walked away into the darkness of loneliness and deep distress and deeper sorrow still.

Let me tell you something. If you don't meet Jesus Christ you will go on to the grave. You will go on to the sorrow. You will go on to the separation. You will go on to the grief. You will go on to the blackness of darkness forever. It will be a sorrow that no one can alleviate and the terrors of hell which no one can relieve you from.

MEET JESUS

Will you meet Jesus? I don't ask you to join the church. I don't ask you to get baptised. I don't ask you to become a church member or to sign a card. I ask you to meet Jesus Christ. Just meet Him. Salvation is in Christ. It is contact with Christ that wakes the dead and gives life to those who lie in the grave clothes of their iniquity. You can meet Him. The procession of your funeral to the blackness of darkness forever can be stopped. You can be raised from that tomb of your sin.

"You have been quickened," said the book. "Who were dead in trespasses and in sin".

I trust the mighty Spirit of God will quicken you and that you will come to the Lord Jesus Christ and receive Him as your Saviour and Lord. May the procession of your life downward be halted. May Jesus Christ stand in this house and may He touch you with his nail-pierced hands and may you call upon Him while He is near and seek the Lord while He may be found. Don't go on in the darkness. Don't let the devil deceive you a moment longer. Don't go on in the night to a lost eternity.

O turn while the Spirit in mercy is pleading,
And steer for the harbour bright,
For how do you know but your soul may be drifting
Over the deadline tonight.

AMEN AND AMEN!

13 The man who kissed the door of heaven *but went to hell*

MY TEXT FOR THIS message is, *"And forthwith he (Judas) came to Jesus, and said, Hail, master; and kissed him."* Matthew 26:49

I have a very solemn subject this evening. I want to speak upon the man who kissed the Door of Heaven but went to Hell, the man who kissed Heaven's Door but was damned in Hell.

The men and women of the Bible were real life characters. All that they said, all that they did and the circumstances in which they lived were exactly as the Bible says they were.

These men are not myths or figments of someone's imagination. They are real life characters. But while that is absolutely so, these men are also representative men. They represent the various types of men and women in every generation of this world. They represent the men and the women of the twentieth century.

This century has its Thomases in the church who doubt the absolute authority of the great doctrine of the gospel, the resurrection of Christ.

This twentieth century has its Boanerges; its sons of thunder.

This twentieth century has its Barnabases; its sons of consolation.

It has its Enochs who walk with God.

It has its Elijahs who cry out against its idolaters and idolatry, and it has its tenderhearted disciples who, like John, repose upon the bosom of the Saviour.

It also has its Judas Iscariots, its traitors; not only in political life but also in religious life.

If you turn to the tenth chapter of John's gospel you will discover that in that chapter Jesus said "I am the Door". Jesus is the Door to Heaven and there is no other door and no other way.

If you turn to the twenty-sixth chapter of Matthew's gospel you will discover that Judas made a pact with the Pharisees. He said "I will kiss the Master and you will know that the one whom I kiss is He, bind Him and take Him away." Yes and Judas kissed the Saviour. He kissed the One Who is the Door of Heaven and yet Judas, this very night, is lost in Hell.

I want to point out some of the characteristics of Judas Iscariot.

ONE: HIGHEST PRIVILEGES NOT CHRISTIAN FAITH

The first thing I want to point out is that the highest privileges, the greatest advantages of Christian faith may be available and yet Christian faith itself may be lacking, In other words, you can have all the privileges of Christianity, all the advantages of Christianity, all the knowledge of Christianity, all the instruction in Christianity, and never have saving faith in a living Saviour.

Judas Iscariot was brought up in what must have been a devout and orthodox Jewish home. He was, no doubt, well acquainted with the Mosaic law and the peculiar tenets of Judaism. He was also fully acquainted with the prophecies concerning the Messiah.

When Jesus of Nazareth started to do miracles, when He started to show forth His glory and when He started to preach and announce the kingdom of heaven among men, one of His most constant hearers, one of His most attentive followers, one of His most zealous adherents was Judas Iscariot. The privileges, the advantages of the gospel were his. Yet gospel light never entered his darkened heart.

How true this is of the men and women of our Province. Nowhere in these isles has the gospel been preached with more fervour and more orthodoxy than in Ulster itself.

Since the plantation settlement, when this Province was carved out by the planting fathers to this present day, this part of Ireland has had the highest privileges and the greatest possible advantages as far as gospel truth and gospel knowledge is concerned.

There are men and women in this service and they, from their earliest years, and from the first moments they can recollect, have had the highest privileges and the greatest advantages that gospel opportunity could bring to them. As it were, they have been cradled in the means of grace. Early were their young feet directed to the house of God. Early did their young lips sing the psalms, the paraphrases and hymns of the church. Early did fall upon their ears the words of the living God. Early were the claims of Jesus pressed upon them.

There are some in this service this evening and this is absolutely true of you. Some of you older people have been up the incline of life, now you are going down on the other side. From your earliest years you have been taught the gospel. You understand it. You know the great basis of the doctrines of free and sovereign grace. But, alas, tonight you heart is still dark., Your soul is still unwashed. Your conscience is still unregenerate. My friend, this evening you are still out of Christ. What a tragedy! Cradled in the gospel. Brought up in the truth and still a stranger to the Saviour which it presents.

TWO: ELEVATION NOT REGENERATION

Judas Iscariot not only had the privileges but he had an elevated position. When the Lord chose twelve, Judas was among the twelve. Not that the Lord Jesus Christ was deceived for we read, "The Lord knew who should betray Him". There is a beacon lamp of warning here. And let me tell you that none of the disciples knew the character of Judas until after his death. Every one of them John, Peter, Thaddaeus and the rest of them thought he was the genuine article. At the Passover when they were going to find out who betrayed the Lord they did not say "Is it Judas?" They did not look at Judas and say "Is it him?" They said "Lord is it I?" They did not know who it was that would betray Him! Judas utterly, totally and absolutely deceived every one of the apostles. The whole eleven of them were duped by the duplicity, hypocrisy and deception of this man. He went with them on their evangelistic tours. He preached the Saviour's message. He worked wonders with them. He was a miracle worker along with the rest of them. And when they came back and said, "The devils are subject to us" Judas was among those who rejoiced in evident evangelical victories.

Learn the lesson that elevation in the church of Jesus Christ is no guarantee of eventual elevation in Heaven. Learn that! You can fall from the pulpit into Hell. You can go from the elder's seat into perdition. You can go from the communion Table to drink the cup of wrath among the doomed in Hell forever. You can go from singing the praises of Christ to the wailing, the groans and the terrors and torments of lost souls. Get it into your heart and mind that elevation in Christian work is no guarantee of eventual and eternal elevation in Heaven.

Let me tell you something more, there are men and women in this house tonight who have been elevated in the various churches to which they belong. Some are elders in the Kirk. Some serve in the church committee. Some teach in the Sabbath School. Some sing in the choir. Some are very zealous in various activities of the church. Some excel themselves in their zeal in church activity. But, oh they have never been born again.

Let me tell you friend you can hold the highest office and never have the grace of God in your heart. Let me go further. Let me say tonight you can be instructed in salvation in the head and yet never have sin destroyed in the heart. You can have a head knowledge of the whole scheme of redemption and be able to argue about the covenant of grace from election and predestination to the final preservation of the saint, and yet to have no part, personally, or lot in it. In other words, you can be like those at the judgment who will say "Lord, Lord, we have taught in the streets and done many wonderful works in your Name." And Jesus did not say "You never taught in the streets and you never did wonderful works in my Name." Jesus said "I never knew you." Do you know Christ? Does Christ know you tonight?

The man who kissed the Door of Heaven and went to hell, had all the privileges but he never closed with the Saviour. Are you like him tonight?

I want to tell you, friend, salvation is a real thing. It is radical. It is life changing and, praise God, it is life transforming. When Jesus comes into a life "old things pass away and all things become new." When Jesus comes the tempter's power is broken. When Jesus comes the night is turned to day! It is a real thing! Have you had this real experience in your heart?

THREE: SIN UNCHECKED WILL EVENTUALLY FIND YOU OUT

Something else. Learn this from the life of Judas, that sin unchecked will eventually find you out in the darkest possible experience of that very sin. Yes, sin unchecked will find you out in the darkest possible expression of that sin.

The sin of Judas, the passion of Judas was for property and money. He loved money. After he was dead it was discovered that he was a thief. No one ever discovered it while he was living. But John records it later on after Judas is dead. He was the Treasurer. He carried the bag. There was not the least mention of suspicion about him. The disciples thought he was the man to do the job. A man of integrity and a man of honesty as far as they were concerned. But you know one day the true Judas came out, for Mary took the box of ointment, spikenard, very precious and broke it and anointed the feet of Jesus, and the fragrance filled the house. Judas said "This should not have been done, it should have been sold for so much money and that money given to the poor." But John says he did not care for the poor. No, Sir! "He had the bag and was a thief." And all the time that he was doing the job he was stealing the money from the bag. No one knew! But that sin developed and the passion of it ruled his heart. Oh how many men have started off never intending to do what they did. I talked to men in prison this morning and they did not intend to commit the acts which they have committed. When they started off they thought it was just a little thing and they got deeper and deeper into it and the passion was inflamed and every bit of sin added to the fuel, until eventually they found themselves chained and tied and bound and incarcerated with a cruel rope from which, humanly speaking, there is no escape.

Such was Judas! He was propelled forward with the lust of money. And he said "I will sell the Saviour." The master sin in Judas's life sold Jesus Christ.

Let me tell you, Sir, you will sell Jesus for your master sin. It is the sin which is keeping you from the Saviour. You love your sin so much that you are not prepared to part from it. If I say to you tonight "Sir, come to Christ" you reply "I would but!" What is after the "but" Sir? "Your master sin." The thing which holds you and controls you and dominates you. That sinful thing will drag you to the nethermost of Hell if you are not washed in the Saviour's Blood. Oh, my friend, if this sin is not checked it will be your ruination.

FOUR: OUTWARD REMORSE NOT INWARD REPENTANCE

Let us also learn that outward remorse is entirely different from inward repentance. Do you see Judas? He has got the money. He has it in his purse but it is burning hot. Judas reckoned without a conscience, without a conscience awakened and set on fire. Cursed is the man that carries his own accuser in his breast. Judas is carrying his accuser in his breast. He is like a madman. He wraps his cloak around him and rushes through the streets of the city. He goes to the Temple and there are the Pharisees with whom he has made his bargain. He opens his purse and takes those thirty pieces of burning hot silver and throws them on the floor. I hear them as they jingle on the marble floor of the Temple. And Judas cries an hysterical cry, punctuated with remorse and tears, "I have betrayed innocent Blood."

The Pharisees look at him with a sneer and reply "See thou to that." Judas then goes from the Temple to the field which he had covenanted to buy and which he had long coveted for his own. He goes to the face of the cliff and standing back a little with trembling hands he ties a rope around the base of a tree. The other end of the rope, in his frenzy, he ties around his neck. Then with one mad rush he runs forward and jumps over the precipice. For a moment or two he dangles in the air but his weight is too heavy for the rope and the rope breaks and there is a dull thud as his body bumps against rock after rock in the gully below. Yes and down there the scripture says: "all his bowels gushed out." There is a mass of blood, crushed flesh and bones. But that is not the end of Judas. It is only the end of his life on earth. It is the opening of his eternity. It was a dark door through which Judas entered into an even darker eternity. Remember, a few hours before he had kissed the very Door of Heaven.

Gospel preaching exalts men to Heaven because Jesus said "Thou Capernaum, exalted to heaven shall be brought down to hell." You, this very night, are upon the very border of heaven. You are at the very door. You have your hand on the knob. Perhaps your lips are upon the very door.

Judas kissed Heaven's Door and went to Hell. Are you going to be a Judas tonight? Is the Iscariot's sin going to darken your heart? Are you going to go out into the same Hell into which Judas Iscariot has gone?

Men and women there is a difference between Judas and Peter. What a difference! Peter made his way to the cross. How do I know? He says in his epistle that he was an eyewitness of the sufferings of Jesus. As Peter, who had denied and blasphemed the Saviour, stood under that cross a wondrous change was wrought in his heart, repentance unto life, a repentance not to be repented of.

Will you come to the cross tonight? Will you kneel there confessing your need of Christ? Will you close tonight with the Saviour and be saved for all eternity? Do not have an unready deathbed. Do not go through a dark door to a dark eternity. Enter tonight through the Door into the light and immortality of the gospel.

May it be so for Jesus Sake

AMEN AND AMEN!

14 The pigs that got *a permanent wave*

I HAVE GOT A wonderful story to preach on tonight. It is one of the most simple of the Lord's parables. But it is not only simple, it is celestially sublime. Not a story in the Book brings forth the mercy, and the grace, and the love and the compassion of God like this story we are going to talk about tonight.

In this fifteenth chapter of Luke's gospel there are three stories. They by right should all be taken together. There is the story of the lost sheep. That is in the first part of the chapter. Then in the centre of the chapter there is the story of the lost silver. And now we come to the story of the lost son. The lost sheep, the lost silver and the lost son.

I want you to picture with me the setting for this story. It is a family setting. It is the setting of the home. But you know, my friend, there is something that is missing in this home. There is no mention of the mother. The mother is not there.

You know the mother is the centre of the home. Everything revolves around the mother. The father is the head of the home,. But the mother is the centre of the home. I know with my wee ones, when they are with daddy everything is all right when the sun is shining. When trouble comes, or they fall, they do not run to their daddy it is mammy they want. Why?

Because mother is the centre of the home. And I tell you when you lose your mother everything in the home is different. I miss my mother more tonight than I ever missed her before. And if you have got your mother, thank God she is living. And do the best you can for her, for she is irreplacable. And when she is gone you will never be able to be the same again.

I believe the mother died in this family. That is why the family broke up. That is why the young fellow said, "I am going to leave home." When mother was there, there was an anchor, there was something that tied him there. There was something that kept him there, there was something that secured him there. Aye, when mother is living there is an anchor in that home. When mother is living there is a centre in that home. There is about it a mysterious magnetism that keeps the whole home and the family revolving round her. Mother is gone. There is no mention of her. And we read that the young fellow said "Father, give me the portion of goods that falleth to me. I want my share. I want my portion." He did not say to the father, "Father, what am I going to get?" He did not say to the father, "Father, I know I don't deserve anything. I know I am not entitled to anything. I know perfectly well that anything I am going to get is of your free will." But this greedy young man said "My portion". It should not be his until after the father died. But he wanted to predate the father's death. He wanted his heritage right there and now. And of course the father divided the living between his two sons. You will notice (and this is my first point) the characteristic of ruin by sin.

RUIN BY SIN

What are the characteristics of ruin by sin? Look in the chapter. Let us look at it together and you will find that he gathered up everything. Sin makes men greedy. Sin makes men possessive. Sin makes men take a tight hold on all the worldly goods that they can get their grip on.

I wonder how many sinners are holding on to worldly goods in this house tonight. And their whole affections, and all their love, and all their talents and all their ability is their centre. They are tied to the goods of this earth.

You remember that rich fool. He tried to feed his soul on corn. And he said "I will pull down my barns and build greater. I will say to my soul, "Soul, thou hast much goods laid up for thee, eat, drink and be merry'." As if the soul could eat and drink. As if the soul could be satisfied with corn. As if the soul could be blessed with money. That spiritual part of you cannot be blessed or satisfied with anything less than Jesus.

Some people are trying to satisfy themselves with all their goods. Come look at it again. "He took a journey". Where did he go? Further and further and further away from the father's house.

Where does sin take us? Further and further and further away from the Father's House. Every day, men and women, you are getting further from Heaven. Further from Christ. Further from God. Further from pardon and peace. Some of you are away in the far country tonight. You have been journeying on for years. Oh, what a journey it is to be away from God. It is a rugged road. It is not an easy road to go away from God. It is a rugged road. It is not an easy road to go away from God. "The way of the transgressor is hard". Thank God, He makes it hard for men to go away from Him.

This fellow is on a journey. And he is journeying to the far country. That is where you are sinner. You are in the far country tonight.

Come on, let us have another look at it. And what did he do then. Oh, look at that word. What a word it is, "He wasted". That is what sin does for you. It wastes you, friend. Your life is wasted if you have not wasted. That is a terrible indictment, is it not?

Is that what you are doing? Wasting your soul, wasting your body, wasting your talents, wasting your ability, wasting time and wasting everything that is worthwhile. Putting it to a wrong use. How many men in this meeting are putting their bodies to a wrong use because of their sin? How many people in this meeting are putting their talents to a wrong use because of their sin? Come on, face up to it. You have wasted many precious years, have you not? When you think of all that you could have done for God in purity, in righteousness, and Heaven and Christ. But you have wasted your years. Now you are up the incline. Some of you are old greyheaded sinners going down the decline, and God is saying "That man has wasted his life, wasted his talents, wasted his ability and has wasted all the breath I have given him, and all the energy I have put into his body". What a terrible thing to be just a waster in the presence of God. And that is what you are sinner tonight.

These are the characteristics of ruin by sin.

Let me show you something else. Let us look at it again. "He wasted his substance with riotous living." In rebellion, yes! You are a rebel. You are a law breaker. You are in rebellion against the King. You are breaking His laws, rejecting His Word, trampling under foot his commandments. Riotous living!

It is not a nice picture, is it? That fine young man stepping out from home. His feet are firm on the path. He is upright, he has a look of innocence about him. But we meet him in the far country. Is this the young man that left home? Is this the young man with innocent look and upright figure? Yes! What has come over him? He has wasted his life, wasted his talents in riotous living. What a change the devil makes. What a change.

You say "I never intend to be like that". No, you do not. I know you do not.

I sat in Sunday School in this very town, with a young boy in Sunday School. The teacher asked us to receive Christ as our Saviour. Some of us said "Yes". This young boy said "No". And, my friend, I followed that young boy and I saw how he lived. I visited him when he was doing time in jail. And he finished a tragic, and sad and ruined soul. He was my Sunday School companion. He was as good and as honourable a lad as I was, but he rejected Jesus. He wasted his substance. He went into the far country. And the end of the story is tragedy piled upon tragedy. And sorrow and darkness piled upon sorrow and darkness.

Do not say "That will never happen to me". It will. Sin is far too strong for any one of us.

Take Samson, the strongest man in the world. Sin said "Come down here, I will fight you in the arena of life." And when sin had finished with Samson, his eyes were out, his hair was cut, he was a prisoner grinding the meal for his enemies. He was the strongest man on earth, but sin was stronger than him.

You cannot fight sin and get away with it. Sin always wins except Jesus comes.

Solomon was the wisest man that ever lived. What wisdom he had! Sin said, "Solomon come off your throne. Come and fight me in the arena of life." Did you ever read the end of Solomon's life? It is the most tragic ending of any life's-story. Sin finished him. And the wise king became a dottering fool. And what a fool he was at the end of his day.

If sin destroyed the strongest man that ever lived. If sin destroyed the wisest man that ever lived, you have not a hope of fighting the battle of sin in your own strength.

Come on, look at it again. That is not the end of the story. "There arose a mighty famine in that land."

I tell you, when sin starts paying its wages, it pays overtime. A mighty famine in the land. In the place where he had his enjoyment, he started to reap his disillusionment.

I want to tell you, sow to the flesh and of the flesh you will reap corruption. There are sinners in this meeting tonight, and you have been sowing to the flesh all your life. You are going to reap what you sow. It is coming. The harvest day sir, is coming. The harvest day, madam, is coming. You will not escape it. The mighty famine will come and will leave you empty and lonely in your sin.

What did this young prodigal do? He went to get a job. And he took a job that was most obnoxious to a Jew. He went to the swine herd. Down among the pigs and the swine. Down at the swine trough. It says here, "he fain would have filled his belly with the husks that the swine did eat".

I tell you, sin will bring you low. It will bring you low to the swine trough. And, if God prevents it not, it will bring you into a lost hell. Sin never finishes until it brings forth death. Do not be bluffing yourself friend. Do not be fooling yourself. Do not say "It will never happen to me." It will happen to you!

This is the story of the characteristics of ruin by sin. Look at it, "no man gave unto him". There is a day coming when no man will be able to help you. That is where sin takes you. To a place where no man can help you.

Listen friend, I have seen men, I have seen women, and no man could help them. And that is you tonight. Oh, if God does not help sinners what will happen to them? They will fall into hell. Only God can save. That is why we are praying for you. That is why forty men and women were out of their beds at six o'clock this morning. That is why our own church and brother McCrea's church have the early morning prayer meeting because only God can save men.

"No man gave unto him." I hope you have got the picture. It is a picture of yourself. The characteristics of ruin by sin. Oh, how sin ruins men and women. It is ruining your soul, destroying you friend, wasting you and you are perishing.

REPENTANCE OF SIN

I want to show you something else. Thank God, we do not close the Book there. Thank God, there is something more in this story. Look at it. There is the characteristics of repentance of sin. There is not only the characteristics of ruin by sin. But there is the characteristics of repentance of sin.

Look at verse seventeen, "And when he came to himself."

I was telling you about old Christmas Evans. He had a great sermon on the prodigal son. A great descriptive wise old preacher. He said "Of course when things got bad, this prodigal went to the pawnshop. And he took off his overcoat and handed it over the counter. He said 'Give me some money on that.' He never redeemed his overcoat. And some days afterwards he took off his other coat and took it to the pawnshop. And he threw it over the counter and got some money for it. And then a few days afterwards he took off his shirt and took it to the pawnshop. And he put it over the counter and got some money for it." And then the old preacher said "he cane to himself. He had nothing else to take off. He came to himself."

Yes! There was a lot of truth in what that old preacher was trying to get at. And I tell you, until you come to yourself, until you come right down to the real naked truth, you will never be saved. And if you think you will make it through the church door, you are bound to wake up in hell. If you think you will make it through the baptismal font, you will be in hell. If you think you will make it by the Lord's Table, you will be in hell. If you think you will make it by singing in the choir, or teaching in the

Sabbath School or doing the best you can, you will be in hell. You need to come to yourself. You need to face the naked truth. That is the first characteristic of repentance of sin. "He came to himself".

Let us look at it again. What else did he say? He said, "I perish." It is great when a sinner says "I perish". He is on the way. When man learns he is a perishing sinner, Jesus is ready to save him. "I perish."

Do you see yourself tonight as a perishing sinner, friend? I want to tell you, you are tonight under the dark clouds of God's wrath. Underneath your feet are the slippery slopes that lead down to hell. Before you are the caverns of the damned. Behind you are the sneering, deceiving devils of the pit, pushing you on and on and on until you come to the frightful edge, and one day they will push you over. And you will scream "Lost" as you fall into the flames of brimstone and fire for evermore. That is what the devil wants to do with you.

Happy the man who says "I perish. I am a perishing sinner. There is nothing good about me. I cannot save myself. I am a lost soul. Lord, it is up to you to do the job."

Mr Nicholson came to the Ravenhill Road in the early twenties. That was the year of the great revival. "From Civil War to Revival Victory" was the book that was written of those campaigns. It was a time of trouble just like now. Men were being shot. Snipers were on the roof. Men were being killed. The gunmen were there, the killers and the bombers were there, and the evil people were there. And that preacher, he was a young man then, came to the Ravenhill Road and preached in what we call Ross's Church, the Irish Presbyterian Church on the Ravenhill Road. Down where my old church is there was a row of whitewashed cottages. It was called Lagan Village. And there was an old ex-army fellow lived in one of them. They called him Jimmy McVeigh. And Jimmy McVeigh was the worst sinner on the Ravenhill Road. When Jimmy McVeigh was drunk it took four policemen to tame him. And the policemen in those days wore the helmets with the long points on the top of them. If you had gone into Jimmy's home you would have seen nothing but holes in the ceiling where these big policemen wrestled with him. As he pushed them about those points went up into the ceiling. Jimmy was a scoundrel if ever there was one. He was a low down reprobate, a swearing hard living, hard drinking man. One night the men from the Island came to hear WP Nicholson preach. They were led by a Salvation Army band.

Jimmy McVeigh, drunkard, wastrel, sinner, ungodly blasphemer, stood on the kerbstone on the Lagan Village. He was an old soldier, and when he heard the marching music he started to swing his arms and march with the crowd. That night they shifted the pillar that held the gates, so great was the crush. And Jimmy McVeigh was carried into the front seat of the gallery facing the preacher. As WP Nicholson preached the gospel, that man got up and he said "I will take Jesus if he will have me. I will take Jesus if He will have me." He became transformed by the grace of God. What a change. My, when Jesus saves you, He changes you. Jimmy was changed. He got a job. And the neighbours decided that they would give him a surprise. So when they got him away to work early one morning they got into that house, and they painted it and papered it from top to bottom. And when Jimmy came up the road that night, marching along and singing that old hymn that Nicholson used to sing "Don't forget there is a house to let". And he was singing that hymn at the pitch of his voice. When he put the key in the door and opened it, man what a change! He did not know the house. And then suddenly he took about six leaps into the middle of the Ravenhill Road and shouted "glory to God, the house is converted too. Glory to God, the house is converted too."

Oh, I tell you when Jesus comes there is a mighty change.

I was preaching at a meeting some months ago in Rathcoole. A woman shouted out, "Preacher, that story is true." I said, "Sure, it is true." She said "I am Jimmy McVeigh's daughter. I know all about it."

Let me tell you friend, when you learn you are a perishing sinner, Jesus can deal with you.

"I perish." Is there a man here tonight and he is saying "Preacher, it is true of me. I am a perishing wretch. If I go on the way I am going I will certainly reach hell. Oh, preacher is there hope for me?" Thank God, there is hope for you. Come on, cry out "I perish." That is what the prodigal did.

These are the characteristics of repentance of sin.

Look at it again. What else do we read here? He said "I will arise." That is the second step in repentance. Man as a repenting sinner does not stay put. He arises. He rises up out of the muck and away from the swine trough and away from the evil companionships. He says "I will arise."

Thank God, there have been men and women in this mission and they have said, "I will arise." And they have come down this aisle. Why? Because they are coming to the Father's House. "I will arise".

Then there is the last one. "I have sinned." The three cries of a repenting sinner, "I perish!" "I will arise!" "I will say I have sinned."

Please God, scores of men and women will say that in this meeting tonight. That is the way Home. If you say those things from the depths of your soul, you are coming Home. You are on the way Home.

Do you see him? Come on, look at it. He gets up from the swine trough and he walks out, and he walks up the hill, and he turns round and, praise God, he gives the pigs a permanent wave. He says "Cheerio," forever. It is a permanent wave all right. He never waved good-bye to them again. He has gone from them for evermore. Hallelujah! That is what happens when God saves a man. "Good-bye". Good-bye to sin. Good-bye to the world.

You young converts, you know you are a mystery to yourself, are you not? You do not understand what has happened, sure you don't? You are saying "I could never imagine it. Imagine me going to a prayer meeting. And imagine me praying, and testifying, and loving the Bible. I used to love old filthy books. I used to run with old filthy companions. But now I love Jesus. I am changed." Who did it? God did it in your soul. You have said "Good-bye" forever. You have given the pigs a permanent wave. Hallelujah! I trust there will be a lot of waving here tonight. You say "I am quitting forever." Yes!

REDEMPTION FROM SIN

Ruined by sin. Repentance from sin. But there is something even better than that. There is redemption from sin. Look at the characteristics of this. Look here, "and when he was a great way off, his father saw him." Oh, I love that. The old father is up yonder on the housetop. He has never left it since the son went away. Every morning he has climbed the stair and stood on top of the house, and he has looked down that road that he saw his younger son depart from. And many a man came up that road, but the father knew it was not his son. Then one morning, although his eyes are now dim with age, his body is now bent, he is still yonder, the picture of the Father looking for His son, the picture of God looking for sinners. And he sees him. Oh, he recognises him. He sees him a great way off.

Jesus sees you, man, tonight. Oh, you are still a great way off, but Hallelujah! God sees you. He sees there is some little desire in you to get saved. That is why you are at the meeting tonight. It is not by chance you are here. God has got you here. The Spirit of God is here and He sees you afar off.

There is no eye like the eye of Jesus,
Piercing so far away
Ne'er out of sight of its tender light
Can the wanderer stray

What happened? I love this. Come on, let us look at it. Is this not good? "He has compassion." "Oh, that is what I need. Father I am perishing. Father I am coming Home. But I am not the son that left home. I have got nothing now. I have wasted my life. I have only got a starved, soiled, ruined soul and a filthy ill-clad body." But God has compassion. Oh, the Infinite Compassion of Jesus!

I had a gospel campaign many years ago in the town of Lisburn. There was a godly Presbyterian minister in that town by the name of Fullerton. Mr Fullerton said to me, "Ian, if you ever come and preach the gospel in Lisburn I will stand by you. I will attend your first meeting. I will take the chair. And I will call for the people to stand with you in the gospel." So when the Orange Hall was booked for that campaign, that dear man rang me up and he said "I am going to keep my promise." I said, "That is good." Then a few days afterwards he rang me up and he said, "Ian, I am in trouble with the Presbytery." He says, "There is a rule in the General Assembly that you cannot go into another man's parish, unless you have got his permission. The Orange Hall is outside my parish. I cannot go and take the chair. I have found out that. There is nothing against me praying. I will just come and pray then." So he came and he prayed. And he worked in that mission with me as a brother beloved. And one night after all the people had gone away, I was standing with him and we were rejoicing together (That dear man is now in the Glory Land. One of the old men of God who had fire in his soul and loved Jesus with all his heart) and the door at the back of the Orange Hall (I can see it now) opened slightly. Two of the worst women in Lisburn, two of the street walkers in that town, said "Is there anybody here?" I said "No, just Mr Fullerton and myself are here." They said "We are so glad, for we are so ashamed. Everybody knows us. Mr Paisley (and I see now their eyes are drenched with tears) would Jesus save the likes of us? We would not come to the meeting because we are so ashamed. Would Jesus save the likes of us?" I said, "Hallelujah! He will save you." I remember Mr Fullerton and myself getting down with those two harlots of the street, and, thank God, 'though their sins were as crimson, they were as white as snow.' God saved them. God saved them from their harlotry and whoredom and street walking, by the grace of God. Why? God had compassion on them.

Sometimes there is more hope for people like that than for religious hypocrites who darken the church door every Sunday and think they are righteous, and know not that they are poor lost sinners just as vile, as far as God is concerned.

He had compassion. But look at it again. It gets better does it not? "And he ran." God runs to save men. Oh, I love that. God is never in a hurry in the Bible, except to save men. He is never in a hurry to damn men. He is slow to wrath. But here we have the father running.

That is what God has been doing in the Ballymena Town Hall. He has been running to men and women.

RECONCILIATION

"He ran, and he fell on his neck and kissed him." The kiss of reconciliation. "Kiss the Son, lest He be angry and you perish in the way, when His wrath is kindled but a little". He kissed him.

Look at it again. What happened? And do you know what the son said? He only got this out. I like this. He said, "I have sinned." The father never allowed him to say anything more. He had a nice speech made up. He was going to say "Father, I have sinned, and I am not worthy to be called thy son." But all the father wanted him to say was "I have sinned."

You have only to say "I have sinned" and God will save you.

The father said "Bring forth the best robe and put it on him." "I have sinned against Heaven, and in thy sight, and am no more worthy to be called thy son." He never got any further than that. He was going to say "make me as one of thy hired servants". He did not get any further. He had confessed that he had sinned against Heaven, and in the sight of his father. That was enough. "Bring forth the best robe."

Nothing but the best for repenting sinners. I like this. Nothing but the best. I want to tell you, God has nothing but the best for you. The devil has nothing but the worst for you. Serve the devil and he will find you with everything and leave you with nothing. But God finds us with nothing and, bless God, gives us everything. There is a great difference is there not? "Bring forth the best robe and put it on him." I like this. He was without shoes on his feet. "Come on, put shoes on his feet. Put a ring on his hand. And come and let us be merry." There is joy in the presence of the angels of God o'er sinners coming Home. "Let us be merry." And do you know what happens? There are three merriments when a man gets saved. He is merry. The saints of God are merry and the angels of God are merry. My, there is joy in heaven o'er sinners coming Home. "Let the angels bear the tidings, upwards to the courts of Heaven, Let them sing in ceaseless rapture o'er another soul forgiven".

Are you going to be that soul tonight? Come on to Christ. The Devil has wasted you. You are perishing. You are on the wrong road. Come, my friend, Home tonight to thy Father's House. Come and welcome, ten thousand welcomes to Jesus.

May many come tonight, for Jesus' Sake!

AMEN AND AMEN!

15 Quenching the firebrands of hell

THE WHOLE OF NATURE is a great preacher of God's omnipotence and of God's creative power.

The Psalmist says, "The heavens declare the glory of God and the firmament showeth His handiwork." Even the material of this planet on which we are and upon which we move is a preacher in parables to us of the things of God.

The earthly world is an emblem of the eternal and the spiritual world. The sun is an emblem of the greater Sun of righteousness. The mighty rocks and the great mountains lifting up their peaks to the clouds of the heavens tell forth the fact that God is great in His power and His almightiness as shown forth in His creation.

When we see the fading of the leaf we are reminded of the frailty of our own human bodies. The Bible tells us that man doth fade like a leaf. When the harvest time comes we are reminded of a great and terrible reaping time. We will reap whatsoever we sow. That great harvest is most certainly coming and with it the great reaping time.

The element of fire in the universe is most suggestive of spiritual things. The Bible makes it clear that in our mortal everyday world the fire is an emblem of sin. The fire in its conflagration, the fire in its burnings, the fire in its strength and all sweeping power is a type of the consummation and conflagration of this thing called sin.

The old prophet Amos said "Ye were as a firebrand plucked out of the burning" - the burning of sin.

I want to talk this evening about fire, an emblem of sin. I want to draw the parallel between the characteristics of fire and the awful characteristics of sin.

Then I want to talk about the firebrand. The type of the sinner consumed, burning, almost destroyed by sin apart from Divine intervention.

Then I want to talk a little about the fact that God is strong enough and gracious enough and loving enough to lift out the firebrand from the burning and to quench the faggots in the powerful liquid of the blood of the Lamb and to transform them into sons of God and to make them new creatures in Christ Jesus.

The topic is simple but its lessons are solemn and please God they may reach some heart and stir some anxious thought and bring down conviction of the Holy Ghost and lead to the salvation of precious souls.

THE MYSTERY OF FIRE

The first thing I must say about fire is this - there is a mystery about fire.

You cannot weigh it, you cannot measure it, you cannot grasp it. They tell me that the hottest flame is invisible and cannot even be seen. There is something mysterious about fire.

My friend there is something mysterious about the mystery of iniquity working in the hearts of sinners. No human scales can weigh sin. The only scale that can weigh it is the scale in the hands of God. It takes God to put sin into the balance." Thou art weighed", He says to the sinner, "in the balances and art found wanting."

No human measurement can measure sin but the measurement of God has measured the iniquity of the ages. No human hand can grasp sin but, praise God, the nail-pierced hand of Jesus grasped it and dealt with it in all His redeeming work on yonder cross.

Yes, sin is a mystery.

Its seeds are sown in every breast. Its harvest is reaped in every life. There is not a soul in this meeting young or old, rich or poor, educated or illiterate, religious or irreligious, who is not stained by this awful thing called sin. Sin contaminates every birth. We are born in sin and shapen in iniquity. Sin has a right of way into every place, be it the palace of royalty or the hovel of the pauper, sin is there. This mysterious satanic, filthy, diabolical, dirty, degrading, debauching, devilish thing called sin is working in the hearts of every one of us. Sin is a mystery.

THE MAGNETISM OF FIRE

Could I say something else about fire. Fire has a special magnetism.
There is something attractive about the flame. There is something enchanting about the conflagration.
The first place a child will go to is to the fire. There is something which attracts the little one to the fire. Therefore the guard has got to be put on and the protection has got to be placed around lest that child, in its foolishness and in its innocency, should go to that which would destroy him. That poor moth, in its folly, flies to the flame. It will not leave the flame. It goes round and round it until its wings are scorched and instead of fleeing from it, it keeps on at it until it falls, sinks to the ground in ashes. I want to tell you friend there is a magnetism about sin that lures men to their own destruction.
How many men, how many women, in the meeting are captivated by the magnetism of sin.
You cannot get away, drunkard, from the public house. You cannot get away from the bottle. You cannot get away from the booze. It is ruining you. It is destroying you. It is going to damn you but it has a satanic magnetism about it which draws you again and again and again to its awful place of woe and darkness.
I am thinking of one man. He used to attend this church. He used to listen to the Gospel preacher but he was tied up in his cups and he could not leave them. He went on, on and on. He used to wring his hands and he used to shed tears and he used to say "Ian this thing will destroy me."

Friend, one day I lifted the paper and I found that his sin had destroyed him. He fell asleep in a drunken stupor not to awaken in time but to awake in the great dark eternity.

Sin has a magnetism. How magnetic is it in your life? What hold has it got upon you? Drawing you to its destruction and you are circling in its flames. My friend of sin, you are destroying your body and you are destroying your life and you are going to damn your immortal soul for ever in the magnetic fire of sin.

Oh sinner heed the warning voice.
Make the Lord your final choice.
Then all heaven will rejoice.
In God's name, be in time.

THE MIGHT OF FIRE

Fire has a magnetism and so has sin. Fire is a mystery and so is sin. Fire is terrible in its might and so is sin. My how fire consumes. If you start a fire in this hall, the appetite of that flame is unquenchable. It will eat all before it. It will leave in its wake a mass of ruin, a mass of ashes and a mass of cinders.

Oh the might of the flame once it gets a grip.

Tell me what about the might of sin. It takes the young life and it burns evil habits into the soul. It takes the heart of youth and twists it and perverts it and distorts it until the young man grows up with a crooked mind and crooked thoughts and a perverse crooked walk. As he goes on growing he is growing in a thwarted perverted manner. Sin is consuming him. It consumes his ambitions. Once he wanted to prosper.

Once he wanted to live clean and do right and be decent and be respectable and be honest but sin destroyed his ambition. Sin blighted his mind. Sin spoiled his prospects. Sin ruined his body. Sin marred his family and sin, when it is finished, bringeth forth death. That is what sin does. Oh the awful might of sin.

SEARED BY SIN

I sat in a Sunday School class many years ago and there was a group of boys in that class and we all sat in a circle on the Lord's Day morning. We had a faithful and godly Sunday School teacher and he used to talk to us about the necessity of personal faith in Jesus Christ.

There was Billy and Billy was a Christian. There was myself and I was a Christian. There was a bright eyed lad called Jim, one of the best lads in the class. A lad you would look up to. A lad who was likeable but he was not saved. He said to the Sunday School teacher, "Mr McCrea, not now. I want to live. I am going to grow up. I am going to see things. I am not going to limit myself by old ways that are Christian. I want to see things. When I have seen the world I will talk to you about getting saved."

IMPRISONED

The Sunday School class broke up as all Sunday School classes do. We all went our separate ways. I came to this city 21 years ago to minister in Ravenhill. I was only there a few months till I got a telephone message one day. It was from the Crumlin Road Prison. I did not think then that I would be jailed there myself some day. The telephone call intimated that a young man urgently required my attention.

I went straight to the prison. I went into that little room where they interview prisoners. Two warders walked in with a prisoner between them. They marched him in. Do you know who it was? It was Jimmy. He thought he was beginning to see life. Sin's fires were burning in his soul.

I said, "Jim there is only one answer to your problem and it is Jesus Christ." He said, "I know that. Ian, I ought to be saved. I am doing six months and I will be out in four, I will get two months off for good behaviour. Ian, leave it with me."

I visited him off and on and as his sentence finished he said "Ian, I will be at church and I will come to Christ." I said, "You know you will not because you should come to Christ now and be saved now." He was discharged and I heard nothing more for some time then the telephone rang again one day. The same man wanted to see me in prison. He was now doing a much longer sentence, three years.

Sin had caught hold. I went to see him and he said the same thing. He said "When I come out I will come to Christ." I said, "You know you will not, you will never come to Christ. If you mean business you will get saved now." He said, "I could not do it, I could not be a Christian and be in this prison." I said, "You could be a Christian anywhere. Jesus Christ does not recognise prison walls or prison bars. You can be saved anywhere. You can live for God anywhere."

RUINED AND LOST

I visited him for three years. He came out and went to England. Sin broke up his home. His wife had to leave him. His daughter had to forsake him and he went down the quick road to the pit. One night he was cut off in his sin. There was a Sunday School scholar in the class that I sat in my father's church in Ballymena and tonight he is in hell. It could have been different.

Cut off without a moment. Cut off tragically in his sin. Yes sin consumes. You say you will manage it all right. Will you? There is not a man in prison, and I talk to scores of them, that ever intended to be there but they found themselves there.

WHAT WOULD THE DAMNED SAY?

If I could draw aside the curtain that divides time from eternity and talk to the damned in hell there is not a damned soul that intended to go to hell. They all intended some day to repent and be saved. But they are lost. Why? Because sin consumes. It ruins men in its consummation.

Oh my friend, could I tell you that sin is like the fire in its conflagration. It is a spreading sin. Ah it spreads. Father, let me tell you, your sin will spread to your family. A drunken father will raise drunken sons. Billy Sunday tells in one of his sermons of a man who went out in a snow storm and he decided he would go to the public house and the marks of his footprints were left in the snow. After he was out about ten minutes he looked round and he saw his little boy. The little boy was coming and he was putting his tiny feet into the footprints of his father. Where were the footprints taking him? Taking him to the public house. Taking him to the death chamber. Taking him to the vestibule of hell. Unsaved father if your son follows your footprints will they take him to hell?

Remember that you do not sin to yourself you know. You don't go to hell on your own. You don't just damn your own soul but you damn every man that you have any influence over.

There is one thing the grave digger's spade will not cover when you die and that is your influence. My influence will live on when I am gone. I trust it will be an influence for God and for truth and for righteousness and for souls. Your influence will live on if it is an influence that is evil and sinful and hellish, it will live on to curse generations following.

THE CURSE WHICH LIVES ON

Remember the old prophet shouted in Samaria and said, "There is the son of Nebat that caused Israel to sin". That was hundreds of years afterwards but that man's sin was still there. Jeraboam, the son of Nebat, his sin went on. Your sin will live on. Sin is terrible in its conflagration. Sin is awful just like fire in the agony that it inflicts.

It is a terrible thing to see a body that has been badly burned. You know some time ago there was a great tragedy.

A ship went out of Harland and Wolff's and there was an explosion on board and there were men badly burned. I had to go to the hospital to visit them and talk to them. What a sight it was to see their bodies. I am thinking of one man now and all you could recognise were his eyes. His nose was shrivelled away. His ears were burned off his head. His cheeks were one great scar. Awful to look on. But oh the agony that that man suffered!

He told me, "Mr Paisley it was terrible down there in a veritable furnace." In the burning, in the burning. My friend sin brings agony and pain. How many scars has sin burned into your soul. How many pains has sin convulsed your physical being with. It brings pain in time. It brings pain at death and it leads to the eternal pain of a screaming hell forever.

THE MAULING OF FIRE

Sin inflicts agony. Oh the agony that comes because of sin. It does not only inflict agony on you but it inflicts agony on everybody else. There is many a mother who has a broken heart because her son is living in sin. There is many a wife who has a broken heart because her ungodly husband is bringing dishonour on the name. There is many a boy and he sheds in the secret place a silent tear because his father and mother are stained with sin. Yes. Sin brings agony.

Oh the defacing power of fire! Set fire to this building and come and look at it after the fire is over and it will not be recognisable. It will be just a charred, dirty, stained, defaced ruin.

My friend that is what sin does with a soul who was built to live with God. You know the soul was never built to be damned in hell. God is not the architect of hell for you. He made hell for the devil and his angels, so the good Book tells me and the good Book is true.

Your soul was built to live with God. Your soul was built for the heaven of heavens. Your soul was built to stand upon the sea of glass and take the golden harp and join in the eternal celestial hallelujah chorus to the Redeemer. But instead of your soul, rising on its pinion to the celestial hills above it is going to sink and sink and sink to the bottomless pit of hell. What defaced it? What destroyed it? What ruined it? What stained it? What damned it? It was sin that did it. It is like a fire, it defaces all who are burned by it.

Let me tell you something else. If you wait too long to put out the fire you will never put it out. Just let the fire get a grip. Just let the fire have its flames fed. Just let the fire get the hold on any person or any place or any city and friend, it will never be put out. Even the firemen themselves let it burn and they seek to save other buildings around it. The original building is too far gone and is left to be completely destroyed.

In God's name sinner, let me tell you with the Holy Book in my hand, there is a time when sin goes too far. Yes, there is such a thing as having this burning starting the unquenchable burnings of hell. Yes sir. You can go on too long, you scoffers of the Word of God. You procrastinators who have sat under the Gospel and rejected it over and over again.

You rejecters of Jesus Christ. You sinners in this meeting who have gone your own way for years and years and years and years. Too late, too late, shall be your cry. Jesus of Nazareth shall forever pass you by.

THE FIRE BRAND

Fire gets too great a hold. There is nothing you can do. That is the fire.

What about the firebrand?

I want to tell you something about the firebrand. All it is good for is the burning. Do you know all you are good for is just your sin. That is all you are good at friend. You say, "Mr Paisley, that is a terrible statement." It is true about sinners. All sinners are good for is their sinning. That is what you live for. Some of you are prepared to die for it and take the great risk of losing your immortal soul just for sin. All the firebrand is good for is sin and until you learn friend that all you are good for in the eyes of God is your sin, God cannot save you.

God does not save respectable people, God saves sinners. That is who God saves. Christ died for church members - I never read that in the Bible. Christ died for good people - I never read that in the Bible. Christ died for those decent, respectable people - No sir, Christ died for the ungodly. That is for whom He died. If I don't recognise that I am a poor, guilty, lost firebrand no good for anything but the burnings of hell, God will never save me. Thank God for men who found that out in this house. Thank God for souls in this meeting who found out they were only firebrands, only good for sinning.

THE FIREBRAND IS ALWAYS BURNING

I will tell you something else about a firebrand, it is already burning.

Yes sir.

Do you know what is happening to you friend, you are already in your sin. The fires have got a grip on your heart. There is not a young person in this meeting that the fires of sin are not burning in their souls.

There is not one exemption in this meeting. The fires have got a hold upon you. You are not a faggot outside, you are a faggot burning in the fire. Your destruction has started. The defacing of your soul has commenced. You are on the lost road at this present time. Lost, lost, and going on to be lost forever. Terrible, those who be here going down the road to eternal hell.

I will tell you something else. A firebrand cannot resist the flames. It has got to burn. You put it in the fire and there is no resistance in that brand. It cannot say it will not burn. It will burn all right.

Put the coals up around it. Set it alight and my it will blaze from end to end until the fire creeps down its fibres and sets on fire its very heart until every fibre is kindled and the whole thing is a mass of flame. It cannot resist it. My dear sinner friend you cannot resist the power of sin. You will go on sinning. I am telling you. I don't believe there is power in any man to save himself. No sir, I don't believe that. It is utter nonsense. Men are lost. They are lost. No resistance.

You know all you need to do with a firebrand to destroy it is to just let it alone, let it burn on.

I CANNOT LET YOU GO

Please God I am not going to let you alone. There are men and women here and their prayers are not going to let you alone. We are out after your soul tonight and we are not going to let you burn easily. We want to take you and lift you out of the fire, disdaining even the garment spotted by the flesh.

THE REDSKIN HAD THE ANSWER

You say, "Preacher, can the firebrand be saved?" I am reminded of the story of an old Indian to whom a white man said "Redskin, how do you know that Jesus saved you? How did He save you anyway?"

The old Indian said, "Come out to the woods and I will show you how Jesus saved me." He brought this unbelieving white man into the woods and he got a worm and he set it upon the ground. Then he gathered all the dry leaves and all the dry little bits of twigs he could find and he made a circle around the worm. Then he set the leaves on fire. Soon that worm was encircled in a flame and it went one way to escape and it could not, and it came up against the wall of fire. It went another way to escape and it could not and again it came up against the wall of fire. It went another way to escape and it could not and it came up against this ring of fire.

He said, "That was like me. I was surrounded by the fire and I tried like this, that and the other and I was going to perish. Let me show you something.He put his hand into the circle and lifted the worm out. A big hand came into the ring and it lifted me out."That hand was the nail-pierced hand of Jesus."

I want to tell you, men and women, there is a hand that can lift you. I want to tell you there is a power can save you. I want to tell you there is blood that can wash you and there is grace that can keep you. Hallelujah to Jesus! He is the One who can save you. The church could not get you out of the fire. The sacraments could not get you out of the fire. But Jesus can get you out of the fire.

Plucked as a brand from the burning.

WHAT MUST I DO?

He can rescue you tonight. He can save you. You say, "Preacher, what will I do?" There is only one thing you can do, cry to this Christ to save your soul. Cry. That is what you do when you are in trouble.

It is about time you started crying is it not? May God help you to cry.

You say "Preacher you don't know me. I have come into the Ulster Hall tonight and I am a sinner and I can't quit it. Oh I have made new resolutions this year. I said I would not booze and I have been boozing ever since. I said I would not gamble. I said I would not go on in my old way and I have been going on."

Yes and you will go on. It is Jesus you need tonight. A real living Person. I can introduce you to a Person who can break every fetter. I can introduce you to a Person who can free you from every habit. I can introduce you to a Person who will lift you and cleanse you and save you and keep you forever. His name is Jesus. May you meet Him and may He meet you at the cross and may you be plucked as a brand out of the burning and become a brand quenched in Jesus blood.

May God bless His truth.

AMEN AND AMEN!

16 Four black *Roman nones*

I WANT TO TALK with great plainness of speech upon these four black Roman nones.

"There is none righteous" Romans 3:10. *"There is none that seeketh after God"* Romans 3:11. *"There is none that understandeth"* Romans 3:11. *"There is none that doeth good"* Romans 3:12

You know there is a lot of talk today about the nobility of man. There is a wee programme comes on at a quarter to seven in the morning on the radio, it is called "Lift Up Your Hearts." And my, you get good and bad on it. An odd time you get a man who loves Jesus and you know he does. And it is not very long until you feel a unity with him. He is telling the truth, he is saved by grace and he is washed in the Blood of Christ. And there is something cheers your heart.

I like to get up about half past six or a quarter to seven to get the sleep out of my eyes. And I have a little radio a dear brother gave me, and I set it just on the time and when a quarter to seven comes it just starts "Lift up your hearts". And I lift up my eyes and look around, and rub the sleep from my eyes. And my wife says, "Get that tea, Ian" and as an obedient husband I get up and get her a cup of tea every morning. I have a tea-making machine right beside my bed. I just press a button and the job is done!

I am sure you have heard that programme and they talk about the nobility of man, what a noble thing man is. They talk about the dignity of mankind. How dignified mankind is. They talk about the inherent goodness of men. And they talk about man's quest for the things that are lovely and true. Man's desires to forward the kingdom of God, the universal brotherhood society. Oh, it is a lot of lies. My friend there is not a vestige of truth in it.

Man, because of sin, is half beast and half devil. You say, "Preacher, that is strong language." That is what George Whitefield says. He said "Man that has sin is half beast and half devil. His body is half a beast and his soul is half a devil." That is what sin has done to man.

If you go to a church and the preacher talks about the dignity of man, talks about the purity of mankind, talks about the universal Fatherhood of God and the common brotherhood of men, do not believe a word of it friend. It is not true. It is a lie. Imagine saying those murderers are children of God.

I have been in some of those homes where murder has been committed. I have seen, the other day, the son of one of my members who was shot in his home. I was in that home. The IRA assassins came and mistook him for his cousin of the same name who was a sergeant in the RUC and had given evidence at a court case which led to the locking away of some IRA killers. And the IRA was out for that man's life. They went up to his door, and they said, "Good-day" to a man working in the garden and they shot him through the glass of his front doorway.

You say people that do that are people of God? Do not believe it. They are children of the devil. No lie is of the truth. The devil is a murderer from the beginning, and he abode not in the truth for no lie is of the truth. They are not children of God.

Let me tell you, some time ago Jim Callaghan came to Ulster. Jim Callaghan is a Baptist. He was brought up in evangelical Baptist circles. I did not know that at the time. He invited me to see him. I looked him straight in the eye and he said to me, "You know Mr Paisley, all people in Ulster are children of God, every one of them." I said, "You are wrong." He said, "What do you mean?" I said, "I believe in Jesus Christ. I do not believe in Jim Callaghan. Jesus Christ said 'You are of your father the devil, and the works of your father ye will do. He was a liar from the beginning and he abode not in the truth.'" He said, "I am not going to argue with you from the Bible." I replied "You brought it up. You bring up anything from the Bible and I am able for you, thank God." He has a sister who is a converted woman. She sent word to a friend of mine who is a Baptist minister in London, she said, "Tell Ian Paisley he really hit him in the sore place." Jim Callaghan professed to be saved and was baptised as a young man. He knew what I was talking about.

I want to tell you friend, that you are not a child of God, men are not dignified, men are not pure, men are not noble. Man in sin is a wretched, God-cursed rebel. And if he dies in rebellion he goes to the place that God has prepared for the devil and his angels.

THE FIRST BLACK ROMAN NONE

There are four very important truths here. "There is none righteous, no not one."

How is a man righteous? He is righteous when he comes up to God's standard. What is a standard of righteousness? It is not man's righteousness. It is not the church's righteousness, it is not the law, man's law idea of righteousness. God has a standard of righteousness. How far short do we fall from God's standard today. There is not much righteousness in our lives.

Do you know what the Bible says? "Righteousness exalteth a nation." This nation is going down. There is not much righteousness here. Man, they have got away from God. They laugh at the Bible. They laugh at those that keep the Lord's Day holy. They laugh at the Christian. They laugh at men who stand up for God. See that Prime Minister in Australia, what he said about a Christian politician, he used a filthy expression about that politician because he believed the Bible. Man, I tell you the carnal mind is enmity against God, not subject to the law of God, neither indeed can be.

The Bible says "There is none righteous." You say "That is a sweeping statement." That is what the Bible says. I tell you what, that takes you in, and it takes me in. That takes the best person in, and the worst person in. It takes the educated person in, and the literate person in. It takes the religious person in, and it takes the irreligious person in. It takes the drunkard in, and it takes the man that is sober in. It takes the moral man in, and it takes the immoral man in. It takes the pure man in, according to the standards of men, and it takes in the impure men, by the standards of their fellows. There is no escape from it. You cannot get away from it. There is not a man who can put himself outside the sweep of God's word, "there is none righteous." You have not reached God's standards.

GOD'S STANDARDS

What are the standards of God? You will find them in the twentieth chapter of Exodus, "You will not have any other Gods before Him." No other Gods before Him. How many gods have you put before Him, the Holy God of Heaven? Some of you have put various other things before God. There are men who have put their business before God, put their lusts before God, put their sins before the God of Heaven, put their companions before their God, put their wives and their families, and their husbands and their friends before God. God says, "Thou shalt not have any other gods before me." What do you put first in your life? Yourself. Your sinful habits. Your enjoyments. Your recreation. Your rest. Your business. Your money. Your home. What is it? Come on, face up to it. There is not a man here can say, "From the day I was born, I never put any other god before the God of Heaven." We are all guilty. There is none righteous.

You can go through them all. You are not only to have no other gods before Him. It is not only the poor benighted Romanists who bow down to false gods. Man, there are many Orangemen who bow down to false gods. Many Apprentice Boys of Derry, and Blackmen and Masonic men who are just as great idolaters as those who are caught up in the darkness of Roman Catholicism. Yes sir! and they put things before God and bow down to them and serve them. God is a jealous God, He will not have it. He will not let you off with it. It says in the Book, "Be not deceived, God is not mocked, whatsoever a man soweth that shall he also reap."

I started to preach the gospel when I was sixteen. I am in my fiftieth year. I know I only look like twenty, I cannot help it! I have seen a few things in my day. And I have seen men put things before God and bow down to them and serve them. I have seen God judging them. I have seen God judging even His people who put things before their God.

"There is a sin unto death, I do not say you should pray for it." Who commits that sin friend, the unsaved? Never. You see, a brother can sin a sin unto death. A good Christian? Yes, Well saved? Sure. Indwelt by the Holy Spirit? Yes. Saved everlastingly. There is no other salvation. Salvation is all everlasting. No other salvation. Let me tell you this, God's people can sin sins unto death. Listen to His Word, "because many are weak and sickly among you and many sleep." That is the sleep of death. "But if we would judge ourselves we should not be judged, but if we are judged we are chastened of the Lord, that we should not be condemned with the world." If God judges His people with death, because they put other gods before Him, what will He not do with an ungodly man who has not got the Blood on him, has not got the Spirit of God in his heart? He will consign you friend into the blackness of darkness forever.

You say "Preacher, do not talk like that." But that is true. That is what God's Book says.

We could go through them all. You are not to take the Name of the Lord thy God in vain. How many times have you thought vain thoughts about the Name of God? How many times have you stifled an oath that you were about to utter? How many a time did you allow that oath to come out through your lips and profane your lips with the blasphemy against the God of heaven? He will not hold you guiltless. He marked them all down in His Book. Every time you have broken the first commandment, since you were born until this day, God has them written down. He has not forgotten about them. I tell you, God has a record in the unfailing tape in the memory of Almighty God, and every sin is recorded. Every act of violation of God's commandments, keeping holy God's Day. You have turned God's Holy Day into a holiday. Have you said, "Well I will go to church in the morning and if it's a nice day I will take the kids to the shore. I will not bother going to church in the evening." There are a lot of

Christians up to that today are there not? They do not keep holy the Lord's Day. You know God blessed Ulster when the Sabbath was sanctified. We need to return to the sanctification of the Lord's Day. Let me tell you, it is God's Day, it is not the Ballymena Town Council's day. Put your hand to something that does not belong to you and you are a thief. If the Town Council says to you, "I will cast my vote for the desecration of the Lord's Day" they are thieving. They are putting their hand to something that does not belong to them. It is the Lord's Day. And I believe if we got back to keeping holy the Lord's Day, what a different nation we would be. Oh, we need to get back to that. Those were the days when Ulster kept holy God's Day.

These are the commandments of God we are talking about. I did not make them up, They were not made up by some fundamentalist Bible thumper. It was the Lord that said it. They are right you know. They are not right because they are in the Book, they are right because they are in the very nature of God, they are part of God's laws, from His very being and He sent them from Heaven, wrote them with His own hands on two tables of stone and gave them to Moses. He wrote them Himself, they are the law of God.

You will not commit adultery. This is an adulterous age, is it not? The man that looks after a woman to lust after her, he is an adulterer. That is what Jesus said. Just as much as if he went and lived in immorality with her.

I tell you friend, God's law is a terrible thing. It is a terrible thing to be exposed to God's laws.

You look righteous tonight. Oh, you look well with your Bible in your hand. You were at church on Sunday. You were baptised when you were a child. You have been catechised. You were received into the church. You sing in the choir. You teach in the Sunday School. You are church elders, church committee men, You are well known with a Christian profession. But I want to tell you man, you are not righteous. God says it, not Ian Paisley, not Jim Beggs, Willie McCrea or Billy Kelly, God says you are not right. You are unrighteous. "There is none righteous." That takes in old Cardinal Conway. "You should not say those things Paisley." But the Bible says there is none righteous. The old Pope too. He is not righteous either.

You would think to hear some people talk that he was the next thing to God Almighty. I do not believe that. If you want to know what I believe about the Pope, read Revelation chapter seventeen and you will hear what God says about him. Yes!

Mr Spurgeon, that great English preacher, said after he read the second chapter of Thessalonians, "Arrest the Pope on suspicion of being the anti-christ." That is what he said.

GOD SAYS NOBODY IS RIGHTEOUS

Let me tell you something and let me rub it into your heart tonight friend, God says there is nobody righteous.

The Queen on the throne, she is a sinner. Harold Wilson is a sinner (I need not tell you that. Everybody knows he is a sinner) "All have sinned." The Moderator of the General Assembly, he is a sinner. Archbishop Simms, he is a sinner. Ian Paisley is a sinner. Everyone one of us, "There is none righteous."

You do not often hear that in the pulpits today. You do not often hear men telling their congregation "There is not one of you righteous in God's sight. Standing in your own shoes you are absolutely soaked in your sins."

I remember Mr Nicholson saying, "you are so filthy you would put a spot in a bucket of tar." This is pretty dirty is it not?

"There is none righteous." That is to do with the standard of God.

"Thou shalt not covet thy neighbour's house."

You have coveted that woman's house next door, have you not? Now come on. You coveted her grand piano did you not? Yes! You coveted her Hammond organ. You coveted her coloured television set. You did covet it. I know you did. And you know you did. "Thou shalt not covet."

I know two men in Belfast and if one gets a new car, the other gets a better car. And if the other fellow sells his car and gets a better one, the other fellow gets a better one still. And they are cutting one another's throats. And if one of them sells his house, the other fellow sells his. If he gets a double garage at his new house, the other fellow gets three garages at his house. I was talking to a friend of one of them the other day and I said, "I do not know what they will do when they are going to be buried." Man, if one fellow has a tomb, the other fellow will want twin tombs. Just to beat him at the end of the way. How foolish it is friend. He can only stay in one room at one time. He can only sit in one car at one time. I would not care what sort of car I drove so long as it gets me where I am going.

I had a friend of mine who bought a very expensive car and he said to me. "Any time you are going to a meeting I will take you." I said, "Well, my Ford, it gets me there. I am a Ford man I cannot afford livery, I drive a Ford. My Ford gets me there." "Oh," he said, "I have got a great car, Ian, now you come." I said, "Well I will test him out." So I rang him up and I said, "Brother, what about your car?" He said, "Oh, I will take you." And I got down the M1 in this grand new car and it stopped. I said. "That is not much of a car." You never saw a fellow more ashamed. That knocked the pride out of him. God has to knock the pride out of us at times, has He not? Yes!

Let me tell you friend, there has been a verse that has been with me all my ministry, and I can say it has burned itself into my soul, "The things that are seen are temporal, the things that are unseen they are eternal. Set your affections on things above, not on things on earth, for ye are dead and your life is hid with Christ in God."

Everything that you have will pass away. You are going to leave it all some day. They say, "How much did he leave?" He leaves it all. A foolish question, "How much did he leave?" You leave it all.

"There is none righteous."

THE SECOND BLACK ROMAN NONE

Look at the second one. It deals with the revelation of God. "There is none that understandeth."

There are three things that the natural man cannot understand. He cannot understand the great manner of his own being. His own being is a shut book to him. You cannot know yourself if you are a carnal man.

You cannot read the Book of life. You cannot even read the book of your own life. How foolish the readings that carnal men have made of their lives.

A second thing, they do not know the great meaning of Christ's work. It is hid from their eyes. They might have degrees, they might be educated, they might be university dons or professors but I want to tell you if they are carnal men, they will not know anything of the meaning of Christ's work. They won't even know the meaning of their own being. They do not understand the meaning of Christ's work.

There is another thing they do not understand. They do not understand the great message of the gospel, it is hid from their eyes. They cannot understand. And many a man has come to the house of God and he could not understand.

I was preaching a few weeks ago at the funeral of a great man of God, Alex Dunlap, who was known as Mr Protestant of the USA. And what a Protestant he was. What a man of God he was. I went to the funeral in Philadelphia.

Dr Jones was there and he said, "Ian, I am having meetings, I want you to join me." And we went up to a town in the north of Pennsylvania, and that night there was a man in the meeting. Do you know who he was? He was the ex-president of Rotary International. A businessman from Florida. And with all his business acumen, with all his intelligence, with all his education he was absolutely dark and blinded to God's truth. He did not know a thing. A young child at Sunday School who loved Jesus knew more. And you know as we preached, God enlightened that man's eyes. At the end of the meeting I had the great privilege of kneeling down at the front of that Bible Church with the ex-president of Rotary International, a big business man from the millionaires' paradise of Florida, and he said to me, "I have seen it for the first time. I see I am lost. I see that Jesus can save me."

I am telling you, there is none that understandeth. You cannot understand it in your own strength. That is why God sent the enlightenment of the spirit of God.

Blessed Holy Ghost, enlighten men's eyes tonight in the Town Hall! Open their eyes! I cannot open your eyes. Praise God, God can do it. He can open your eyes.

"There is none that understandeth."

THE THIRD BLACK ROMAN NONE

Look at the next one. "There is none that seeketh after God." That has to do with the Person of God. Man is looking to get away from God.

Adam sinned, but before he sinned he ran to God every evening. When he heard the voice of the Lord God walking in the garden in the cool of the day, he ran, did he not? He ran to be in company with God. But when he committed one sin, the first thing he did, he ran away from God.

"There is none that seeketh after God."

"Oh, I go to church," you say. You do not seek after God. "I read my Bible." You are not seeking after God. "I am religious." You are not seeking after God. "Why do you say that preacher?" It says here "There is none that seeketh after God." It is all a vain show. You draw near to God with your lips but your heart is far from God.

What a tragedy it is that men are not righteous, that men do not understand and that men do not seek after God.

Every preacher has a sore heart after he preaches. I have a sore heart every night in this hall when I see scores of men going away from Jesus. It breaks my heart to see men and women I know, and men and women I am pleased to call my friends, and they are pleased to say they have a friend in me, and they go away every night from Jesus. It breaks my heart! "There is none that seeketh after God." Why do men go away from God? "There is none that seeketh after God."

There is One that can draw you and that is the Spirit of God. Happy is the man who can say, "He drew me and I followed on, charmed to confess the voice divine."

Do you remember that night Christian when you heard the voice of God? Oh you had heard the gospel of Christ for years. You had heard what the theologians call the general call of the gospel. Everybody hears that who hears the preacher's voice. But one night you heard the effectual call. Oh, that was a different business. And when you heard that effectual call, praise God, it was irresistible.

When I went to the Ravenhill Road thirty years ago one of the worst drunkards on the Ravenhill Road, who had a business on My Lady's Road attended the Sunday evening services. I had an old elder, JL Harbinson and JL used to go up for him every Sunday night. He used to say "I am away to get Joe." We would be on our knees and we would be praying. JL would come back about five to seven and say, "I have got him. He was in bed when I got there. I got him out of bed and got him shaved and brought him down to church." And Joe came to church. He sat Sunday after Sunday after Sunday and my heart was broken, and those that prayed for him were brokenhearted. And then I had a mission in Crossgar., the mission out of which the Free Presbyterian Church of Ulster was born. And one night in that mission Joe came along and heard the effectual call of the gospel. It was irresistible. And when I made the appeal, he was down the aisle. He did not need any coaxing. Why? God had drawn him by the power of God.

Oh, Blessed Spirit draw men to Jesus tonight. Let the drawing power of God be felt in the Ballymena Town Hall. Then we will be able to stop preaching and start praising. We will be able to quit the preaching and start the praising.

God, for God is drawing men to Jesus. Oh may He draw you tonight. That is what I am praying. May He draw you away from the world. There is nothing in it friend. There is nothing in the world.

You remember Lord Byron, he had everything. At thirty years of age he said, "My days are in the yellow leaf. The flowers and fruits of life are gone. The worm, the canker and the grief are mine alone."

Oh, you could have everything but you will have nothing if you have not Jesus. Friend, if you have nothing and you have Jesus, praise God you have everything you need. "All my lasting joys are found in Thee, Jesus Thou art everything to me." Oh that you may seek Him tonight by the power of God.

"There is none that seeketh after God."

THE FOURTH BLACK ROMAN NONE

What is the last one? "There is none that doeth good, no not one." You say, "I do not believe that, preacher. I know people who do good turns.

I know ungodly people who do good turns." The Bible says there is none that doeth good. Ah, this is doing good in order to merit salvation. That is the difference. Of course there are people who do good turns. I know people and they do not like me, and they do not like my preaching, but they would do me a good turn. And there are people I do not like too much, and I would do them a good turn. I would. Let us be honest about it. You do not think the same about everybody, sure you do not? That is true. We would do them a good turn and if we could help them we would, and we ought to. But that does not merit salvation. There is not a thing good you can do that can get you to heaven. You can do everything the church asks. You can do everything the church demands of you. You can go the second mile. My friend, you can obey to the full the letter of the law to your utmost extent. Old Paul said, "As touching the law, blameless." He was talking about the traditions of the law, ceremonial practices of Moses, touching the law, blameless, and yet there is none good, no not one. You cannot earn salvation. You cannot buy it. You will never merit it. Oh, praise God, it is a gift.

You know friend, I could turn this text around now, and say it is true that there is none righteous. But it is also true, praise God, there is One righteous. It is true there is none that doeth good. It is also true that there is One Who doeth good. Yes! It is also true, I could say there is none that understandeth. But, praise God, we can say there is One Who understandeth. It is true to say there is none that seeketh after God. But, praise God, there is One Who sought after God with all His heart, with all His soul and all His mind. Who is the Blessed man of Psalm one? Do you know? The Blessed Man of Psalm one is the Lord Jesus Christ. He is the Man Who never walked in the counsel of ungodly men, or sat in the seat of the scornful or stood in the way of sinners. He was the Man Who day and night delighted in the law of God. He is the Evergreen Tree, Hallelujah! Thank God I know One Who has done good. He has done enough good to save me from hell, Hallelujah! He has enough righteousness to cover all the unrighteousness of His people. "Jesus, Thy Blood and Righteousness, My beauty are, my glorious dress, Midst flaming worlds in these arrayed, With joy shall I lift up my head."

REMEMBER THE CROSS

Do you remember Christian at the cross? What did He get at the cross?

He got a new suit. And he wore it forever, and it never frayed, it did not need any patches on it, it never needed to be mended. It was like the children of Israel when they came out of Egypt, they never needed to patch their clothes for forty years. That would be lovely mother, you would never need to patch up anything!

And the children as they came out, two years of age, and as their feet grew their shoes grew with them. That is what the Bible says. Do I believe it? Sure I believe it! God can do anything. When He saved Ian Paisley, He could do that. Making shoes grow is nothing to our God!

Let me tell you, I got a coat one night at the cross and I have been wearing it ever since, and I am going to wear it in Heaven. There is not a spot on it, and there is not a patch on it, it is the Righteousness of Jesus.

Come on, old ungodly sinner tonight, strip off your rags and wash in the Blood and put on the garment.

> *"Have you been to Jesus for the cleansing power?*
> *Are you washed in the Blood of the Lamb?*
> *Are you fully trusting in His grace this hour?*
> *Are you washed in the Blood of the Lamb?"*

Happy the man that can say, "Yes I am washed in the Blood, the soul-cleansing Blood of the Saviour." You can be washed tonight.

> *"I know a Fount where sins are washed away,*
> *I know a place where night is turned to day,*
> *Burdens are lifted, blind eyes made to see,*
> *There's a wonder working power*
> *In the Blood of Calvary?"*

Come on and test it tonight. Taste and see that the Lord is good.

There is One that doeth good. There is one that seeketh after God. There is One righteous., There is One that understandeth, and His Name is Jesus. Will you meet Him tonight? Take Him home with you. Come on friend, get saved tonight. Let the angels bear the tidings upward to the courts of Heaven. Let them sing in ceaseless rapture o'er many souls forgiven. God grant it tonight. Make it a salvation night Lord. For Jesus's Sake!

AMEN AND AMEN!

17 The gospel antidote *to L.S.D.*

IT WAS ANNOUNCED in the press that the title of my message this evening was L.S.D. To those of an older generation L.S.D. stood for pounds, shillings and pence. To modern youth L.S.D. is the name of a drug, a dangerous, death inflicting and damning drug.

The world, of course, has gone crazy and escapism from the circumstances that surround modern youth is imperative to their living. So modern youth and older folks too, caught up in this hazy, crazy, sinning, licentious and adulterous age, they go for what they call L.S.D. trips.

They take this drug and they go on a trip of fantasy. They forget about their circumstances. They forget about their environment. They forget about the battles that men and women have got to face as they face up legitimately to life's struggles, to life's sorrows, to life's temptations and to life's hardship.

One young woman said, "I turn off about twice a month. I like to take the trips. Not liking my own surroundings, I create my own. Seeing things as I have never seen them before. We hippies find ourselves in a society we do not like and want to change. We seek more love and place values on personal worth rather than on material riches." What is the trip like? "It is anything you make it but exaggerated, expanded, intensified, you see things as your unconscious mind sees them. You turn inside out, sort of way." This is the testimony of those addicted to this drug. Across our land there are thousands of young people who have fallen prey to this drug addiction.

What is the antidote to L.S.D.? Having a coffee party on a Sunday night? Giving the youth as many cigarettes and as much of the pleasures of the world that they want on church premises after the Lord's Day services? The only answer to every sin and to every pleasure of this world is the answer of the Gospel of Jesus Christ. I am sold out completely on this fact - that Jesus Christ alone can meet the need of the human heart. There is not a person in this meeting and I don't care what your addiction may be, what your pleasure may be, what your habit may be, what your circumstances may be, what your environment may be, what your past may be - Jesus Christ can completely satisfy you.

I have been thinking on those letters L.S.D. and I find that the Gospel antidote to L.S.D. is L.S.D. I want to take four of the L.S.D.'s of the Gospel.

A LONG SUFFERING DEITY

The Gospel, first of all, proclaims a longsuffering Deity. That is the first one. If you have your New Testament turn with me to II Peter 3:9. A longsuffering Deity. *"The Lord is not slack concerning his promise, as some men count slackness; but is longsuffering to us-ward, not willing that any should perish, but that all should come to repentance."* A longsuffering Deity.

My dear sinner in this meeting tonight you are a living monument. You are a living testimony. You are an every day testimony to the fact that God is longsuffering. He is longsuffering for He has restrained you in sin's follies. There were sins that the Devil wanted you to commit but by the grace of God sinner, although you are still in your sins, you did not commit them. God was good to you. There were things that you planned to do and roads which you planned to travel and paths that you planned to walk along but God, in His great mercy, restrained you in your sins.

Do you remember the man that purposed to do sin in the Old Testament and his testimony was this - God withheld me from sin? You say, "Preacher do you believe that God restrains unregenerate men in their sin?" I do. I believe that that drunkard would have finished in a drunkard's grave but God restrained him, preserved him when his feet made haste to hell. That is what God has been doing with you. He has been longsuffering to you. He has restrained you from doing sins, my friend, that would have darkened your soul with the blackness of hell's midnight forever. He has restrained you in the path of sin's folly. Why? Because He is longsuffering.

I will tell you what else He has done. He has retained you in life and He has preserved you to this day. We live in a word of accidents. We live in a world of sickness. We live in a world of tragedy. You know yourself there have been deaths in your family circle. You know yourself there are vacant places among the associates in business and in the particular environment in which you move. You are in the meeting tonight sinner because God has retained you in time. That accident that you were in, you could have been cut off. That tragedy that overtook your friends could have overtaken you. That sickness that cut down your nearest and your dearest it could have cut you down but God was longsuffering. He was longsuffering.

I want to say not only has God been longsuffering in restraining you in sin's folly, in retaining you in time and preserving your life. He is longsuffering in renewing another offer of the Gospel to you. You know what is happening to you? You are hearing the Gospel tonight another time. God is good to you isn't He?

Yes, last Sunday night the Spirit of God spoke to you, young man. The Spirit of God, young woman, laid hold upon you and you hardened your heart, didn't you? You went out resisting, refusing, rejecting, but you are back tonight and the Gospel is being renewed to you once again. Why? Because God is longsuffering, not willing that any should perish but that all should come to repentance.

Then friend, God is longsuffering for He is refraining from His swift and terrible judgment upon your soul. You don't deserve, my friend, to be where you are. It is only the mercy of God that keeps being merciful to you.

The Bible says, 'Because there is wrath beware, lest He take thee away with a stroke, then a great ransom cannot deliver thee.' The Word of God says he that being often reproved and hardeneth his neck shall suddenly be destroyed and that without remedy. The immutable, unchangeable law of God says, 'The soul that sinneth it shall die'.

You are still in time. God has refrained from loosing upon you His swift and terrible judgment. The Gospel, my friend, proclaims a longsuffering Deity. God has been longsuffering. The Holy Spirit has striven with you when you were young. He has striven with you when you were in youth. He has striven with you when you were a young man or a young woman. He has striven with you in middle age and some of you are old and you are going down and every day is taking you nearer to death, to the coffin, to the Christless grave, to the Christless tomb, to the Christless shroud, to the Christless hell. But He has been longsuffering. He will have mercy on you even tonight if you will call upon His name.

A LOVING SAVIOUR'S DEATH

I am glad God does not cut men off in their sin. I am glad He is gracious. I am glad He is loving. I am glad He is kind. I am glad that He lets a man go a very long way before He cuts him off in His wrath. The Gospel of Jesus Christ proclaims a longsuffering Deity. The Gospel of Jesus Christ points to a loving Saviour's death. That is the second thing in the Gospel.

The hand of the Gospel is always pointing to the death of Jesus. Turn over with me to Isaiah 53. In that chapter we have a wonderful description of the death of Jesus Christ, Verse 10 *"Yet it pleased the Lord to bruise him; he hath put him to grief: when thou shalt make his soul and offering for sin, he shall see his seed, he shall prolong his days, and the pleasure of the Lord shall prosper in his hand."*

Three things about Christ's death. Its origination, it pleased the Lord to bruise Him. Here is man fallen, lost, ruined, hell-bent and hell-deserving. Sin must be punished. Death must overcome and overtake the lawbreaker. What is going to happen? Is the whole world of sinners to be damned? Have fallen men, like fallen angels, no way back into the presence of God? Then God steps in and the Father makes His Son your substitute and my substitute. Your surety and my surety. Your sacrifice and my sacrifice. It pleased the Lord to bruise Him.

It was the will of God that He should wear the crown of thorns. It was the Father's will that He should be buffeted and spat upon. It was the Father's will that He should give His back to the smiter and His cheek to those who plucked off the hairs. It was the Father's will that He should hang, stark naked, on the cross but my friend, I can describe the whipping and the scourging and the bleeding and the crucifying and the crowning and the buffeting and the battering of the Lord Jesus Christ but there is one thing I can't describe - the darkness. When Jesus Christ went out into the darkness and God put out heaven's light and made the sun to withhold its shining, when God bruised Jesus for me I will never be able to understand that.

Jehovah drew His awful rod,
Oh Christ it fell on Thee,
Thou wast sore stricken of my God
Didst bear all ills for me,
A victim led Thy blood was shed,
Now blessings draft for me.

The origination of Christ's death. It pleased the Lord to bruise Him. Look at this, the propitiation of Christ's death. What did He propitiate? Our sins, *"when thou shalt make his soul an offering for sin."* Jesus Christ was made an offering for sin.

I deserve eternal hell. Down in hell there are thirsty souls among the damned. Every damned soul is crying for a drop of water. Jesus Christ took the dread cup of my hell in His hands and He drank it to the dregs. He cried "I thirst." Why? Because He was enduring the pangs of hell for me. That is why.

Jesus Christ cried, "My God, my God, why hast Thou forsaken me?" God forsook Him on the cross. Hell is the place where men are eternally forsaken by God forever.

Don't you see it friend. With one tremendous draft He drank for me damnation dry. That is what the cross means. That is its propitiation. Thank God it has a consummation *"he shall see his seed"*. What does that mean? That means that He saved that drunkard and made him clean through His precious blood. That means that He has saved that gambler. He has saved that sinner, that unclean person, that poor fallen woman of the street, that religious pharisee and hypocrite, that person who thought the church could take them to heaven and found out, like Nicodemus, that they needed to be born again. Jesus Christ, through the cross, sees His seed. Yonder in heaven by the crystal sea of glass before the everlasting throne there is an innumerable company which no man can number and every one has a white robe and every one has a golden harp and every one is playing the sweetest celestial music that human fingers could bring from that harp that is strung with gold. What are they praising God for? Because Jesus died for them!

He shall see His seed. He shall prolong His days. Thank God Jesus Christ is a living Christ. He died once. He lives forever.

Sinner I am not asking you to put your name at a dead creed. I am not asking you to sign a formula. I am not asking you to consent to a long list of doctrines that you do not understand. I want to introduce you to a living, blessed, life giving friend, Jesus Christ. Oh that you might meet Him. Oh that you might know Him. Oh that you might trust Him. Oh that you might love Him. Oh that you might keep company with Him.

He breaks every fetter. He smashes every chain. He looses from every habit. He sets men and women free and He can set you free.

His blood can make ten thousands clean,
His blood avails for me.
Oh that you might know Him!

A LOST SINNER'S DELIVERANCE

But the Gospel not only portrays a longsuffering Deity and points to a loving Saviour's death but the Gospel proposes a lost sinner's deliverance. Yes.

Lost sinners can be delivered. The sweetest and the simplest verse in the Bible to me is Romans 10:13. What a verse it is *"Whosoever shall call upon the name of the Lord shall be saved."* A lost sinner's deliverance.

The widest possible scope - *whosoever*

There are four things in that verse. There is the **widest possible scope** -*whosoever*. The widest possible scope. That brings you in friend. You are sitting here and you are saying preacher I would get saved but I could not keep it. Do you know who told you that? The devil. No man keeps salvation but Jesus keeps all those committed to Him. That is the devil's lie. He wants to take you to hell. Will you go to hell believing the devil's lie. Whosoever - you say preacher it is not me it is for my mates, it is for my friends, but I could never keep it. God is saying tonight whosoever. That is the widest possible scope, it takes in everybody in this meeting.

You say preacher do you believe that God could save everybody in this meeting. I believe He could save them and a thousand times more. It is the Gospel I believe in.

The simplest possible act - *call*

Let me tell you something else. In this verse you not only have the widest possible scope but you have the **simplest possible act** - *call*. The word in the original is cry. The first thing a child does when it is born it cries. You do not need to teach it to cry, it cries. I never needed to teach my boys to cry, they will cry at four o'clock like clockwork. They get you up to get a bottle and when you get your wife's elbows in your ribs you know you have got to jump. There are no excuses then. They will cry.

It is easy to cry. There is not a man or woman, boy or girl who cannot cry. How do men get saved? By the simplest possible act. It is not baptism or the Lord's Supper or the church, or Bible reading, or believing a set of doctrines. It is crying. That is how men are saved.

The widest possible scope - whosoever - it takes in everybody. The simplest possible act - cry. In God's name sinner, cry tonight and God will save you. That is all you have got to do.

The grandest possible name - Jesus

We have something else in this verse. We have the highest, **the grandest possible name**. What name is that? The name of the church? No. The name of the preacher? No. The name of doctrines? No. The name of a well established scriptural creed? No. What is it? It is the name of Jesus. *"Whosoever shall call on the name of the Lord."* Thou shalt call His name Jesus for He shall save His people from their sins. Wonderful name of Jesus. I am thinking at this moment of people to whom I have whispered that.

I was preaching in a tent in a certain place. One night when I made the appeal I heard a great sob. It was not the sob of a child or the high pitched sob of a woman. It was the deep awful sob of a man in distress. When I made the appeal he stepped forward and we had a little curtain in front of the tent and I drew it aside. He stepped in and I shut him in. When the others had gone he just sat there sobbing. He said, "Mr Paisley, I have committed a terrible sin. Last week you preached in this tent and I have been in hell ever since. I am sobbing now but I have sobbed since last Sunday behind the hedges of my farm. I have gone out and left my bed and I have lain down in the gutter and I have sobbed. My God how I have wrecked myself, I have wrecked my family, I have wrecked my name." He shook like a sally rod shaken by the wind. He said, "Mr Paisley is there hope for a villain like me, a criminal like me, a sinner like me. I not only sinned but like David I covered up my sin so no one would know. But you put your finger on it." I never knew the man, I never saw him before. He said, "You uncovered it and my God it is awful."

I said to that man "There are certain things about your sin that are public and public sins must be repented of publicly." Private sins should be repented of privately. Public sins need a public putting right. He said "Mr Paisley I will do all I can to put it right. But even if I do that it will not help me." I said, "No, it will not. But there is a name that will help you. It is the name of Jesus."

Do you know what it did to that man? It soothed his sorrows. It healed his wounds. It drove away his tears.

I was at a meeting in that district some time ago and there he was with his wife and family and he was singing the songs of Zion with all his heart. He had put everything right. It was a hard battle but he did it. I said to him "How about it?" He said, "It is just Jesus who has done it, He has done it for me."

The greatest possible fact - *shall be saved*

The Lord Jesus, friend, is who you need to call on. The grandest possible name. Then there is something else - the greatest possible fact - whosoever shall call on the name of the Lord might be saved. It does not say that. Whosoever shall call on the name of the Lord can be saved. It does not say that. Whosoever shall call on the name of the Lord probably will be saved. No, sir. It says *"Whosoever shall call on the name of the Lord shall be saved."* It is done and it is done eternally.

I want to tell you friend God stakes His character on His own Word. I am going to heaven on the word of Jesus Christ. God's character is at stake.

Some of you people who believe in me would come forward and if I said something to you you would believe me. But friend I am only a poor, faltering, sinning, imperfect human being. Listen friend, you can trust the Word of God tonight. Oh that you might trust Him. Oh is there some man here torn with strife? Is there some heart that is sore? Is there some soul that is darkened? Is there somebody here with a burden? Jesus lifts the burden, don't carry it any more. Put it in the sepulchre like old John Bunyan's Pilgrim and you will see it no more. Praise the Lord. Praise the Lord Oh my soul. The greatest possible fact, you will be saved.

You say "Preacher what about tomorrow?" You come back here next week friend and look up Romans 10:13 and it will still be the same. You come back here in a fortnight and look it up and it will still be the same. Come back in 50 years and it will still be the same. Friend, turn up the Word of God when the heavens are no more and the stars are forgotten and the earth's planet is forgotten and the Word of God stands forever. It shall be the same. No change Jehovah knows.

I have often told the story and I will tell it again for it is worth repeating, of the little boy and his mother who came to Christ in Major Whittle's meeting. Major Whittle was a contemporary of DL Moody. They came to the verse John 6:37 *"Him that cometh unto me I will in no wise cast out."* They went home and got up the next morning. The little boy got his breakfast and went off whistling to school. The mother started to do her work and the devil came and told her she was not saved. He sowed his doubts and instead of the woman trusting in the Word she started to doubt and feared and looked in. She lost assurance, she did not lose salvation, she lost assurance of salvation. When the boy came home for his lunch his mother was weeping. She said, "Johnny I am not saved." Johnny was a very wise little boy. He went to the cupboard and got the old Bible down and turned it to John 6:37 and then he started to laugh. He said, "Mummy it is still in the book. It is still in the book."

Someone said to WP Nicholson , 'What have you got for salvation but a bit of paper with writing on it. 'Correct,' says Nicholson, 'but it is God's writing that is on the bit of paper.'

I have got God's writing for my salvation, that will do me. It will do you and it will do every man that will come.

THE GOSPEL PORTRAYS LIFE'S SURE DESTINY

One last word friend. The Gospel portrays life's sure destiny. Oh yes. What is life's sure destiny? I can tell you. Every man and every woman is on a trip of no return. You are taking a trip of no return.

'Straight is the gate, narrow is the way that leadeth unto life. Few there be that find it. Wide is the gate, broad is the road that leads to destruction and many there be that go in thereat.' 'It is appointed unto man once to die.'

You are all dying men and women. I am nearer to preaching my last sermon that ever I have been before. You are nearer to listening to your last sermon than ever you have been before. We are all dying and we are all going to the judgment. Friend, if you died and appeared at the judgment bar how would it be with your soul, now answer it honestly? Answer it honestly. How would it be with your soul? Would it be a Christless soul? A Christless deathbed? A Christless shroud? A Christless coffin? A Christless judgment? A Christless hell forever? Alas, alas, scores and scores of men and women in this very meeting and if death came and if judgment came their destiny would be hell, eternal hell for evermore.

I have one appeal to make to you friend. Don't listen to the devil's lies. Don't listen to the devil's arguments. This night come, get the Gospel antidote for every ill, for every sickness, for every habit, take Jesus as your Saviour and walk out of this meeting in the company of the Friend who will never leave you. A Friend who will be with you in time, in death, with you for all eternity. In God's name sinner be saved tonight.

AMEN AND AMEN!

18 It is only
a matter of dress

THE SCRIPTURE READING for my message is found in the Gospel according to Matthew 22:1-14

"*And Jesus answered and spake unto them again by parables, and said, The kingdom of heaven is like unto a certain king, which made a marriage for his son. And sent forth his servants to call them that were bidden to the wedding: and they would not come. Again, he sent forth other servants, saying, Tell them which are bidden, Behold, I have prepared my dinner: my oxen and my fatlings are killed, and all things are ready: come unto the marriage. But they made light of it, and went their ways, one to his farm, another to his merchandise: And the remnant took his servants, and entreated them spitefully, and slew them. But when the king heard thereof, he was wroth: and he sent forth his armies and destroyed those murderers, and burned up their city. Then saith he to his servants, The wedding is ready, but they which were bidden were not worthy. Go ye therefore into the highways and as many as ye shall find, bid to the marriage. So those servants went out into the highways, and gathered together all as many as they found, both bad and good: and the wedding was furnished with guests. And when the king came in to see the guests he saw there a man which had not on a wedding garment. And he said unto him, Friend, how camest thou in hither not having a wedding garment?*

And he was speechless. Then said the king to the servants, Bind him hand and foot, and take him away, cast him into outer darkness: there shall be weeping and gnashing of teeth. For many are called, but few are chosen."

'It is only a matter of dress.' How often have we heard that expression. But that expression spells out the principle of the saving Gospel of Jesus Christ.

If you turn to chapter 22 of Matthew you will find that the king said in verse 12 *"Friend, how camest thou in hither not having a wedding garment?"* It is only a matter of dress. How did you get in here without the wedding garment?

The king made a great feast to celebrate the marriage of his son. He sent the royal invitation to the great men of his kingdom, to the cities over which he lived and to the representatives of the royal power in those cities. But they treated the invitations with scorn and ridicule and they treated them lightly and the king was wrought. He sent again and said "I have made my feast. I have killed my oxen. I have laid the table, Come, for all things are now ready." Those invited refused to come.

Some went to their business and some went to their farms and others took the servants and killed them. The king was wroth and he sent forth his army and he killed those who had murdered his faithful royal servants who had carried the wedding invitation.

Then he said "Go out into the highways and all that you find bring them into the marriage." They brought them in and the marriage supper was furnished with the guests.

Then at the end of the eating and the feasting and the banqueting the king came in to see his guests and he saw a man there who was not attired in the specially prepared and available marriage garment. He said to the man "How didst thou come in hither not having a wedding garment?" The man was speechless. He could not answer.

The king said, "Bind him hand and foot and take him away. Cast him into outer darkness, there shall be weeping and gnashing of teeth."

What is a parable? A parable is an earthly story with a heavenly meaning. In this story we have the heavenly meaning of the Gospel. The King of heaven had a Son whose name was Emmanuel, Prince Emmanuel.

He decided that He would have a bride for His Son. That from the ruined ranks of Adam's fallen race He would summon the people to become the church which would become His Son's bride.

He sent the invitations to the wedding, to His subjects. What has happened? Men have made light of the Royal invitation. Men have turned upon the kings heralds who brought the invitations. They have smitten them, they have killed them, they have reviled them, they have rejected them. God has had to turn His wrath upon those who treated lightly His Royal invitation.

Not only has He to turn His wrath on them but He has had to turn to another place to find His guests. So He turned to the highways and in the highways they found both good and bad people some clothed with respectability and people with none. The gracious King gave the same invitation to them all and the banquet was filled.

But there is only one garment that makes you accepted at that banquet. That is the wedding garment. I want to discuss, first of all, the discernment of the King as He came in to view His guests. Then I want to look at the indictment of the intruder because there was an intruder among the guests, a man who ought not to have been there, a man who had climbed up some other way the same as a thief and a robber. Lastly, I want to look at the punishment of that speechless individual.

I have already described the banquet. Let me say that the highlight of the banquet was the advent of the King as He revealed Himself to His guests. After the royal table which was filled with the good things of the royal bounty had been cleared away, the King came to walk among His guests. To reveal Himself, to mingle with the crowd and to talk with those that had eventually come to the wedding feast.

That, of course, was the highlight of the feast. The appearing of the King. The King came graciously and lovingly and majestically and gloriously to communicate with those whom He had invited. To grace the wonderful celebration by His own presence and by His mingling with the guests. The revelation of the King.

If you look at the portion you will find the emphasis - the king came and it says he came in to see the guests. But the marvellous thing was this, that the King came to be seen by His guests, to be one of them, to join with them in the celebrations. This was a manifestation of His grace. He wanted to be acquainted with them. They had come from the highways and byways of the city. They had come in response to an invitation and the strength and power of the King's command. Now He deigns to show Himself in grace and favour among them. The advent of the King.

As the King came in He saw the white robes of all the guests, because in the marriages of the east every visitor and every guest was supplied with a white robe. There was a vast white-robed multitude. But among them the King saw a black spot. Could it be that a guest had come in and had refused the wedding garment? Could it be that among the hundreds of these guests one man crept in unawares and the audacity and he has the villainy and criminality to appear as a guest without the wedding garment? The discernment of the King. So He went through that crowd and I see the King in His splendour. That crowd parts before Him and He comes to the man who has no wedding garment. He says "Friend," notice His term of address, He wanted to be the man's friend but the man, by his own sin, had become His enemy, "how camest thou in hither not having a wedding garment?" The man was speechless. Every mouth will be stopped and the whole world will be declared guilty before God. A guilty man.

There was only one thing that man needed, it was not wealth or breeding. It was not the strength of his own intelligence that gave him the right to a place at the King's table. He needed the wedding garment. That is what he needed and he had not on the wedding garment. Every one that came to the marriage was offered the wedding garment and it was the custom for every one to take it. They were given without price, all sizes of garments were available so as large and small people, thin people and fat people could all have their wedding garments, all carefully prepared. But this man turned with disdain and walked in the midst of the white robed throng without a wedding garment. Then when he is challenged he has not a word to say in his defence.

He had no wedding garment. The wedding garment was the distinguishing mark of a properly accredited guest. This man, unashamedly and brazenly and scornfully, rejected the garment and decided that he would go in his own clothing, wrapped in his own garments.

The true Christian has a mark of distinguishing grace upon him because he has on the wedding garment. 'Who are these that are arrayed in white robes and whence came they. I said sir thou knowest ,and He said these are they that came out of great tribulation and have washed their robes and made them white in the blood of the Lamb.' We were singing about them -

> *Are your garments spotless?*
> *Are they white as snow?*
> *Are you washed in the blood of the Lamb?*

I have one question to press upon you - Have you got the wedding garment? The distinguishing mark of grace, the attire of the child of God. Have you? There is no mention here about baptism or church connection or creed or confession or ecclesiastic al fellowship. No! Have you got on the wedding garment? It is only a matter of dress. Are you attired as a child of the King? Happy is the man, gloriously happy is the man, woman, boy or girl who wears the distinguishing mark of the child of God.

My Dad used to say to me, "Ian, I wear the garment God gave me the day I was saved and there is not a spot on it. It is the spotless garment of the righteousness of His Son." Happy is the man who has the blood and righteousness upon him. It does not matter what your past was. These people came from the byways and the highways. God said some of them were good and some of them were bad but they all had to get the garment because it is not by works of righteousness that we have done but of His mercy He saves us, by the washing of regeneration and the renewal of the Holy Spirit. Tell me, my friend, have you got that mark of grace?

That garment was a badge of respect for the King and for the King's commandment. 'Not everyone that saith unto me Lord, Lord, shall enter into the Kingdom of God but he that doeth the will of my Father which is in heaven'. God's will is that if you are going to be saved from hell and be in heaven you must have the wedding garment. The child of God wears that garment with pride because it is a badge of respect for the King.

How glad I am I have a garment that has been washed in the blood of the Lamb. That is my passport to heaven. When I get to the door of heaven they will not say, 'Is that a preacher at the door?' Is that a baptised Christian at the door? 'Is that a Free Presbyterian at the door?' No. They will say has he got on the wedding garment and I say hallelujah! I have on the wedding garment and I will sweep through the gates of the new Jerusalem singing washed in the blood of the Lamb.

My friend it is the badge of respect for the King. It is the sign of acceptance by the King's Son. The King's son has accepted me and he has given me His own white robe. Because the white robe I wear is the white robe of the Lord Jesus Christ. We were singing about it in the hymn:

> *Jesus, Thy blood and righteousness,*
> *My beauty are, my glorious dress,*
> *'Midst flaming worlds in these arrayed,*
> *With joy shall I lift up my head.*

Bold shall I stand at that great day. When the heavens are on fire. When the oceans are on fire. When this old world burns out to ashes I shall lift my head because I have on the wedding garment. That is why. I am accepted by the King of kings and Lord of lords.

My, when I meet you in heaven I will show off my wedding garment. It is beautifully tailored, It is absolutely right fitting. You know in the old days when we were boys we went to a tailor and he used to make our suits. I had a tailor and he was a very fussy wee man. I passed his place of business the other day in Ballymena and I remembered that fussy wee man, making a waistcoat took him nearly an eternity. He had to have it absolutely right. I want to tell you the Lord Jesus with His own hands and with His own ingenuity and wisdom has made us that blessed coat and He has given it to us to wear because we are accepted with Him.

The wedding garment is a declaration. I have conformed to the rules of the Kingdom of God. The Bible says, 'Except a man be born again he cannot see the kingdom of God.' When you tell people they need to be born again they get really mad, they do not want to know about it. Say to a man, 'Are you born again?' He will say he is a church member. That is not what God says. Except you are a church member - it is not in the Book. They want to tell you about all their good deeds and all their good works and their righteousness is, according to God's book, as stinking rags in His sight. But the man who has the wedding garment has conformed to the rules. You cannot get into heaven except you conform to the rules.

Last of all, that garment says I have submitted to the Royal command of the King. I am a friend of the King because I have submitted to His command.

Let me ask you the question my friend. Have you got the wedding garment? Have you got the distinguishing mark that you are a child of God? Have you got the badge of respect for the King of kings? Have you got the sign of acceptance in your heart by the Lord Jesus the Prince Emmanuel? Have you got a clear declaration in your life that you have conformed to the rules of God and submitted to the Royal law of heaven? If you have you can say, 'I have got on the wedding garment. It is well with my soul.'

But the King looked at the man who was speechless. If you have not on the wedding garment on the day of judgment you will be speechless. All your puny little arguments that you would put to me, you will not put them up there on the great judgment day. You will stand aghast at your folly. You will stand miserable and you will hear a voice and it will not say, 'Come in.' It will say, 'Depart from me ye cursed, I never knew you.' That is what you will hear.

Oh my friend what a terrible face to face encounter with the King took place. This man, unclothed, uncovered and unwashed, a rejector of the Gospel. It was only a matter of dress. Do you remember when Naaman was arguing about dipping himself in Jordan the servant said, 'If the prophet had asked you to do some great thing you would have done it, but the prophet said wash and be clean.' That is all God is saying to you. Wash in the blood of My Son and be clean and I will bring you into heaven.

This man repudiated the righteousness of Christ. He reviled the grace of Christ. He caused a barefaced affront to the King and to the King's Son. The King said, 'All right you have made your choice - bind him hand and foot. He would not put on my garment. Therefore I will bind him hand and foot. I will bring him into eternal bondage.' When God binds a man it is forever. When God puts the chains on a lost soul it is forever. Take him away, take him away, take him away. Is that what you will hear sir on that last day? From the throne, the order, 'Take him way, take him away.' How dreadful will the state of your soul be if those words pierce your ears on that day. 'Cast him out into outer darkness, there shall be weeping and gnashing of teeth.'

Have you been to Jesus for the cleansing power? Are you washed in the blood of the Lamb? That is my final question to you. May you make sure you can say, 'I have on the wedding garment.'

AMEN AND AMEN

19 Moon *madness*

SOME YEARS AGO there was a little poem written. It was handed to me this morning. It would make a fitting introduction to this subject.

> *'I am sure you have heard or read about the satellites in space,*
> *and how Russia and the United States are in the rocket race.*
> *"To hear them talk, it won't be long for space they'll conquer soon,*
> *And then what next will man attempt, if he should reach the moon?*
> *If man should ever reach the moon there's one thing that is clear.*
> *He'll ruin everything up there just as he's done down here.*
> *With sin and crime, with lust and greed he's got enough to do,*
> *To cleanse the mess he's made on earth, and you know that is true.*
> *The sickness and the want and fear, the broken hearts and shame,*
> *And hungry millions cry each day, and man is all to blame.*
> *I think we'd better set our sights above the moon and space,*
> *And look into God's eternity while there is time and grace.*
> *It's not the moon we need to reach, it's the God Who placed it there,*
> *The One Who went to Calvary, a rugged cross to bear.*
> *For sins of men with wicked hearts, He died one afternoon -*
> *With faith in Him you'll have no fear if man should reach the moon.'*

Could I comment that in India they are making a sacrifice of thousands of pounds worth of relief food parcels in an offering to their Hindu gods. We are supplying money to feed the hungry and they are burning it. That is what happened in India this past week. Could I just break in here and say that in Biafra there are four hundred separated fundamentalist churches in membership with the International Council of Christian Churches and they are not getting any relief because the relief is being channelled through World Council agencies and it is going to the Roman Catholic church.

Now we are having retiring offerings next Sunday to help our Biafran brethren. The leader of the Biafrain churches is in prison. Do you know why? Because he will not co-operate with the rebellion which is Roman Catholic inspired. Why is the Pope worried about Biafra? Because the Pope has a hand in this revolution, He is talking about justice, think of it, and Rome itself a seething cauldron of injustice.

Man has reached the moon. Man has put his foot upon another world. This is a momentous happening for all humanity and it has an effect upon every one of earth's millions.

Now I want to turn you to the Scriptures for the only basis for my message is the Word of God. I want to point out, first of all, God's purpose for the moon. God has a purpose for the moon and if I read this Bible aright it was never God's purpose that man should walk upon the moon, never. I am convinced about that. God has permitted it.

GOD'S PURPOSE FOR THE MOON

As I have said, God has permitted many things, and maybe before we begin we should turn to a little verse over in Ecclesiastes, chapter 7:29. If you want to do your wife a favour, husband, when you go home, read her verse 28. Be sure and do it. Ecclesiastes 7:29 *"Lo, this only have I found, that God hath made man upright:* (I want you to notice this) *but they have sought out many inventions."* This seeking for power, this lusting for power, this desire to glorify man is an evil thing.

I will just show you how evil it is. A cartoon appeared in the Daily Mirror on Tuesday last, and it is utter blasphemy. It depicts man sitting on the moon with his feet upon the world. "The heaven is my throne and the earth is my footstool." That is how far man goes in his blasphemy against God. I want to tell you that heaven is the throne of God to which man would like to climb. The devil's first sin was the sin to be like God. The devil said, "I will climb up, I will sit where God sits." There is a coming great world ruler and he is going to say the same," I will sit where God sits."

Let me say something. In this Word we have clear instructions concerning the moon. The Bible is right up to date you know. We turn to Genesis 1 and we find that God made these lights, that is the sun and the moon and the stars. He made them to divide the day from the night and for signs. I believe that these things will be the means of prophetic signs. God will use them to mark in the very heavens definite prophetic signals or storm signals as this old world rushes to its final and everlasting consummation.

Take the book of the Revelation for a moment or two and you will find in that book in chapter 8 the moon is mentioned. In fact there are a lot of mentions of the moon in the book of the Revelation. We have not time to fully expound them but in Revelation 8 it says in verse 12 *"And the fourth angel sounded, and the third part of the sun was smitten"*. There is going to be a time when a third of the sun is going to be smitten by the power of God in judgment. Look at it, *"and the third part of the moon, and the third part of the stars; so as the third part of them was darkened, and the day shone not for a third part of it, and the night likewise. And I beheld, and heard an angel flying through the midst of heaven, saying with a loud voice, Woe, woe, woe, to the inhabiters of the earth by reason of the other voices of the trumpet of the three angels, which are yet to sound!"*

So here we have a time when the moon shall mark off in a third of darkness a particular interval in God's judgments upon this world. Then if you turn back with me to chapter 6:12 you will find that at the final judgment the moon will give a signal in the heavens that the judgment has come. Look at it. Revelation 6:12 *"And I beheld when he had opened the sixth seal, and, lo, there was a great earthquake: and the sun became black as sackcloth of hair,"* God's blackout forever of the sun. That is something that man will never do. Let me tell you something friend, man will never, never, never destroy this world. God is reserving it to judgment from His own hands. I want to make that clear.

Some people get terribly worried and they think man is going to blow himself up on this earth. Don't you believe it. God is going to deal with man. God will have the final word in the whole situation. I am glad God is on the throne tonight. I am glad I can look up and say God is still on the throne and He will remember His own. Of course, when this old world is burning up I will not be here. I will have flitted before that time, praise the Lord for that.

THE MOON SHALL BECOME AS BLOOD

Now let us look at it again. It says that the moon shall become as blood. I am not going to try and tell you how that is going to happen. That is not my business. I am not a prophet nor the son of a prophet but I know this that the book says it and I believe it. The moon will bleed itself to eternal death in the very heavens. What a day that will be. When the sun is dark and the moon is as blood and the stars leave their orbits in the heavens and fall to the earth. What a terrible day that will be. Thank God for those that will be safe that day, safe in the arms of Jesus and safe on His gentle breast. My, I am glad I am saved. I am glad I will not be calling on the rocks and mountains to fall on me because I have hidden in the eternal Rock of Ages.

Rock of Ages cleft for me
Let me hide myself in Thee.

Yes, there are going to be prophetic signs on the moon. I will tell you what else. The moon is the symbol of the church's power. It is linked with the church. Turn over to Solomon's Song 6:10 *"Who is she that looketh forth as the morning, fair as the moon, clear as the sun, and terrible as an army with banners."* It is a type of the church. You get the same type again over in the book of the Revelation with the two women. You have the scarlet woman of Revelation 17, the harlot bride of the antichrist and you have the bride of Christ, the church, in chapter 12 *"And there appeared a great wonder in heaven a woman clothed with the sun and the moon under her feet and upon her head a crown of twelve stars."* Do you know what it means? It means that God has given the dominion of his heavens to the church, that is what it means.

I am not talking now about mere aerial heavens or the moon but I am talking about the symbols of the celestial worlds above. Praise God we are going to be clothed in all the glory of the work of His mighty and unfailing and totally availing redemption.

So the sun and the moon are for signs, have you got that. Let us look at it again. They are for seasons and for days and years. That does not need much explanation. The old day and the old year and the old season was reckoned on the lunar calendar. That is quite simple. We understand that.

A SIGN FOR SEASONS

Now tell me what was the Divine purpose for the moon? The Divine purpose is set out here. Is the Divine purpose for man to walk its surface and conquer it? No sir. The Divine purpose for the moon was to be a sign for seasons, for days and for years. Now turn with me in the same chapter to verse 26 and when God comes to make man He made man to rule. What did He make man to rule? He made man to rule in a three-fold dominion. This is very important.

You turn over and compare this with the eighth Psalm. *"O Lord our Lord, how excellent is thy name in all the earth! who hast set thy glory above the heavens* [there is the place of God] *Out of the mouth of babes and sucklings hast thou ordained strength because of thine enemies, that thou mightest still the enemy and the avenger. When I consider thy heavens, the work of thy fingers, the moon and the stars, which thou hast ordained; What is man, that thou art mindful of him? and the son of man, that thou visitest him? For thou hast made him a little lower than the angels, and hast crowned him with glory and honour. Thou madest him to have dominion over the works of thy hands; and hast put all things under his feet:* [What all things?] *All sheep and oxen, yea, and the beasts of the field;"* There is man's dominion on the earth. Man was called upon to rule the earth. Here is man's dominion over the air and the seas *"The fowl of the air, and the fish, and whatsoever passeth through the paths of the seas."* Now God said to man "Rule the earth. Rule the aerial heavens and rule the seas."

Here we have man's dominion. Of course man's sceptre has been smashed. Man's throne has been defaced and in chapter 3 we see man broken, soiled, scarred and ruined by sin. Man has not the dominion that he ought to have or God planned him to have or God was mindful for him to have. Man, unable to conquer the depths of the sea for there are depths that he has never conquered. Man unable to subdue this earth and this earth is torn with wars that no NATO or any other so-called peace keeping organisation shall ever settle. Man unable to deal even with the aerial heavens that are his. He has gone to other worlds. He has sought out other places. He has gone across the boundaries of heaven-set dominions.

You know what it is all for? It is all for his own self-glorification. Now there are three things that moon madness has done to this world.

MOON MADNESS PUTS THE TEMPORAL BEFORE THE SPIRITUAL

The first thing it has done is it has put the temporal before the spiritual, do you know that? You know there were more people interested in the world during that space flight and the coming of the astronauts on to the moon's surface and what they did there than ever were interested in things that were spiritual. Do you know that? Let me turn you to one verse, II Corintians 4: 18 *"While we look not at the things which are seen, but at the things which are not seen: for the things which are seen are temporal."* That moon is only temporal. It is an amazing part of God's creation, so is this earth, but it is only temporal *"but the things which are not seen are eternal."*

I know people who sat up half the night to see it but they never sat up half the night to consider where they will be in eternity. What fools they are. They have time to leave their bed, time to leave their sleep just to dwell upon a temporal thing no matter how fascinating or entertaining it may be. My friend have you taken time to consider the things which are not seen, the great things concerning judgment that is to come. Listen friend, consider your latter end and be wise.

MOON MADNESS PUTS THE WORK OF THE CREATURE BEFORE THE WORSHIP OF THE CREATOR

Secondly, moon madness puts the work of the creature before the worship of the Creator. The greatest week in man's history was the great week of redemption, and the greatest day in man's history was when Jesus rose from the dead and He brought in a new creation, which will last longer than the sun and the moon shall endure in the heavens as we see them today. Praise God we look for a new heaven and a new earth in which dwelleth righteousness. Moon madness puts the temporal before the spiritual. It puts the work of the creature before the worship of the Creator. One thing I did not like about it was this boasting confidence that they would make it. My friend, just let one little thing go wrong and they would not have made it. Then they have the blasphemy to say "Heaven is my throne and earth is my footstool."Don't you believe it friend, you are only just a puny wee bit of clay and if God blew on you tonight you would perish for all eternity. Do not think you are anything. A box and six feet of earth will do you friend, and it will do me as well.

MOON MADNESS PUTS MAN IN SPACE BEFORE GOD IN GRACE

Then the last thing I want to say is that moon madness puts man in space before God in grace. They are interested in them going up and landing and coming back, but I am interested in the great excursion that God took out of eternity into time. We hear a lot about visitors from space but praise God this world had a visit from God's throne. God's Son came, Jesus Christ came from beyond the moon and beyond the stars and beyond the planets that human eyes have yet to see, and no telescope ever made by man has ever pierced the gloom to see those burning orbs that revolve in their own orbits away out in the far flung reaches of the great space beyond this world. Praise God Jesus came. I am glad Jesus came. He came to deal with the rupture and the cancer and the curse of humanity. He came to deal with that thing called sin.

*"One day they led Him up Calvary's mountain,
One day they nailed Him to Calvary's tree,"*

One day, one lonely day, one dark day, but one wonderful day for me, Jesus Christ accomplished my salvation. I am going to tell you something and every believer will agree with me no matter whether you are a Baptist, a Brethren, or a bound Presbyterian or a Free Presbyterian, or whatever sort of Presbyterian you may be you will agree with me, that because Jesus died and rose again and we believe it and we are washed in the blood, we are going to go up to meet our Lord. The trumpet is going to sound. Yes I am going to put on a space suit that day. I am going to put on an incorruptible body. It will not need any oxygen pack in the back of it either and it will not need any tubes through it, hallelujah, and we will rise to meet the Lord in the air. Say, if that trumpet sounded now, if the great shout that is going to shake the world sounded now, if at this moment the trump of the archangel, the trump of God sounded, what about you? You are not saved. You are not redeemed. You are not ready to meet your God.

I have a verse to leave with you. *"Be ye also ready for in such an hour as ye think not the Son of Man cometh."*

AMEN AND AMEN

20 How Pilate *lost his soul*

I WANT TO SPEAK on the subject 'How Pontius Pilate lost his soul.' No name is better known, next to the name of the Lord Jesus Christ, than the name of Pilate.

Since the writing of the apostle's creed which probably took place at the beginning of the second century, those who believe the doctrines of the Gospel have emphasised the fact that Jesus suffered under Pontius Pilate. In fact the Bible has many things to tell us concerning Pilate.

Four times outside the Gospels there are references to Pilate. Three of them you will find in the book of Acts. If you have your testament and consult Acts 3 you will find that Peter, preaching at verse 13 says, *"The God of Abraham, and of Isaac, and of Jacob, the God of our fathers, hath glorified his Son Jesus; whom ye delivered up, and denied him in the presence of Pilate, when he was determined to let him go."* If you turn to Acts 4:28 you have another reference. *"For of a truth against thy holy child Jesus, whom thou hast anointed, both Herod, and Pontius Pilate, with the Gentiles, and the people of Israel, where gathered together."*. Acts 13:28, Paul preaching at Antioch in the synagogue there says in verse 28 *"And though they found no cause of death in him, [that is Jesus] yet desired they Pilate that he should be slain."* When Paul was giving his charge to young Timothy in I Timothy 6:13 *"I give thee charge in the sight of God, who quickeneth all things and before Christ Jesus, who before Pontius Pilate witnessed a good confession."*

So four times outside the Gospel narratives Pilate is mentioned and his part in the suffering and crucifixion of the Lord Jesus Christ is underlined. So Pilate is a very important character in the Scriptures and worthy of our consideration.

Linked with Pilate in the betrayal and death of Christ was Herod. Herod is a despicable character. A vile, debauched, immoral man. The Scriptures tell us about his debauchery. How to please his mistress he was prepared to cut off the head of John the Baptist, the great preacher of the Gospel and the forerunner of Christ. If there is one sin which will take a soul to hell quickly it is the sin of impunity, the sin of adultery, the sin of fornication and the sin of immorality.

We are living in an unclean age. We are living in an age where morality is taboo. Where Christian standards are mocked. Impurity of the marriage vow is made the object of the pun and of the joke. When alas even Christian young women are trying to model themselves on the standards of Paris and by the fashions of an evil adulterous age. This is an evil age, my brethren. Let us face up to it.

Let me tell you friend you cannot have your uncleanness and have Jesus Christ. Let me tell you you cannot have your sin and go to heaven. Let me tell you, young person, in this permissive society so-called launch your boat on the sea of sin and one day you will be a shipwreck in eternal hell for evermore. No sin will take you quicker to hell than uncleanness.

It was not uncleanness that damned Pilate. It damned Herod but it did not damn Pilate.

PILATE HAS CHRIST BEFORE HIM

Pilate has Christ before him. Don't you see those Jews? They are so religious and sanctimonious. They are so eager to keep the letter of the law that they would not come into the judgment hall. You know why? Because Pilate was a Gentile. In the house of Pilate there was unleavened bread and for a Jew to have any contact with leaven, when he was going to eat the Passover, put him beyond the pale. Of course, they did not mind pushing the Lord Jesus in the door. They did not mind if Jesus Christ should be contaminated in the house of Pilate but they, the religious hypocrites, the whitewashed sepulchres of the religious world, no, they were too holy, too separated, too sanctimonious to be contaminated with the leaven of the house of Pilate. So Pilate has to go out to talk to them.

I see the proud dignitary. The representative of the Imperial Caesar. He goes out and he looks at those Jews and their throats are swelled with their cries against Jesus. Their faces are bloodshot with their hatred against the Christ. He says to them, "What accusation have you to bring against the prisoner?" Of course they had no accusation to bring, no charge that could stick to Jesus Christ. He was the sinless, flawless, harmless, crimeless Son of God. So they turned on Pilate and they said "Do you think we would have brought Him if He was not a malefactor?" Pilate said "What evil has He done?" They cried out "We want His blood. He must die. We reject Him."

Is that not the cry of the religious world? Is that not the cry of many a heart of many a man in this meeting - rejecting Jesus Christ. My friend, Jesus Christ is the door to heaven. Reject Him and you will end in hell. Jesus Christ is the way to God. Reject Him and you will end in darkness. Jesus Christ is the truth, the only One who can enlighten and bring God's truth to your heart. Reject Him and you will die deceived, for the god of this world has blinded the minds of those who believe not lest the light of the glorious Gospel of Christ should shine into their heart.

PILATE FACE TO FACE WITH JESUS

Here is Pilate face to face with Jesus. Then they get Pilate on the sore spot. They say, "Pilate, this man says He is a king. If you let this man go you are not Caesar's friend." Pilate was ambitious. He had got his feet early in his career on the rungs of the political ladder. He was climbing up that ladder. He was now the representative in one of the most important territories that Rome controlled in that day of the Imperial Caesar. He wanted to climb further and further up the ladder of ambition and up the ladder of fame. The Jews knew it and they said, "You are not Caesar's friend if you let Him go."

THE LORD'S ANSWERS TO PILATE

Pilate takes Jesus aside and he says to Him, "Art Thou a king. Art Thou a king." I want you to notice the Lord's answer. It is a very important answer. It is one of the most important answers Jesus gave in all the record of His trial. He said to Pilate, "Do you say this of yourself or did someone tell you to say it to me?" Pilate said, "Am I a Jew? Thine own nation and the chief priests have delivered thee unto me: what hast thou done? Jesus answered, "My kingdom is not of this world: if my kingdom were of this world, then would my servants fight, that I should not be delivered to the Jews: but now is my kingdom not from hence." Except a man be born again he cannot see the kingdom of God. He is not talking about a materialistic kingdom now. He is not talking about a kingdom with an earthly throne or an earthly sceptre or an earthly crown. He is talking about the mystical and spiritual kingdom of God. The only way of entrance to that kingdom is by the mystical and spiritual new birth. It is not by materialistic things. It is not by church worship. It is not by church membership. It is not by baptism. It is not by communion but by a mighty birth of the Holy Ghost. Thank God for people who are born again and are members of that kingdom. Then he goes on, 'Pilate therefore said unto him art thou a king then? Jesus answered thou sayest that I am a king. To this end was I born.' Born to rule, born to be the king, born to wear not a crown of diadems but a crown of thorns. 'We see Jesus, made a little lower than the angels for the sufferings of death crowned with glory and honour.'

Then He goes on. He says, 'To this end was I was I born and for this cause came I into the world that I should bear witness unto the truth. Everyone that is of the truth heareth my voice.' You know what Pilate said? He said, 'What is truth?' Before Jesus Christ could answer he turned his heel and he went out again to the mob.

You remember Lord Bacon, the poet, said what is truth suggesting Pilate and waited not for an answer. There are many people who will come and for a moment or two will consider the Gospel and they will consider the words of Scripture and they will ask a question and before the question is answered they will turn their heel and they will become a Christ rejecter and a rejecter of the truth that alone can set them free and the truth alone that can save.

How many men and women in this hall have asked the question but before the Spirit of God could answer it you have turned on your heel and you have gone out again to the crowd. Because Pilate had the rungs of the ladder to climb, because Pilate had his ambitions to be achieved, he merely asks the question and then closes his ears and goes on down the road to hell. Friend it is hard to get away from Jesus, you don't get away like that. Pilate said to himself, 'Can I get out of this difficulty? Ah', he said, 'I will offer them Barabbas for Jesus.'

WHAT BARABBAS ARE YOU CHOOSING?

Now Barabbas was a robber and he said will you have the robber or Christ. They said they would have the robber. I wonder how many men and how many women in this meeting have said, 'The robber for me.' The thing that robs you of your health, the thing that robs you of your soul, the thing that robs you of heaven, the thing that robs you of Christ, you will have it but you will not have the Lord Jesus Christ. My sin is personified in Barabbas.

I wonder what Barabbas you are choosing tonight. I wonder what sin it is that is going to damn your soul. I wonder what evil companionship, I wonder what vile habit, I wonder what secret thought., I wonder what secret practice you are putting in the place of Jesus Christ. Let me ask you this question - what is it that is going to rob you of your soul? Men are being robbed in this hall of their soul by their sin. I wonder what sin is robbing you tonight.

Through the crowd there comes the slave boy. He has a parchment in his hand tied with a silken thread. He hands it up to his master and the master takes the parchment and pulls a dagger from his embroidered belt and cuts the silken thread and I hear the crinkle of that parchment as it is rolled out and he reads it. It is a letter from his wife, Claudia was her name. She was a Christian. She associated herself with those who followed the lowly Christ of God. And his wife, whom he loved, and there never was a mark of immorality in the life of Pilate. There was never a suggestion that he was an unclean man for he was not. He is visibly moved and he reads "Have thou nothing to do with this just Man for I have suffered many things in a dream this day because of Him" and I see the hand, the strong sinewy hand and it is shaking. He says to himself, 'I must get out of this.'

He calls the slave back again and he whispers something in his ear and the slave goes away and in a few minutes the slave returns and this time he has a fine porcelain bowl in his hands. In it is the clear crystal water from the fountain and he brings it up to Pilate and Pilate takes his hands and he thrusts them under the water and he rubs them together and then he holds them up until the water drops from his fingertips and he shakes them. He says something else to the slave, and the slave produces a towel and he wipes his hands clean.

He says to the crowd "I am clear of His blood. I am washing my hands of Jesus." You cannot wash your hands and put the blame on someone else, friend, you cannot do it.

THE ENDING

You know the way it ended? I will tell you. 'What shall I do then with Jesus which is called Christ?' What shall I do? He allowed someone else to make up his mind for him.

Let me finish with a tragic story. It will live with me in my ministry forever.

Some years ago I preached in Rathfriland. There are people in this meeting and they were saved, thank God, in that mission and they are going on with the Lord and they are members of this church. We started in the Friends Hall in Newry Street. It became too small. The second Sunday night we moved to the Presbyterian Hall and then we finished the mission in the large First Church.

One night I was preaching in that church and I made an appeal and a big man stood to his feet. I invited those who had stood to come forward and publicly declare that they were going to receive the Saviour and I saw that man make a move and then I saw a hand coming up and pulling him by the sleeve and pushing him back into the seat. As the appeal went on I went down the aisle. I had enthusiasm in those days, please God I have not lost that old fire. I went down the aisle and I said to that man "Sir, you stood to your feet. You made an effort to come but something kept you." A woman sitting beside him said "I am his wife and he is not getting saved." That man tried again but in vain and she held him in the seat.

My friend, the meetings finished and both of them went on their mad stampede to hell. Oh the tragedy of it. I can see that hand now. What hand is it that is keeping you from Jesus? If it is the hand of a loved one friend it is the hand of a traitor. If it is the hand of a loved one it is the kiss of a Judas, let me say it lovingly. Let nothing keep you from Jesus Christ tonight. My friend if your eye offends you pluck it out. It is better to enter into life blind with only one eye than to go to hell with your sight complete. If your foot offends you cut it off. It is better to stagger into life than to go with both your limbs into hell fire forever.

Oh friend what will you do with Jesus? I will tell you something. Some day your soul will be asking, 'What will He do with me?' God grant that you will come to Christ. God grant that you will trust Him. I have preached to you for many a year friend. I have prayed for you. I have longed to lead you to Jesus. Please God you will respond and on this 23rd anniversary of this preacher you will say I am coming to Christ, I am trusting the Saviour. Please God that it will happen, for Jesus sake.

AMEN AND AMEN!

THE
❧ IAN R. K. PAISLEY LIBRARY ❧

OTHER BOOKS IN THIS SPECIAL SERIES

♦ **Christian Foundations**

♦ **An Exposition of the Epistle to the Romans**

♦ **The Garments of Christ**

♦ **Sermons on Special Occasions**

♦ **Expository Sermons**

♦ **A Text a Day keeps the Devil Away**

♦ **The Rent Veils at Calvary**

♦ **My Plea for the Old Sword**

♦ **Into the Millennium**

❧ **AVAILABLE FROM** ❧

AMBASSADOR PRODUCTIONS, LTD.

Providence House
16 Hillview Avenue,
Belfast, BT5 6JR
Telephone: 01232 658462

Emerald House
1 Chick Springs Road, Suite 102
Greenville, South Carolina, 29609
Telephone: 1 800 209 8570

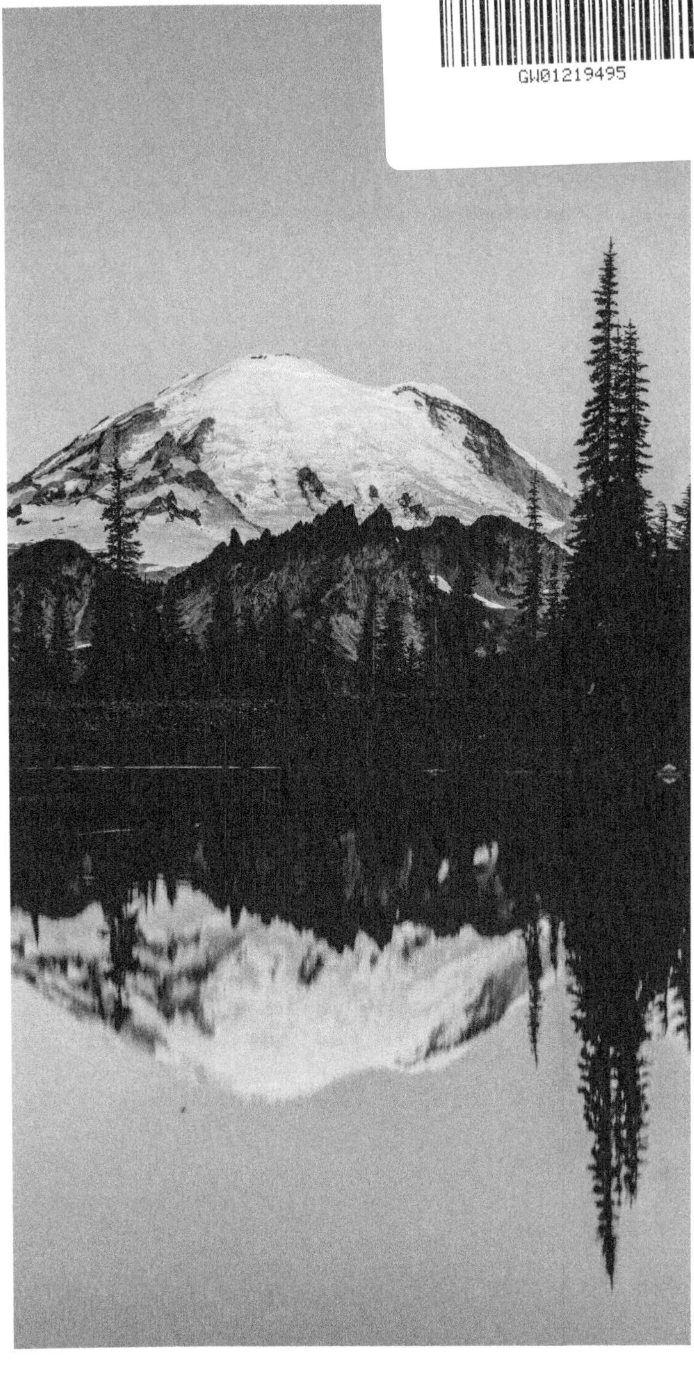

THE PERFECT MAIL-ORDER BRIDE
Book 1 in the Frontier Matches Series

Copyright © 2022 by Regina Lundgren

All rights reserved. Except for use in any review, the reproduction or utilization of this work in whole or in part in any form by any electronic, mechanical or other means, now known or hereinafter invented, including xerography, photocopying and recording, or in any information storage or retrieval system, is forbidden without the written permission of the publisher.

This is a work of fiction. Names, characters, places and incidents are either the product of the author's imagination or are used fictitiously, and any resemblance to actual persons, living or dead, business establishments, events or locales is entirely coincidental.

Printed in the USA.

Cover Design and Interior Format
© THE KILLION GROUP, INC.

THE PERFECT MAIL-ORDER BRIDE

BOOK ONE
FRONTIER MATCHES

REGINA SCOTT

*To those who begged for Scout to have a story all
his own—enjoy!
And to the Lord, who always leads us home.*

CHAPTER ONE

Seattle, Washington Territory, June 1876

SOMEWHERE OUT THERE was the man waiting for his bride.

Ada Williamson swallowed the lump in her throat as she stood on the deck of the steamer *Frances Downing* from San Francisco. The sailor on the helm blew the ship's horn twice, the blasts echoing across the blue-gray waters of the bay until it bounced off the forested hillside beyond. Clapboard houses grew more elaborate as they climbed the hill, stretching across the arc of the town with a line of tall firs behind them, and businesses crowded the waterfront.

"Adds another few establishments each week," one of the businessmen behind her murmured to the balding Mr. Clancy, who had made a point of making her acquaintance on the trip. "I hear they have more than three thousand inhabitants now."

"And nearly forty saloons," Mr. Clancy joked.

Ada shifted farther away from them along the rail as the steamer cruised into port. The rumble beneath her feet slowed, stopped, as the massive engines ramped down. The anchor rattled as the crew released it to splash into the water. Across the bay came the unmistakable sound of a cheer.

Odd. She'd thought steamer service from San Francisco was a regular occurrence. Was the ship carrying important cargo?

She shifted again, clutching her carpetbag in front of her auburn traveling dress as sailors moved past to man the small boats. Her other belongings were already packed in her trunk, which waited to be offloaded.

"Take any dress you like," her sister had said with a toss of her golden curls. "I'm sure Bertrand would be glad to buy me more."

If not Bertrand, then Frank or Peter or George or any one of the two dozen men who had attempted to capture her sister's heart in the last year. It didn't matter that proper ladies would not allow such extravagant gifts. Melinda Williamson deserved better, at least in her own mind.

Ada grimaced at the unkind thought. Melinda couldn't help that she was beautiful and charming, that she could sing to the second A above middle C without trying, that she glided across the ballroom floor like a swallow on the breeze. When she entered a room, everyone knew it. When she left, the very air seemed to follow. Ada had never met anyone—male or female—who didn't immediately want to make her sister's acquaintance. And it was entirely Melinda's doing that many eventually wandered away, disheartened.

"Jealous," her sister would claim of a lady friend's defection.

"He bores me," she had insisted of the man she'd thrown off for another. Melinda went through acquaintances nearly as quickly as gowns.

And nothing Ada had done could convince her sister she must mend her ways now that they had been left nearly destitute.

She patted her black feathered hat into place on her

hair, wishing as she often did that the light brown had half the luster of her sister's curls. At the moment, it felt as dull and heavy as the clouds overhead. Rain would entirely fit with the news she was bringing. Surely Mr. Rankin would mourn.

She swallowed again as the small boats began their way down the side of the steamer for the salt water below. In a moment, the little craft would be ferrying passengers from deep water to the piers that jutted out into the bay like fingers eager to grasp hold. One of the piers looked particularly crowded—people all jostling to stare out at the ship.

Ada glanced around at the whiskered gentlemen, the mothers holding firmly to their children's hands. The steamer only carried a dozen passengers, and many were newcomers to Seattle like her. She hadn't met anyone on the seven-day journey from San Francisco who had claimed a large family waiting. She had sent a telegram to ask Mr. Rankin to meet the ship and a solitary Miss Williamson, for she would be leaving the sister he thought would be accompanying her in San Francisco. He couldn't know that the sister left behind was the one he intended to marry.

What, or who, were those people on the dock expecting?

The second mate stopped beside her. "Would you care to take the first boat, Miss Williamson?"

Her? She glanced at the businessmen. One was frowning as if he couldn't understand why she'd be given such an honor. Mr. Clancy was regarding her as if she must hold hidden depths. She should demur, allow those with more important business to disembark first.

But the sooner she got this over with, the better, and the less likely she'd beg a return passage to San Francisco instead.

"Thank you, Mr. Tilden," she said. "That would be

lovely."

A short time later, she was seated with chubby Mr. Clancy, his colleague, and three other men as two sailors bent the oars to send them bobbing across the waves. Her hat was securely pinned, but already the tangy sea breeze tugged at strands of her hair, whipping them about her face as the boat approached the pier. She should try to tame them, but it didn't really matter what she looked like. She'd come to break Thomas Rankin's heart. He'd soon despise the very sight of her.

Which was such a shame! The letters he'd written in response to the ad Ada had convinced Melinda to place as a mail-order bride had been so heartfelt, so poignant. He deserved the charming beauty he thought he was marrying.

Melinda didn't seem to care. She'd been certain a letter would suffice to inform him she had changed her mind. He'd paid her passage from New York, but she preferred to stay in San Francisco rather than the rural hamlet she considered Seattle. Because of Ada's respect for him, she had used a good portion of her remaining money to come tell him the truth. And after that, she prayed she could start a life of her own.

Another cheer went up as the boat bumped the pilings. Hands reached down to help secure the ropes. A band started playing, brass melding with strings.

"Someone important must be on the boat," Mr. Clancy told his colleague.

Burley dockworkers bent to offer Ada their calloused hands. They both grinned as if it were a great honor. Mystified, she allowed them to lift her to the planks.

The cheer that went up this time was deafening, drowning out the music from the band. Dozens of faces, male faces, beamed at her. From senior fellows with grizzled locks and gap-toothed grins to lads with barely the scruff of a tawny beard, they clapped their hands, stomped their feet, and whistled, until the pier trembled.

Ada glanced back into the boat, where Mr. Clancy and the others waited their turn to climb onto the pier. They frowned back at her. And no one reached down to help them ashore.

Her gaze was drawn to a movement in the crowd. A lean man with deep brown hair brushing the collar of his fine wool coat stepped forward. She didn't need to see his smile to know his name. She'd read about the bump on the bridge of his nose, how he'd gained the faint scar that marked his left cheek. She knew his hopes for marrying and had shared his dreams for a future.

He must have planned the band, the crimson carpet that stretched up the pier to the golden-yellow carriage on the shore, and the banner overhead, hand-painted with blue and yellow iris and the words "Welcome, Melinda Williamson." He'd done all this for the woman he'd hoped to wed.

The lump in her throat felt as large as the snow-capped mountain in the distance.

He stepped forward, a bouquet of red and gold blanket flowers in one long-fingered hand. "Miss Williamson?"

Those two words held so much hope and so much doubt. Around him, men doffed their hats and waited for her answer. How could she tell him, shame him, in front of them all?

Ada pasted on her best smile. "Yes. You must be Mr. Rankin. It's a pleasure to meet you at last."

Thomas "Scout" Rankin blew out a breath, then hastily bowed to cover it. She was here. She'd come. He hadn't really believed she would.

"You mustn't judge Miss Williamson by Mrs. Jamison,"

Beth McCormick had insisted when she'd come by this morning to check on him. She'd carefully straightened the trailing ends of the blue silk bowtie at his collar, her own pink skirts impeccable as always. "She sounds quite reasonable from her letters."

He should have trusted Beth. They'd known each other since they were children, and she had a knack for matchmaking, having helped each of her five brothers find love. She'd been one of the first to cast doubts on the beautiful widow he'd been drawn to last year. But Evangeline Jamison had proved herself false. That didn't mean Miss Williamson would do the same.

He still remembered the ad Beth had drawn to his attention.

Interested in matrimony to a kind, considerate gentleman who is a good provider: Boston beauty of fine family and education. Hoping to make a family and share a faith. Willing to travel for the right man.

He wasn't so much interested in beauty as character. The Good Book said that beauty was fleeting, but a woman of good character was to be praised. It was the character of Melinda Williamson, as expressed in her letters, that had made him believe love stood a chance. Still, the photo she'd sent hadn't hurt.

And the woman standing in front of him now resembled that photo very little. Instead of bright, thick curls, her hair was sleeker and a warm brown. Instead of a rounded-cheek face, hers was nearly as narrow as his. And she seemed to have lost weight, for there was no sign of her lush figure.

But that smile—tremulous, full of awe—he could bask in that admiration for quite some time.

The other men around him weren't so willing to wait. Despite his best intentions to keep this meeting private, word had gotten out. Beth's insistence on adding the carpet up the rough planks, as if he was ushering

Miss Williamson to a coronation rather than a possible wedding, and the presence of the Seattle Brass and String Band had guaranteed notice. Now half the male population of the town was crowding the wharf and lining the shore. Sawmill workers in flannel and denim, merchants in calico and wool, and even a local banker in a tall beaver hat stood around him, watching his every move.

"What are you waiting for, Scout?" someone shouted. "Give her the flowers!"

"Forget the flowers," someone else yelled. "Give her a kiss!"

The word flew through the crowd, until they all sounded like a flock of geese hissing at a stranger. His cheeks felt hot.

Her cheeks turned pink, and she thrust out the hand that wasn't holding her carpetbag. "Thank you for the flowers."

Thomas handed her the bouquet, picked from the hillside near his house. Then he took the bag from her and offered her his arm. "May I escort you to the carriage?"

"Why are you asking her?" someone demanded. "You paid for her to come. Tell her who's boss."

"You may be a Rankin, but you can still act like a man."

"Act is the right word!"

He ignored the gibes. So did Miss Williamson as she placed her hand on his arm.

"Will they know where to send my trunk?" she asked.

"I've left word at the booking office," he assured her.

Several men moved to block their way, hands on their hips and grins cocky. What, did they think they deserved to kiss the bride too?

Thomas hardened his face as he met their gazes. Their grins faded, and they stepped aside with respectful nods. He led the woman he hoped to marry up the pier for his waiting carriage.

Bobby sat in the driver's seat, holding the horses ready, eyes wide, as they approached. Why was his seventeen-year-old ward nervous? He wasn't the one contemplating marrying a stranger.

Only she wasn't a stranger. Through her letters, Thomas had felt her sorrow on the loss of her parents in a carriage accident, her eagerness to travel around the Horn to meet him. He enjoyed the same books she did—adventure stories of valiant men and visionary women. They both shared a passion for maple sugar candy, nearly impossible to get out here on the frontier. They both believed in a merciful God, who stood by to help in times of trouble.

That woman—that warm, kind, intelligent woman—was who he hoped to make his bride.

"Melinda Williamson," he said, "allow me to introduce my ward, Robert Donovan."

He'd told her about Bobby in his letters too, though not everything. Bobby deserved to be judged on his own merits, not those of his conniving older sister, who had been convicted of instigating the murder of three men.

Bobby removed one hand from the reins to yank his tweed cap off his black hair, leaving strands sticking out at odd angles. "Ma'am."

"It's a pleasure to meet you, Mr. Donovan," she said.

The tops of Bobby's ears turned red.

"Bobby offered to drive so I could devote my attentions to you rather than the horses," Thomas told her.

Her color seeped away. Were his attentions unwanted at the moment, or was she daunted by the hill rising behind them? The streets of the town were steep, and those streets were more mud than hard-packed dirt some days. At least they'd had good weather this June, the gray skies today notwithstanding. That boded well for the upcoming Centennial Celebration.

"Very kind of you," she murmured, and he wasn't sure if she was thanking Bobby or him.

He motioned with his hand, and she nodded permission for him to help her up into the carriage. The movement set the black silk fringe on the skirts of her dusky red gown to swinging. Mindful of the men still watching from the wharf, Thomas went around to the other side of the carriage to climb in beside her. The Seattle Band played them down the street and around the corner to the Occidental Hotel as his other impromptu guests began making their way back to their homes and businesses and Mr. Mercer, the longshoreman, began rolling up the carpet before taking down the banner Beth had painted.

"I booked you a suite," Thomas explained as she looked right, left, straight ahead at Bobby's slender back, anywhere but at him. "I thought that would be easiest for you. And I asked my friend, Mrs. McCormick, to act as chaperone."

"I remember Mrs. McCormick," she said, look brightening. "She answered the ad for you. She was ever so nice."

"She is," Thomas agreed, admiring the way the black lace lining the edges of her hat called attention to her fluttering lashes.

Bobby pulled up the team of dappled grays in front of the white-washed two-story building. "Here you are, Scout."

Thomas shook his head. No matter how he'd tried, he couldn't seem to outgrow his childhood nickname. Some—like Beth, her brothers, and Bobby—used it fondly. Others held it over him.

He hopped down and came around to offer a hand to Miss Williamson. She had little hands, dainty, like the rest of her. He hadn't expected that. He'd been a little afraid she might tower over his five-foot-seven frame. But her head came just about to his shoulder, and his arm would have fit around her waist easily. He made sure not to confirm that as they entered the lobby.

The Occidental was one of Seattle's finest hotels. Wingback chairs with crimson, tufted upholstery dotted the lobby, and the clerk's stand was of polished mahogany. Thomas led her up to the clerk.

"We have Miss Williamson's suite all ready," the fellow assured them as he handed her the brass key. "I'll have a porter show you right up."

She glanced at Thomas, smile slipping just the slightest. "Will you be coming too, Mr. Rankin?"

The clerk was watching avidly, and Thomas felt as if everyone in the lobby had stopped and held a breath to hear his response.

"No," he said. "A lady deserves her privacy. But I'd love to have dinner with you later, after you've settled in. Say six?"

"That would be lovely," she said.

He handed her bag to the porter and watched until they disappeared up the stairs, then turned to go.

"I thought she was supposed to be a great beauty," one of the other guests said to another. At least his friend had the good sense to look abashed, gaze flitting away from Thomas. He ignored them and headed for the door.

She might not be a great beauty, but if she was the woman who had written those letters, she was the perfect mail-order bride.

Now he just had to convince her he needed a little time before becoming her groom.

CHAPTER TWO

ADA GAZED AROUND at the suite of rooms Thomas Rankin had arranged for her. The sitting room overlooking Elliott Bay had elegant, flocked wallpaper and was furnished with a camelback settee and two satin-striped chairs, all of cerulean blue, nestled close to a stone fireplace. The room next to it held a brass bed large enough to sleep a family of four, a desk and chair of polished walnut, and wardrobe space where her few gowns would likely look lonely. The blue and white carpet patterned with lilies sank under her feet as she crossed it.

She had never stayed in such fine surroundings. Guilt shoved on her shoulders. She shook it off.

It was only for one night. At dinner, she would tell him the truth. At least, most of it.

She ventured to sit on the horsehair settee, the cushion as firm as her convictions. Truly, it would be a relief to stop finding excuses for her sister's selfish behavior.

"She's high spirited," their father would say, gray head up as if proud of the fact.

"She draws every eye in the room," her mother would put in with a doting smile.

Melinda certainly did, but it hadn't been until their older parents had died, leaving a pile of debts behind, that Ada realized her sister not only drew attention, she craved it. In the end, she had been unwilling to surrender it, even if it meant going back on her word and stealing a man's money.

The memories pushed her to her feet and set her to pacing. Melinda's betrayal had been nearly as bad as their father's. He'd inherited a small fortune when he'd been younger, enough that her parents needn't work. But he'd never learned to manage money properly. After indulging every whim of Melinda's, they'd gone into debt, then kept spending to keep up appearances. In the end, they'd left their daughters with little choice but to seek employment or marriage. And only Melinda had held any hopes for marriage.

Ada shook her head. If she kept ruminating about the past until six, she'd go mad. But there was no sense in unpacking her carpetbag, or the trunk that would shortly follow. Tomorrow, she must find work and a boardinghouse.

Her limited skills had prevented her from competing in the workforce in Boston, but this was the frontier. There must be jobs here. She might not be polished enough with a needle for fine work, but she could hem and mend. She tended to overcook or undercook her meals no matter how hard she tried, but she could clean vegetables and wash dishes. She had no experience with children—unless dealing with her sister's tantrums counted—but she could clean houses and launder clothes. Surely someone would hire an honest, hardworking woman.

Honest—ha!

Would the people of Seattle hold it against her when they learned that she'd misled one of its finest citizens, if only for a few hours? Perhaps she really was mad to think she could leave Melinda behind and start a new life.

She stopped in the middle of the plush carpet. No. She refused to think like that. Against all odds, she'd gotten herself here. Now she must take the next step and apply for a position. An ad had brought her here. An ad could see to her future.

She marched herself downstairs and requested a newspaper from the obsequious clerk, who introduced himself as Thaddeus Carter. She nodded her thanks and clutched the paper close, all the while trying to ignore the number of gazes pointed in her direction. Thomas Rankin was clearly a man important enough in Seattle that everyone wanted to take a gander at his supposed bride.

Once safely back in the suite, she opened *The Puget Sound Dispatch*, published the previous Saturday by Brown and Son. The front page of the weekly carried news from around the country as well as the territory, including a story about a sixteen-year-old girl who had killed a wildcat.

"That is the kind of a girl for new countries," the editor opined.

Ada sucked in a breath. If that was the sort of woman men expected in Seattle, she would never find a position.

She thumbed through the eight pages nonetheless but found few positions advertised and none that might fit her dubious qualifications. Well, there would be another paper on Saturday. In the meantime, she noted names of boardinghouses and other businesses to approach.

By half past five, she was ready to be done with her confession. She changed into a dinner dress her sister had never liked. It was a little behind the current fashion with wider skirts and a less-fitted bodice, but that made it easier to hide the fact that it had been made for a woman with a more expansive figure. Ada had spent most of the trip up from San Francisco hemming and tucking the gowns. When it came to new dresses and things, Melinda had always come first. Ada was used to hand-me-downs.

Still, she thought she looked rather well in the gown

the color of a summer sky as she descended to the lobby, the pleated ruffle at the hem brushing the stairs. Several gentlemen lounging on the tufted chairs glanced her way. Why were they smiling? Her hand went to her hair, which she'd combed to spill down behind her past her ruffled collar, but everything seemed to be in place. She twisted to make sure the waterfall skirts were laying properly and the hem hadn't come undone. No, good there too. Perhaps she should simply keep moving.

She recognized the door to the dining room by the neatly lettered sign beside it and the tantalizing aromas wafting from it. A fellow standing near it was bold enough to speak to her as she approached.

"A pretty lady like you should not have to dine alone," he said, pulling off his hat from his straw-colored hair.

Pretty lady? Was he some sort of charlatan to think she'd dive into his butter sauce? Ada raised her chin, prepared to skewer him with a sharp retort.

"Miss Williamson won't be alone." The tenor voice was surprisingly firm as Thomas came up to them. "She'll be dining with me." He offered her his arm.

With a regretful smile, the other man moved ahead of them into the dining room.

"I'm sorry I wasn't here when you came down," Thomas said.

"I was a little early," Ada admitted, accepting his arm. He led her through the two wide doors into the dining room.

Tables draped in white dotted the expanse of polished wood floor, with palms, no doubt imported at great expense, sheltered in scarlet pots against the paneled walls. A waiter hurried forward to show them to a table in the corner. Candlelight gleamed on heavy silverware. The aromas were stronger now—melted butter and garlic and fresh-baked bread.

Thomas held her chair for her, then went around to

take his own seat opposite.

"Was the suite to your liking?" he asked.

"Oh, yes," Ada managed, mindful of the hovering waiter. "It's lovely."

"The Occidental is the best hotel in Seattle," the waiter bragged, broad face wide in a grin. "Though rarely has it been graced by so lovely a lady."

Ada had to stop herself from snorting. Someone was hoping for a fat tip.

Thomas leaned back in his chair. "What do you have for us tonight, Roy?"

Roy stood taller, slicked back brown hair shining in the light from the center brass chandelier. "Mussels in a cream sauce, dilled salmon, and prime rib in its own juice." He waited expectantly.

So did Thomas.

He wanted her to choose? Usually Melinda decided what they would eat, and Ada went along, knowing anything else was sacrilege. But to make her own choice? A little bubble of happiness rose up inside her, like a balloon soaring into the sky.

"Mussels," Ada said. "I haven't had them in ages."

"Make that two, Roy," Thomas said, and the waiter hurried off, white apron flapping about his long legs.

"A shame it's not the season for strawberries," Thomas said.

Strawberries? Oh, right. They were Melinda's favorite. Ada had written to tell him that. She scooted closer to the table. "Or huckleberries. Do they really grow everywhere here?"

"Hillsides, forests," he agreed.

Do it, Ada. Just tell him.

"My friend Levi and I used to gorge ourselves on them," he continued, gaze soft. "We even grabbed one of his mother's pies off the cooling rack. We weren't gentlemen in those days."

But he was now. His dark hair was neatly combed, his chin freshly shaved if the scent of bay rum cologne was any indication. He wore a yellow-checkered cravat at his throat and a green watered-silk waistcoat inside his tailored jacket. With that kind look and considerate attitude, he was everything a gentleman should be. She ought to tell her sister a thing or two about abandoning him.

And she ought to tell him the truth.

"Actually, Mr. Rankin," she started.

"Thomas, please," he said. "And I hope you will allow me to call you by your first name."

She nodded. Why not? In a few minutes, it wouldn't matter. He probably wouldn't want to set eyes on her again once she confessed.

"Thomas, then," she said, surprised by how nice it felt to say the name that had been on her mind for months. "We must talk."

He reached across the table and took her hand where it had been balled on the cloth. The touch warmed muscles that had gone tight. "Yes, we must. I know we've shared a lot through our letters, and you agreed to marry me, but I feel as if we need to become better acquainted before making any lasting decisions."

Ada blinked, feeling as if those gray clouds outside had opened up and doused her. "You don't want to wed?"

His smile widened. "I am intrigued by the lady who has been writing to me, but I want her to be very, very sure before she commits her life to mine. With your permission, I'd like to court you, say for a month. If, after that time, we both agree we do indeed suit, we'll marry. If we find we don't suit, we'll go our own way, friends. What do you say?"

What could she say? He could not know the person who'd written most of those letters had been her, not her far-too-busy sister. He said he liked that woman. He was offering her a month, a glorious month of courting, where she could show him who she was, how much she admired him. Could she, perhaps, win his affections away from her sister?

She nearly snorted again. No man ever looked at her after seeing her sister.

But Melinda wasn't here. This wasn't Boston or even San Francisco. Ada had a chance, perhaps the only one she'd ever be given.

"Look at me, Thomas," she said. "Do you really want to court me?"

He met her gaze without hesitation. "Yes, I do."

Ada took a deep breath. "Then I agree to your proposal."

He nearly jumped up and ran around the room, shaking hands with the other diners who had come in. Melinda Williamson was going to let him court her—with his crooked nose and scarred face and rough life and all. He wouldn't have been surprised if his heart hadn't leapt right out of his chest.

Oh, he knew she'd agreed before. She wouldn't have accepted his money and made the long trip otherwise. But Seattle extolled in a letter and Seattle experienced in person were two different things. And so was he. He had to be sure of her.

"Thank you," he said. "I hope that makes things a little easier."

She smiled. "You'll never know how much. So, where do we start?"

"Dinner tonight," he suggested, suddenly eager to eat every entre the hotel kitchen had to offer. "Tomorrow, Beth, Mrs. McCormick, will join us for a tour of Seattle. A lot's changed since I wrote you. It changes every day."

"But the Pastry Emporium is still here?" she asked.

Thomas shook his head. "I can't believe you remembered."

"Well, you mentioned it several times," she allowed. She had a dimple to the right of her mouth. It showed every time she smiled. It was like a sign saying *kiss me right here*.

He forced his gaze up to her eyes. Funny, he'd thought she'd said they were blue. These looked closer to gray, like the mists that rolled down from the mountains or up from the Sound.

What were they talking about?

"The Pastry Emporium," he answered himself aloud. "Yes, it's still here. I'll be sure we stop tomorrow for a treat."

The fingers on her free hand plucked at the napkin, and he realized he still held her other hand, which had relaxed under his fingers. It felt warm, supple. He ought to let go.

He didn't.

As if she knew it, she dropped her gaze, and he waited for her to pull away.

She didn't.

"You shouldn't spend so much money on me, Thomas," she murmured instead.

"I have money to spare," he assured her. "And don't worry about food either. I left an account open at the hotel for you. If you're hungry, eat."

Roy returned with their dinners, then, steamed mussels nestled in a cream sauce over rice, with flaky rolls and asparagus tips. It was almost worth removing his hand from hers.

Almost.

"Tell Pete the garden is paying off," Thomas said to the waiter before he could hurry off.

"I will," Roy promised with a grin. "Thanks for the

loan, Mr. Rankin."

"Loan?" his lovely companion asked as the waiter left them.

Thomas shrugged. "People come to me for help sometimes. I do what I can. Shall I say the blessing?"

She nodded and bowed her head.

"Dear Lord," Thomas murmured, the same feeling of humility stealing over him every time he considered what he'd been given, "thank You for this food and the path You've laid before us. May it bless us even as we bless You. Amen."

"Amen," she responded, but she didn't raise her gaze from the silver fork in her hand.

"I've been thinking about the money you put out for the travel," she said. "Perhaps you could consider it a loan. I could pay you back in time."

"You're an investment in my future," he told her. "If anything, I owe you."

"Nonsense." She dug into her dinner at last. "I haven't done anything."

If only she knew.

He swallowed the urge to tell her. It was too soon. He'd revealed a little about his past in their correspondence, including the fact that she was the second woman with whom he'd corresponded, and she'd still agreed to come. Of the two ladies whose ads he'd answered, he far preferred Melinda.

Over the next month, he'd explain everything, all the matters he rarely shared with others, all the history that made some in Seattle look down on him. It was only her right to know the truth about the man she thought she might marry.

And he'd vowed that, no matter the cost, he would have no more lies or liars in his life.

CHAPTER THREE

ADA WAS IN the lobby of the hotel, waiting, when Thomas and Mrs. McCormick arrived the next day. She'd spent the evening unpacking her things with the giddy hope that she wouldn't have to pack them up again until she went to her own home as a bride.

A bride!

The very thought left her breathless. She'd taken a moment to read through some of their correspondence again, untying the red satin ribbon she'd wrapped around the precious sheets.

Trees so high they tickle the clouds…

Cookies that warm your stomach and your heart…

People who are valued for who they are, not what they can do for you…

The man who'd written those words wanted to court her! Her! She could hardly wait.

Unfortunately, she had to endure more stares and refuse several attempts at an introduction as she waited in the lobby that morning. Really—were all the men in Seattle except Thomas so cruel? She'd been ignored most of her life. Why should she think they'd all find her fascinating now?

Mrs. McCormick, however, was every bit as enthusiastic as her initial letter introducing Ada to Thomas. She too was a beauty—blond curls cascading down her back, blue eyes several shades darker than Melinda's, winsome smile. And her clothes! Pink and white stripes and lace and ruffles. Ada felt as if she was looking at a plate from *Godey's Lady's Book*.

"I am so happy to meet you," she said, pulling Ada in for a hug. The feather on her hat bobbed as she disengaged. "You must call me Beth. And I will call you Melinda."

She would gag if she had to go by her sister's name for a month.

"Perhaps you could call me Ada," she said. "That's what my family called me."

A slight frown marred Beth's face. "I thought the sister you left in San Francisco was named Ada."

Oh, dear. She had mentioned herself occasionally in the letters. Not too often. She'd been afraid he wouldn't want to take on the responsibility for two women. She'd hoped, whoever Melly married, he'd be amenable to supporting Ada too.

"It is a family name," she extemporized, "shared by many Williamson women for generations. Shall we go? I wouldn't want to keep the horses standing."

Thomas offered her his arm, and she took it. It was strong and firm inside the fine navy coat, despite his slender appearance. A lady could learn to feel comfortable leaning on it.

His ward, Bobby, was once more at the reins, dressed in a blue gingham shirt and gray wool trousers. He nodded at her shyly, and Ada offered him a smile of encouragement. Thomas helped Beth up beside the youth, then joined Ada in the second set of seats.

"This is a lovely carriage," Ada said, running a hand over the brown leather seats. "And you drive it very well, Mr. Donovan."

"Thank you, ma'am," he shot back over his shoulder before urging the horses away from the white front of the hotel.

"Scout sent all the way to San Francisco for this equipage," Beth said, twisting in her seat to meet Ada's gaze. "It's the finest in Seattle."

"Well, David Denny might argue with that," Thomas demurred.

"I'd argue right back," Bobby put in, directing the horses up the hill. "And only James Wallin has better horses than Skip and Jack."

She didn't know much about horses, but the dappled grays did look rather impressive with their black manes flying and their coats flashing in the sunlight. They pulled the loaded carriage up the hill with prancing steps, as if as proud as Beth of the carriage they drew, and Bobby turned them onto another street.

"What do you think of Seattle?" Beth asked eagerly.

She should say something warm and witty, but the clapboard buildings seemed to cling to the hillside by sheer determination.

"It's muddier than I expected," she said, eyeing the black, lumpy street.

"You should see it when it rains," Beth teased.

"It's not so bad," Thomas said. He pointed toward the two-story building on the corner. "There's the new store TP Freeman opened."

"Goods on commission," Beth said dreamily. "Think of the bargains."

"Think of wearing Mrs. Horton's hand-me-downs," Thomas countered.

Beth sniffed. "I sincerely doubt the banker's wife sells her clothes on commission. But point taken. I far prefer to make my own anyway."

The bench felt stiffer, and Ada smoothed the skirts of her white sprigged muslin dress. This one was hers, fitted to her figure, with two overskirts edged in ruffles of the same material, material, she feared now, that would turn brown and sodden the moment it contacted a Seattle street. Would Beth McCormick raise her delicately arched brow if she knew most of Ada's clothing was handed down from Melinda?

Thomas pointed out other businesses as they drove along. Ada spotted a number of dry good stores, windows crowded with everything from bolts of fabric to new plows. There were bootmakers, brewers, and banks along with candy makers, carpenters, and coal merchants. An entire district was devoted to Chinese merchants, with wash houses, a drug store, a chop house, and a cigar manufacturer. She was used to the tall brick stores of Boston, crowded along fashionable thoroughfares. Seattle seemed to have found a way to bring as much variety into a far smaller space.

"You have the wealth of the world," she said, and Thomas smiled.

"This is Second Avenue," he said a short time later, leaning closer and raising his head as Bobby turned onto another street. "And there's the Pastry Emporium."

She'd longed to visit the bakery he'd written about so fondly. She turned to tell him, and the words disappeared. With his face close to hers, she could only marvel at the length of his lashes, the golden flecks in the depths of his eyes. The scar stood out white against his tan, and she had to stop herself from reaching up to trace its route across his cheek.

Bobby reined in, causing Thomas to lean back, and Ada drew in a breath before forcing herself to look out at the building. The two-story structure boasted windows overlooking the street and a cheery sign proclaiming its wares.

Thomas jumped down, the mud squelching beneath his boots, then came around to help first Beth and then Ada alight onto the boardwalk. Bobby busied himself putting feed sacks on the horses and tying the team to the hitching rail, before following Thomas and the others into the bakery.

Inside, wrought-iron tables and chairs dotted the space, leading up to a glass-fronted counter where an untold wealth of cookies, pastries, pies, cakes, and bread awaited. Ginger and lemon seemed to float in the air.

A woman with fiery red hair was putting some money in the cash drawer at the counter. She glanced up as the bell over the door tinkled, then grinned at them all.

"A very good day to you, Beth and Scout," she said, voice hinting of Ireland. Her brown-eyed gaze drifted over Ada. "So this is your lady, is it, now? Tis honored I am that you'd bring her here."

Red was creeping into Thomas's sculptured cheeks. "Maddie Haggerty, meet Melinda, that is Ada Williamson."

The proprietress came around the counter, green gingham skirts swaying and hand outstretched, and Ada shook it. The scent of cinnamon hung over her, and something sparkled in the depths of those eyes.

"It's a pleasure to meet you," Ada said. "Thomas has told me so much about this place I feel as if I've been here before."

"And will return again," Maddie urged her. "Sit down, now, and I'll be bringing you a treat. Gingersnaps, sugar cookies, or lemon drops?"

"You know what I want," Beth said, sinking onto a chair. "And wrap up two for Hart."

"Sugar cookies," Bobby volunteered with an anticipatory grin.

"Perhaps a gingersnap?" Ada asked.

Thomas nodded. "Good choice. I'll take some too."

"Coming right up," Maddie promised before disappearing through a curtained doorway.

He held out the chair for Ada, and she sat, guilt once more tugging at her.

"You don't have to eat what I choose," she murmured

as he took a seat as well.

"Why not?" he asked. "It's the same choice I'd make."

Was it? From the first time she'd read one of his letters, she'd felt an affinity for him. She'd thought at once that he might be the man to make Melinda settle down. Would he be willing to settle for her instead?

What a treat to see Seattle through someone else's eyes. Thomas had grown up among the towering firs and the gray skies that could give way to brilliant blue. He knew by the amount of brine on the breeze whether the tide was in or out. He told time by the wail of the whistle at Yesler's sawmill.

But this was all new to Ada. Her wide-eyed interest, her delight in seeing things he'd described, were evident. It was nothing to her awe as Bobby drove them up to the house.

"I'll stay with the horses," his ward whispered as Thomas passed him. "You show her the house." He smiled with proprietary pride.

Thomas knew how he felt. He'd purchased the two-story house from a man who had decided to return to San Francisco after running through his gold mining riches. Thomas had taken the lesson to heart. Some of his earnings were safely in Dexter Horton's new bank, the only brick building in Seattle. The bulk was invested where he was all but guaranteed a profit. What remained was his to enjoy.

Which meant he could indulge in one of the nicest homes in Seattle, with scallops along the eaves and multipaned glass in the windows that overlooked Elliott Bay. He hurried to open the lacquered front door for Ada. Beth had helped him decorate, so he knew the furnishings in the parlor, including a curved-back sofa in emerald brocade, the mahogany side tables and credenza, and the porcelain-based oil lamps, were the height of fashion.

But Ada stood just inside the entry hall—gaze darting from the wood-railed staircase on the right to the parlor on the left—and gaped.

"We can change things," he assured her, concern nibbling around the edges of his confidence. "Anything you like, if you end up living here." Could he sound any more inept?

Her gaze met his, still round and amazed. "I wouldn't dream of changing your things."

He grimaced. "Well, they're new, so they're not really *my* things." Now sweat trickled down his back.

"Yet," Beth added, joining them. "Is there something you'd like better, Ada?"

Was that a hint of defensiveness in his friend's voice? Beth prided herself on knowing the latest fashion, in clothing and furnishings. Did she think Ada would usurp her place?

"It's all lovely," Ada said, and Beth's shoulders came down a little. "I suppose the only things missing are a few personal touches—a crocheted blanket or quilt, a family portrait."

Beth beamed. "Excellent suggestions. We have plenty of Ma's quilts at Wallin Landing, Scout. We'll send back a couple with you when you come out to visit on Sunday."

Warmth wrapped around him, as welcome as one of her mother's quilts. He didn't remember his own mother, but Mrs. Wallin had fed him, physically, emotionally, intellectually, and spiritually. He still missed her, and he knew Beth and her brothers did too.

"Thank you," he told Beth. "If you'll come this way, Ada, I can show you the dining room and kitchen."

He led them across the emerald and blue patterned

carpet of the parlor into the next room. Ada ran a hand along the harp-backed chairs that surrounded the walnut dining table with a smile. Did that mean she could imagine herself sitting there beside him? He could.

He nodded to the door in the papered wall. "That's the kitchen."

Ada peered through the door. The black cast-iron cook stove with its multiple ovens, burners, and warming rack nearly eclipsed the white-washed walls, porcelain sink, and oak worktable in the center.

"The pump's inside," he pointed out as Ada gazed around.

"And that's a new stove," Beth added. "Thomas tells me you're an excellent cook."

She blinked, and now her gaze looked more panicked than awed. "I...I wouldn't call myself more than proficient."

Beth's usual bright smile was tight. "My mistake."

Thomas stepped back to allow them to return to the parlor. "Upstairs are three bedrooms. Bobby has one for now."

"You wouldn't mind mothering an orphaned young man, would you?" Beth asked Ada.

Thomas bristled. That was his place to ask, not Beth's. He and Ada had discussed the matter a little in his letters, but he couldn't know how she'd take to Bobby, or Bobby to her.

"Of course not," Ada said, but some of her color had fled again.

He threaded his arm through hers. "It's a lot to take in and different from Boston, I imagine."

"Very different," she said, gaze now on the door as if she couldn't wait to leave.

He'd hoped that Ada might relax a little once they were in the carriage, but, despite all his efforts to turn the subject, Beth kept peppering her all the way back to the hotel, asking about Ada's parents, her schooling, her church affiliations. Ada answered readily enough, but her shoulders seemed to squeeze in on themselves in her pretty frock.

"Oh, Scout!" Beth cried as Bobby reined in the horses at the front of the hotel. "Remember how Ada told you she was an accomplished singer? You should invite her to perform for the Centennial Celebration." Before he could respond, she turned to Ada. "Scout's on the committee making all the arrangements. It's terribly important to Seattle. Even the Territorial Governor has been invited."

She overstated, but not by much. Seattle was planning a major celebration for America's one hundred years—orations, a parade, fireworks, and a dance. Local entrepreneur Clay Howard had recruited him to the committee, but Thomas was under no misconceptions as to why the other members had agreed. They knew the amount of money he could donate. He didn't mind that his wealth opened the door. It gave him a chance for people to see him for himself, not as Benjamin Rankin's son.

"If you'd like to sing, Ada," he told her, "I'll make sure there's a place on the program."

She was whiter than the sheets hanging outside Mrs. Werner's laundry. "I wouldn't dream of taking the place of one of Seattle's singers."

"Oh, no one sings as well as you do, I'm sure," Beth said.

Ada hunched in on herself even further.

Anger licked up him. How many times had he reacted the same way—at a raised fist from his father, at the taunts of the boys in town?

"Ada doesn't have to sing to impress me," he told Beth. "I already like her."

Beth's brows shot up at his vehemence, but Ada's lips trembled. "Thank you, Thomas. And I like you too."

The adoration on her face was enough to set a fellow to preening.

He resisted the urge and came around to help her down. "Dinner tonight?"

"That would be lovely," she said. With a nod to Beth and Bobby, she hurried inside.

Thomas offered Beth his hand to help her alight as well. "Take the carriage back, if you would, Bobby. I'm going to walk Mrs. McCormick home."

"Sure thing, Scout." Bobby clucked to the horses and left them.

Beth eyed Thomas. "Walk me home, eh? What don't you want Bobby to hear?"

Thomas started up the hill toward where Beth and her husband had a house and some property. "Whatever's got you so angry at Ada."

Beth sighed, falling into step beside him. "I'm not angry, Scout, and I'm sorry I got your back up. But I am concerned. I haven't read all the letters you exchanged with Melinda Williamson, but you've told me enough. Are you wondering at all about this Ada?"

Thomas shoved his hands into his pockets. "Nope."

Beth stopped on the hillside. "Nope? Nope! Scout, she said she'd won prizes for her pies, but she showed no interest in that amazing stove of yours."

He shrugged. "Maybe a stove that's amazing in Seattle is nothing to sneeze at in Boston."

"That stove would be amazing anywhere," Beth insisted. "And she claimed to have performed for the mayor and she was tired of having men vie for her hand. This woman can't or won't sing before others and acts as if she's never been courted in her life. And she looks nothing like the picture she sent."

"I know." Thomas set out walking again.

Beth scurried to keep up. "Then why are you allowing her to carry on this ruse? Confront her! Demand that she tell you the truth."

"Nope."

"Arg!" Beth grabbed his arm and pulled him to a stop. "Scout Rankin, explain yourself!"

He met her outraged gaze. "All I have are letters, Beth. Letters that spoke to me, touched my heart. If Ada wrote them, I trust her to tell me why she pretended to be someone else."

"And if she didn't?" Beth challenged.

"Then she knows who did. And that's the woman I want to court."

Beth sighed. "I just don't want to see you hurt again."

He pulled away. "Don't worry, Beth. I won't let another woman pull the wool over my eyes, not even someone as sweet as Melinda Ada Williamson."

CHAPTER FOUR

OH, BUT TODAY had been so good and so challenging! Thomas had shared his city with her, pride in his voice and love in his smile. The way he looked to her, clearly hoping for approbation, told her he wanted her to make Seattle her home as well.

And then there had been his attentions, everything planned as if with her in mind. The meeting of gazes, the brush of hands, had thrilled her. She was being courted by a gentle, good man.

A man who had no idea who she was.

Beth suspected. Her questions had grown ever more pointed as the day went on. Perhaps Ada should have lied, yet how could she claim Melinda's talents? Her sister might have won a prize at the city-wide contest for her cherry pie, but Ada's pies always looked like craters with blackened edges. Melinda's voice with its multi-octave range might hold men in thrall. Ada struggled to carry a tune. If she'd been asked to prove herself, she would have failed. She couldn't embarrass Thomas.

Yet how could she accept his proposal in her sister's name?

Her chest felt tight in her gray silk evening dress as she descended the stairs to the lobby for dinner that evening. Three gentlemen were lounging on the upholstered chairs. None were Thomas, but all looked up as she reached the plank floor. They stood and bowed.

Ada glanced behind her to see who else had come down. The stairway was empty. Facing front with a frown, she found one of the men approaching her, hat in hand and look eager.

"If your escort hasn't arrived, I'd be proud to wait with you, miss," he said, gaze ranging from her toes to her top.

Perhaps it was being on her own for the first time, perhaps the conflict within her, but Ada was ready to speak her mind for once. She squared her shoulders and met his gaze. "I do not appreciate being made a joke of, sir. Take yourself off."

He reared back, then spun on his heels and stalked away to one of the other men.

"Why is it the pretty ones always think they're above everyone else?" he complained loud enough for his voice to carry.

"Spoiled by all the attention," his friend commiserated.

Spoiled by all the attention? That was Melinda, not her. She'd never had the least attention before she'd come to Seattle.

The two men put their backs to her, but she could not doubt she remained the topic of conversation. She'd apparently hurt his feelings. How? He wasn't the one who had been insulted.

Unless it hadn't been a joke.

She pressed a hand to her heart, but it kept up its rapid beat even as heat flushed up her. He thought she was pretty. She glanced around again. This time, the other men avoided her gaze, more than one stubbled cheek turning pink.

She'd embarrassed them.

Ada picked up her skirts and hurried across the lobby to the man who had approached her.

"Pardon me, gentlemen," she said when they paused

in their conversation to eye her warily. "I fear the stress of travel and the strange surroundings have served to sharpen my tongue. What I should have said is that I very much appreciate your kind offer to wait with me, but I am expecting my betrothed shortly, Mr. Rankin."

The man she'd offended stood taller. "Mr. Rankin's a lucky man."

Ada's cheeks felt warmer still. "Thank you. Good evening, gentlemen." She went to wait closer to the door of the dining room.

And still they watched her. Her! As if she were a bird of rare and gorgeous plumage or an orchid blooming in the wild.

No one had ever looked at her that way before. Certainly never after they'd seen Melinda. Few noticed the moon when the sun was up. Was it possible the moon had a beauty of its own?

Her parents hadn't seemed to think so. Ada had been the second child, and both she and her sister had been unexpected, as her mother had been nearing fifty when Ada had been born. After the angelic Melinda, who apparently had never fussed as a baby, never kept her parents up at night, and rarely been ill, Ada had been a letdown.

"Thrush, croup, and an acute inflammation of the bowel, and all before three years of age," her mother would lament to doctors, ministers, and other mothers she met. "I live in fear that she will infect dear Melinda."

It had only worsened as Ada grew older.

"You must work harder at your studies, Ada. Do you want to reflect badly on your sister?"

"Surely you can cook better than that, Ada! How will you help Melinda in the kitchen?"

"Do stop sniffling, Ada. I cannot hear your sister sing."

And the very worst, "I'm sure you don't try to be a burden on the family, Ada, but perhaps you could attempt to be a little more pleasant about the matter."

Tears threatened, and she blinked them back. Her parents hadn't meant to hurt her, any more than the man who had attempted to befriend her. Though the moments her mother and father had encouraged her were small in number, they had happened, and she was grateful for the home she'd been given. Still, at times, she wondered what it would have felt like to be her sister.

She glanced up to find that Thomas had entered, dressed in a gray wool coat and trousers with a long-tailed black bowtie at his throat. He came straight to her side.

The words flew out before she could stop them. "Do you think I'm pretty?"

With her eyes wide and speaking, slender figure shown to advantage in the fitted gown, there was only one way for him to answer. "Yes. Very pretty."

And that smile made her beautiful. It set the gray of her eyes to sparking and her skin to glowing, as if lit from inside. He wasn't sure how long he stood admiring her before a polite cough reminded him that there were others in the room.

Turning, he found Roy standing at his elbow.

"Table for two?" the waiter asked hopefully.

"Yes, please," Thomas told him. He offered Ada his arm, and together they followed the waiter to the same table where they'd dined the previous evening.

"We are pleased to serve salmon almondine, a very fine beef stew, and clam chowder with fresh biscuits," Roy offered, glancing from one to the other.

Ada dimpled up at him. "Now, how could Seattle's clam chowder ever compare to Boston's?"

Roy winked at her. "You'll only know if you try a

bowl, miss."

Was he flirting? Something poked Thomas between his shoulder blades, and he shifted on the chair before realizing the source wasn't outside him, but inside.

He was jealous.

Ada looked to him. "I think the salmon. What do you think, Thomas?"

I think I'd follow you to the ends of the earth if we weren't there already.

"Salmon, definitely," he said.

Roy bowed and left them.

Ada rearranged the silverware before her. "Thank you for the tour today. I found it fascinating. I had no idea Seattle had so many shops, so much industry."

He pulled the linen napkin off the table and whipped it to release the fold. "Then you could see yourself living here?"

She bit her lip a moment, and his heart sank as quickly as the napkin across his lap.

"I wonder," she murmured. "I believe it important, particularly on the frontier, to contribute to one's community. Back home in Boston, I visited the sick and bedridden, took care of the house and M… my sister. What would I do here?"

Thomas shrugged. "Whatever you like. Unless my investments fail utterly, I'll never have to work again, at least, not at anything I don't enjoy, so neither would my wife. I know Beth and Mrs. Howard belong to a group of ladies who sponsor good works. They helped found our library and supported the new hospital. No doubt there are other groups you could join with similar aims."

She nodded. "Perhaps I should talk to Beth about that."

Her light was fading, and he thought he knew why. He reached out, covered her busy fingers. "I hope you weren't offended by Beth's questions today. She's trying to become better acquainted, and she likes to talk."

Her smile fluttered into view again, setting up an answering flutter inside him. "I'm used to people who like to talk."

"But you don't talk much yourself," he guessed.

"I suppose I haven't found too many receptive ears," she said. "It's easier to allow people to talk about themselves than take the risk that you might say the wrong thing and offend someone."

He squeezed her hand. "Seattle's not like Boston, Ada. It doesn't matter to most folks where you came from, what you did, or how you phrase things. Everything needs doing here. If you're willing to pitch in, you'll find plenty of things that need doing, and people grateful for your efforts."

She glanced up, and once more he couldn't look away.

"Evening."

Ada pulled her hand out from under his. Clay Howard stood beside the table. The strapping entrepreneur was something of a legend in the town, having come here after journeying through nearly every state and territory in the Union. Like Thomas, he'd earned his fortune in the goldfields, but in California, and, like Thomas, he invested in those who had dreams and weren't afraid to work to achieve them. Little of that would be evident by the buckskin coat he wore over brown work trousers and a chambray shirt.

"Sorry to interrupt," he said, cool green eyes watchful.

"A visit from a friend is never an interruption," Thomas managed. "Ada Williamson, allow me to introduce Clay Howard. He's a businessman here in Seattle."

He inclined his head, red-gold hair and beard catching the light. "Miss Williamson. I've heard a great deal about you from Mrs. McCormick. Welcome to Seattle."

"Thank you, Mr. Howard," she said.

He turned to Thomas. "Kellogg called a meeting for tomorrow morning at ten. He's concerned he hasn't heard back from the governor."

"The lieutenant governor promised to attend if Governor Ferry couldn't," Thomas reminded him.

"He's also worried about those fireworks he ordered. They still haven't arrived from China."

"They're coming in on the *Pride of Baltimore* next week, I hear," Thomas offered.

"Just come to the meeting, Scout," Clay urged. "You're usually the most level-headed in the room." As if he took Thomas's attendance for granted, he nodded to Ada. "Enjoy your dinner, ma'am." He strode off.

"This must be the committee Beth mentioned," Ada ventured. "About the centennial."

Thomas nodded, more than glad to focus on her. "Clay arranged for me to join the committee, but I've found the whole process a bit frustrating. There are three things that are never in short supply in Seattle—rain, fir trees, and opinions."

She laughed, the softest, warmest sound he'd ever heard, like the glow of a fire on a cold day. On the wings of it, Roy brought them their dinner.

She waited as Thomas said the blessing. Thankfulness made the words easy. How many times had he and his best friend Levi Wallin, Beth's brother, dreamed of making their fortunes and being able to afford such fine surroundings? Levi had been the youngest in his family, and a bit spoiled, truth be told. He'd been sure he was meant for finer things than a cabin in the wilderness. Thomas had just wanted something to call his own—a home, a family. Barely eighteen, they'd run off at the rumors of a gold strike in the Canadian territories, certain they were about to make their marks.

But panning had been hard, slow work in impossible conditions. They'd run out of food, supplies, and still with nothing to show for all their efforts. He hadn't realized his friend had been even more desperate than he was for fame and fortune until Levi had done the unthinkable.

He'd moved the markers between their claim and the one next to it.

The goldfield camps had been wild and lawless, but there had been one rule no one violated without consequences: you didn't mess with another man's claim. When the miners had discovered the markers had been moved, they had come gunning for the culprit. They'd found Thomas instead. And when Levi had stumbled upon the group, he'd been too frightened to tell them he was the one they should have been beating.

It had been the first time someone had betrayed him. Thomas had earned the scar on his cheek and nearly had his neck stretched before the timely intervention of a preacher there to minister to the souls of the miners had stopped them from stringing him up.

Ashamed of his deeds, Levi had left with the minister, leaving Thomas completely alone. It had been terrifying and thrilling. He'd learned to defend himself better and taught himself any number of skills before finding that pocket of gold in the stream.

"You're a rich man, Mr. Rankin," the assayer had said when Thomas had carried the gold down into the nearest town after selling his claim. "What are you going to do with all that money?"

Thomas had squared his shoulders. "I'm going home."

And he had come home, to find that Levi had made his peace with God and only wanted to make it with Thomas too. He smiled every time he thought of his rambunctious boyhood friend as a minister.

Pain and betrayal notwithstanding, at the moment, he couldn't regret a minute of it, not when it had led him to the lovely lady seated across from him.

"Mr. Howard called you Scout," Ada ventured as if she noticed him smiling at her. "Others have as well. Is that because you scouted for your gold?"

Easy to let her think the name came from such a respectful association. But if he wanted her to be comfortable telling him the truth, he had to share his own truth, at least as much as he dared.

"It's a family nickname," he said. "My father called me Scout. I didn't realize I had another name until Mrs. Wallin, Beth's mother, told me. She'd known my mother a short time before Ma died. Ma named me Thomas."

She swallowed her bite of salmon. "Why did your father choose Scout?"

"I asked him once." He hesitated. Could he tell her? *Should* he tell her? There were still any number of people in Seattle who remembered his father and not fondly. They'd be more than happy to educate her about the blight on the territory that had been Benjamin Rankin. She ought to hear it from him first.

He stuck his fork into the salmon and let it stand there a moment, quivering as much as his insides. "He said he couldn't remember my name, and Scout was easy."

"Was that a joke?" she asked, clearly confused.

"No," Thomas said. "It wasn't. I realized later that it wasn't a name, either. It was my role in my father's life. He had shady dealings, and he'd send me out to keep watch for the sheriff. His little scout."

She must be able to hear the bitterness in his voice. It resonated inside him, for all he tried to forget it most days. She set down her fork and reached for his free hand.

"Parents can be cruel to their children," she said softly. "I think they love us, deep down. But some aren't prepared to raise a child."

It was a kinder view of his father than most people had. Than he often had.

"Some folks think that all acorns grow into oaks," he murmured, gaze on her hand and relishing the warmth. "I try to tell myself I grew into a willow instead, bendable, adaptable, with my roots in the water of life."

"I can see that in you and in the things you wrote about," she assured him. "When you couldn't find work in Seattle, you headed north. When tragedy struck on the goldfields, you didn't give up. Look where that led you. You can have anything you want, be anyone you like. Yet you're still humble, still kind."

She saw all that? He wanted to hug her close, soak in the words. When was the last time anyone had admired him?

But she didn't know him, not really. And, much as he hated to admit it, she might be saying things she thought he wanted to hear.

No, until he understood why she was spinning a tale about her own life, he could not feel comfortable sharing all of his heart.

CHAPTER FIVE

EVERYTHING IN SEATTLE was more than Ada had expected. The town was bigger, more settled, than she and Melinda had been led to believe back home and in San Francisco. The people were friendlier. Even the salmon was richer in color and flavor than the fish she was used to eating from the Atlantic.

And Thomas was more than she'd expected as well. His letters had talked of his present. She hadn't realized there had been little about his past aside from some stories about Beth and her family and his time on the goldfields. Now she could see why. Besides a fondness for maple sugar candy, they shared a challenging childhood.

And still, he hoped for a brighter future.

If she wanted to be part of that future, she had to tell him the truth. She kept trying to think of the best approach all through dinner, but every time he gazed at her so fondly, dark eyes brimming with admiration, the words scrambled back down her throat. How could she jeopardize the bond growing between them?

"It seems I have a meeting tomorrow morning," he said as he walked her across the lobby to the stairs. "But I'll ask Beth to keep you company."

Beth, whose sharp ears had already detected something different between the Ada who was here and the woman promised in the letters.

"I wouldn't want to inconvenience her," Ada murmured.

"I'm sure it's no trouble," he said. "But I'll leave word at the front desk either way. Good night, Ada." He took her hand from his arm and gave it a squeeze.

"Good night, Thomas," she murmured, and she watched his lean form until he was out the door.

"Glad to see you have friends in Seattle."

Ada started, then turned toward the voice. "Mr. Clancy."

The businessman from the steamship doffed his hat, bald head gleaming. "Sorry to intrude, but I couldn't help noticing you as you came out of the dining room. That was Scout Rankin, wasn't it?"

Ada nodded.

His smile tipped up. "Smart lady, cozying up to one of Seattle's richest bachelors."

He made it sound as if she'd somehow taken advantage of Thomas.

Didn't you?

The voice in her head was condemning. She'd come to Seattle with a noble purpose and allowed herself to go along with a charade. Thomas thought he was courting Melinda Williamson, celebrated beauty.

Well, he was clever enough to figure out that was a lie.

The truth slammed into her, and she took a step back, her heel banging against the last tread of the stairs. "Forgive me, Mr. Clancy. I find I'm not feeling well. Please excuse me."

She turned, lifted her skirts, and fled up the stairs before he could say another word.

Her fears chased her into her suite. She shut the door and leaned against it, sucking in air. Across from her, the windows looked out on a darkness where the only spots of light were the glimmers from ships riding at anchor.

Could it be true? Could Thomas know her secret?

She set about pacing the room, going over every

conversation and each look in her mind. He'd never questioned her comments. He hadn't probed or prodded, like Beth. In short, he'd never given her any reason to doubt that he accepted her story.

She blew out a breath and made herself perch on the settee. He was willing to believe her, for now. Perhaps she really was prettier in Seattle than in Boston. Perhaps, for once, she would be enough.

Even if her heart told her that too was a lie.

Ada's struggling confidence only slipped further when she met Beth in the lobby the next morning. Ada had donned one of her sister's dresses. It might not fit her as well, but it was made of finer material and trimmed with patterned ribbon. Beth's smile said Ada looked well, but her deep blue eyes seemed harder, as if she intended to pry out any irregularities.

"We have all morning together," she told Ada, linking arms with a swish of her frilly pink skirts. "Scout showed you his Seattle. Let me show you mine."

It was easy enough to go along. Beth's personality was fully as engaging as Melinda's on a good day. They stepped out into the little square in front of the hotel. It had rained during the night, and puddles gave back a reflection of the sky. Ada breathed in the crisp, cool air.

"It's different here, isn't it?" Beth asked as they started up the hill on the boardwalk.

Thomas had asked her the same question. At the moment, Ada was trying hard not to gawk at the broad-shouldered men standing by the buildings, the dusky-faced natives crossing the street, and the wagon rolling past piled with logs bigger around than she was tall. "Very different."

"Different, good?" Beth pressed.

Ada brought her gaze back to Beth's with difficulty. Was that compassion along with the curiosity in the blue depths?

"Definitely a change for the better," she assured her.

Beth grinned.

Thomas' friend led Ada first down Second Avenue to Kellogg's, where a narrow-faced clerk named Weinclef proudly extolled the wares of the dry goods store. Beth bought two lengths of blue gingham, a spool of thread, several lengths of ribbon, and pins, asking that they be delivered to her home before whisking Ada down the street to another shop.

"A jeweler's?" Ada asked before the blonde dragged her through the door.

Inside, watches gleamed from a few glass-topped cases. Beth skimmed along them, head bent as if in perusal. A middle-aged man came out from a curtained doorway, graying hair a rough halo around his head. His lined face broke into a smile.

"Ah, Mrs. McCormick," he said, voice thick with a German accent. "How good it is to see you again. May I be of service?"

"Mr. Naeher," Beth said, beaming. "Allow me to introduce you to my good friend, Ada Williamson."

"Miss Williamson, but not for long, *jah?*" He waggled his finger at her. "You are Scout's bride."

Ada's smile froze to her face. "Mr. Naeher."

He beckoned to her. "Come, I have some marvelous wedding rings."

Ada clutched Beth's arm to keep her from following him to one of the cases at the back of the shop. "Beth, we shouldn't."

Beth frowned. "Why not? Scout will want to know what you favor. I'm sure he'll ask my advice. This way, I'll know exactly what to tell him."

Ada's mouth was dry, but she allowed Beth to lead her over to the case.

The jeweler looked her over. "Something simple," he mused, "elegant, I think." He took out a key and opened the case to pull out a gold band etched with vines.

"I think Scout could do better," Beth said.

For a moment, Ada thought she meant in a bride, and heat flamed up her. Then she realized Beth meant in a ring.

"No," Ada said, reaching for the ring the jeweler held. She turned it slowly, and light gleamed from the surface. She could imagine Thomas slipping it onto her finger.

With this ring, I thee wed.

"It's perfect," Ada murmured. "Simple, elegant, just like you said."

"A lady who knows her mind," the jeweler said with a nod. "Very good. I will put it aside for the right time."

And that decision, apparently, necessitated a stop at the Pastry Emporium.

There was no sign of the red-headed owner, but a woman about Ada's age stood behind the counter. She had dark brown hair braided around her head and a slim figure swathed in a blue chambray gown covered by a white apron. Her face brightened when she saw Beth, and she came around the counter for a hug.

"Ciara O'Rourke," Beth said as they disengaged, "meet Ada Williamson."

Ciara's brows went up. "Scout's bride?"

Had he told everyone in Seattle? "Miss O'Rourke," Ada acknowledged. "A pleasure."

"Scout has a meeting of the Centennial Celebration Committee," Beth explained. "So I thought I'd show Ada the best places in Seattle. Can you join us for a cup?"

Ciara twisted this way and that, as if trying to spy someone through the front windows. Then she grinned at Ada and Beth. "I might have a minute before the shift change at the mill. Have a seat, and I'll bring out the tea and lemon drops."

"Gingersnaps too," Beth warned. "They're Ada's favorite."

"Mine too," Ciara confided with a wink to Ada. "But Beth must have her lemon." She disappeared through the curtain.

"I'd be happy to try the lemon drops," Ada said as she followed Beth to one of the little wrought-iron tables by the main window.

"You'll love them," Beth predicted. She arranged her pink skirts. "Truth be told, everything's delicious here. Maddie is an amazing baker, and Ciara has improved on her genius."

"Do not say that in front of my sister," Ciara scolded, returning with three steaming cups balanced on a wooden tray, along with a plate brimming with cookies. "She still thinks I need tutoring before I can handle cooking on my own."

Something inside Ada unfurled, like a cat stretching before the fire. How easily they joked. Few joked with her sister. They were either too awed or too jealous. And Ada had never had a friend who hadn't been Melinda's acquaintance first.

Beth shook her head. "It's terribly hard for them to see us grow up." She selected a lemon drop and snapped a bite.

"Them?" Ada couldn't help asking as Ciara nodded for her to choose a treat. She took a gingersnap, the scent sharp and warm.

"Our family," Ciara clarified. "Maddie pretty much raised me and my brother, Aiden, after our parents died, and Beth's older brothers took care of her and her mother after her father died."

"But I paid them back," Beth said, wiggling her brows. "I found them all clever ladies to take care of *them*." She grinned.

"Beth's the local matchmaker," Ciara explained. "Dozens of couples owe their marriages to her."

And Beth had selected Melinda for Thomas. The cookie was suddenly hard to swallow. Ada reached for the cup of tea.

The bell tinkled as six burly gentlemen crowded into the shop.

Ciara sighed. "Sorry. Duty calls." She rose to return to the counter, even as the ravening hoard surged up to her like a wave.

"The Emporium is very popular with the workers at Yesler's Mill," Beth told Ada as she watched.

So was Ciara. The men were jostling each other in an attempt to be first in line, and Ada didn't think it was just the food they found enjoyable. She was surprised when several glanced her way as well.

"If they come over, be kind but firm," Beth advised.

"Don't they know you're married?" Ada asked.

"Oh, yes," Beth assured her. "They wouldn't dare approach me. Hart, my husband, has that effect on people. He's the deputy sheriff. When these men come over, it will be to make your acquaintance."

"Because of Thomas," Ada said with a nod.

Beth peered closer. "You really believe that, don't you? Surely as the beautiful Melinda Williamson, you've had gentlemen chase after you before."

Ada ran her hand over the white top of the table, willing her fingers not to tremble. "Perhaps not as often as you would think."

"Morning, Mrs. McCormick."

Ada looked up to find two of the gentlemen beside the table. Both wore flannel shirts with no coats, and suspenders held up their rough wool trousers.

"Who's your friend?" the auburn-haired fellow with the big nose asked.

"Miss Williamson," Beth supplied with a look to Ada.

This is what Melinda faced every time she went out in public in San Francisco. It had been less obvious in Boston, where she had other belles with whom to compete, but even there Ada had seen the avid looks. Melinda would have charmed these men, led them on, made them think they were each special to her.

Before breaking their hearts for the next handsome fellow who came calling.

"Gentlemen," Ada said. "I'm new to your city. What do you recommend at this fine establishment?"

"A cinnamon roll," the brunette said, long beard hitting his chest as he nodded.

His friend elbowed him. "Lemon drops."

"Cinnamon rolls," the other said, frown forming.

"They must both be delightful," Ada put in. "I'll be sure to let Mr. Rankin know your opinions on the matter."

The brunette slumped. "Oh. *That* Miss Williamson."

His friend knuckled his brow respectfully. "Enjoy the day, ladies."

Ada watched them go with a smile, then turned to find Beth eyeing her again.

"That was nicely done," Beth said. She leaned across the table. "I like you, Ada. You're kind, thoughtful, and you have excellent taste."

"You say that because I agreed with your purchases," Ada couldn't help teasing.

She smiled. "In part." She lowered her voice. "So why are you lying to Scout about your identity?"

"I still say we should have held a picnic and been done with it," Walt Kellogg complained, leaning back in his chair. Half-owner in the city's most popular dry goods store, he was used to getting his own way, Thomas had noticed.

Now Thomas stifled a yawn. Yesler's Hall was darkly paneled and dimly lit, which worked well for the theatricals held there on occasion, but not for a meeting that went on for hours. He caught Michael Haggerty's eye across the long plank table.

The big, raven-haired blacksmith shrugged. He was here because he knew his way around a fire and a crowd. Even though the fireworks would be let off from a scow in the bay, there was still the chance a live ember might fall in the wrong place. The Irish Brigade, a group of immigrants Michael led, had been known to put out a fire or stop a riot.

"We don't have a clearing big enough to host everyone in the territory," George Butterby, a new shopkeeper keen to make his mark, pointed out.

"You still think everyone in the territory is going to come to Seattle," Clay Howard countered, arms crossed over the chest of his gingham shirt.

"We can't even get confirmation from the governor," Kellogg agreed.

"He's a busy man," Butterby said, stiffening. "Unlike some."

They all started arguing at that.

It had been like this every step of the way. Once such a task would have fallen to the founding families—Denny, Yesler, Maynard, and Bagley. Now the citizens of Seattle looked to the next generation. This celebration was an opportunity to shine, to show the territory that Seattle was in good hands and here to stay. But most of the men on the committee were so aware of the fact they couldn't allow anything to be less than perfect.

Which meant nothing got done.

Thomas raised his voice. "How about I write to Governor Ferry, see if I can get confirmation one way or the other? Just in case he or his lieutenant can't come, we should think of someone else to give the main address."

"There isn't anyone more important than the governor or his lieutenant," Butterby insisted.

"More important to the territory, maybe," Thomas allowed. "But not to Seattle. We could ask David Denny or Henry Yesler. Or the sheriff, for that matter."

"Nobody wants to hear from the sheriff," Kellogg sneered. "And Yesler talks at every civic event."

They started bickering again.

Michael rose. "Let me know about the next meeting." He nodded to Thomas and strode from the hall, the sound of his boots barely audible above the noise of the debate.

In the end, the others agreed to let Thomas try his letter.

"If this comes off, it will be a miracle," Kellogg said as they headed for the door.

"If it doesn't, I'll disclaim all involvement," Butterby muttered.

Thomas shook his head, blinking as he stepped out into the sunlight and the noise of machinery buzzing at the nearby mill. Here he'd thought they'd agreed to let him join because he had the money to contribute. It seemed that, like his father, the Centennial Celebration Committee needed a scapegoat if things went badly.

Unless he found a way to convince the governor or his lieutenant to join them, he was it.

CHAPTER SIX

ADA MET BETH'S gaze, seeing confusion and frustration written in the deep blue. Beth had been the one to answer the ad, introducing Thomas into Ada's life. Beth had welcomed her to Seattle and was trying to help her make friends. How could she lie to her?

How could she tell Beth the truth when she hadn't found the courage to tell Thomas?

"Thomas deserves a beautiful, talented bride," she said instead. "I'm trying to be that person."

Beth's face fell. "But doesn't he deserve the real you?"

Ada's heart jerked as if it had been pierced. "I may not be beautiful or talented, and I may not light up a room when I walk in, but I have some good qualities."

Beth looked as stricken as Ada felt. "Oh, Ada! Of course you do."

She managed a breath. "I came to Seattle to meet the man who wrote those letters. I promise you, Beth, I would never do anything to hurt him. I hope you will trust me in that."

"I don't want either Scout or you to be hurt, Ada," Beth assured her. "I hope you can trust *me* in that."

"More lemon drops," Ciara announced, blowing a lock of hair off her face as she plopped down on the other chair and set a plate with golden cookies on the table. She glanced between Beth and Ada. "Have I missed something?"

"Nothing," Ada said, rising. "I should go. Thank you for your understanding, Mrs. McCormick."

Beth nodded, and Ada escaped the bakery.

At least Beth had been willing to trust her a little. If only she could earn that trust! If only she could be more like her sister. Melinda never failed to charm. But even with her sister hundreds of miles away, Ada still felt lacking.

She headed back toward the Occidental, fists in her skirts. Why couldn't she have been born with some talent? If she could sing or paint or sew, if she had anything she did better than others. Was she truly such a nonentity?

The men following her didn't seem to think so. She noticed them as she turned the corner off of Second Avenue. Their gazes seemed fixed on her figure, and, when she caught their eyes, one smiled. It wasn't the grin that had lit the millworkers' faces when they'd approached her. This one was calculating, as if the man knew he held all the power.

Ice crept up her spine.

The next business was a shop. She grasped the door handle, ducked inside, and bent behind a display of brass bedsteads. Out the window, she saw the men stopping, glancing about, then continuing on their way. She sagged with a sigh.

Another man dressed in a brown wool coat with a neat linen shirt and simple tie came forward around the beds. "Someone troubling you, miss?"

Ada straightened. Her eyes came only to his shaven chin, the black skin gleaming in the light. Two dark eyes gazed down at her from a strong-boned face.

"I'm sorry," Ada said. "I didn't mean to intrude."

"Why apologize?" he asked. He waved a hand. "Now that you're here, why not shop? I bet you'll find your heart's desire."

His urging and the smile he offered couldn't help but banish the fear that had gripped her. Unfortunately, she sincerely doubted the shopkeeper could sell anything that would meet her heart's longings. At the moment, her heart's desire was tangled up with Thomas. Still, it was only polite to do as he asked, especially since she'd taken refuge in his store, so she turned and took stock of her surroundings.

And what surroundings! This was the shop Thomas had pointed out and Beth had extolled on their first tour, the Pioneer Variety Store run by TP Freeman. All manner of goods were scattered about as if by a giant's hand—bedsteads, dressers, stoves, sofas, and upholstered chairs. A maple dining table waited for a family of eight, if the chairs around it were any indication. Gilded mirrors hung on the walls as if begging someone to glance their way. Rugs stretched out and crisscrossed each other underfoot, and brass and crystal chandeliers hung from the rafters. At the back, a table was barely visible under the dresses piled on it.

"Where do you find it all?" she asked, gaze coming back to him.

"Some I order from companies that send a catalog. Others I get from people who want to sell. I like those pieces best. They have a story."

He picked up a fat-bottomed lamp from the edge of a counter as Ada wandered closer. "See this? Came all the way from Persia."

"Really?" Ada peered closer, seeing her wide-eyed expression in the gleaming brass.

"Yes, ma'am. And that table over there was brought from China. Seems folks will buy the furniture even if they won't welcome the people."

Ada glanced at the black-lacquered table painted with pearly white storks. "What do you mean?"

"You're new here, aren't you?" he asked.

When she nodded, he continued.

"There are coal mines on the other side of Lake Washington. Hard work, good money. All kinds of folks want to make a fortune. Miners recently rounded up all the Chinamen and marched them out of camp."

"That's terrible! Where did they go?"

"Hard to find anywhere they're welcome." He shook his head. "Hard for anyone who's different."

"It shouldn't be that way," Ada said, chin coming up.

He nodded. "I agree. We do what we can to make things better. But you see why I say everything has a story. Everyone, too. Don't suppose you'd tell me yours?"

He leaned closer, as if he could catch the scent of her past, like cinnamon at the Pastry Emporium. It would be easy to unburden herself to a ready ear, a person willing to commiserate. But Seattle was a small town.

And Beth loved to shop.

"I came to Seattle as a mail-order bride," she said. "But my groom wants to court me before we wed, and now I wonder whether I've made a mistake."

He pulled a rag from the pocket of his brown wool trousers and gave the lamp an extra polish. "He not what you expected?"

"He's more than I expected—successful, kind, sweet."

"Sounds like a keeper." He spit on the lamp and rubbed harder.

"Yes, but am I the right person to keep him? Doesn't he deserve better?"

He chuckled. "You *are* new. How many unmarried gals have you seen wandering the streets?"

Ciara hadn't been wandering, but she was unmarried as far as Ada knew. "One."

"Uh-huh. How many unmarried men?"

Ada smiled. "Dozens."

"And there you go. Last time the *Dispatch* put out the figures, there was one unmarried lady to eight and a half bachelors around Puget Sound. Your groom is being gentlemanly not to rush you to the altar before you have more offers."

The very idea that eight or nine bachelors might line up for a chance at her hand was so amazing, she gaped at him.

He chuckled again and pointed into the store. "Don't you have some shopping to do for your trousseau?"

A short while later, Ada exited the Pioneer Variety Store feeling lighter, for all she was carrying a brass lamp from Persia with a paisley shawl from England draped over her shoulder.

"You tell your sweetheart he's welcome here too," Mr. Freeman had encouraged as she'd left.

It seemed she'd made a friend.

What she hadn't expected was an unwanted acquaintance.

Mr. Clancy, who had been sitting on one of the velvet chairs, popped to his feet as she came into the hotel lobby and hurried to meet her, plaid coat flapping about his ample hips.

"Miss Williamson, allow me to be of assistance and carry that up for you."

If Thomas had felt it inappropriate to escort her to her suite, she certainly wasn't going to invite this man to do so.

"No need," she told him, making for the stairs. "But thank you for the thought."

He moved to block her path. "Then just a word will do."

Ada pulled up short rather than plow into him. "A word? What about?"

"About your friend, Mr. Rankin."

It was possibly the only topic that would have prevented her from sweeping around him. But why would he need to talk to her about Thomas? Fear dug in its claws.

"Has something happened to him?" Ada asked, searching his face.

"Not that I'm aware of," he told her. Those baggy brown eyes were so eager, so determined. "Though I hear something nearly happened to you earlier."

Ada leaned back. How had he known about the men who had followed her? Had she been right, they'd intended mischief?

"What do you mean?" she asked.

He shrugged. "Just a rumor I heard. Seattle can be a difficult place for a lady on her own. Lots of men looking to take advantage."

She was beginning to think the most likely candidate to take advantage was standing in front of her. "Thank you for your concern, but I'm not entirely on my own." Once more she made to move around him, but he didn't budge.

"I'm glad to hear that. A lady like you needs to be careful who she associates with."

No one had ever spoken to her that way before, but she'd seen her sister depress a fellow's notions often enough. Ada drew herself up.

"I cannot like your tone, sir. Please step aside."

He shifted just enough to make it appear he was humoring her, but not enough to allow her access to the stairs. "Now, then, no need to be harsh. I only wanted to talk to you because I'd like to make Mr. Rankin's acquaintance about a business deal. I hear he's leery of partnering with folks he doesn't know well. I thought you could put in a good word for me."

She didn't know this man well either, but she didn't much care for his attentions at the moment. What if she told Thomas to hear him out, and the man turned out to be a scoundrel?

"I'm afraid I have no connection to Mr. Rankin's business dealings," she told him. "I wouldn't be the best choice to introduce you."

"Now, I think you do yourself a disservice, Melinda." Her sister's name was a purr of sarcasm.

Cold raced up her. She would not allow him to know it.

"I must go," Ada said, trying to edge around him again.

Once more, he shifted to block her, gaze holding her captive just as surely. "I know an opportunist when I see one. I met your sister in San Francisco. She knew how to make the most of what she'd been given. You're doing the same. All I ask is that you give me an introduction. If Mr. Rankin doesn't like what I have to offer, I'll move on. But if you don't introduce us, and I find another way to make his acquaintance, I just might have to tell him everything I know about you and your sister, in the interest of a fair partnership, of course."

He stepped back even as her stomach churned. "He generally joins you for dinner at six, I've noticed. I'll be in the lobby then. I hope you can bring yourself to see things my way, Miss Williamson."

Thomas had hoped to meet up with Ada and Beth that afternoon. He poked his head in Kellogg's, where Beth preferred to shop for fabric and notions, but he caught no sign of them. Neither were they at the Pastry Emporium, though Ciara assured him they had been by earlier.

He had stepped out onto the boardwalk, intending on heading for Beth's house, when he spotted a wagon coming down the street, pulled by two unmistakable horses. The glossy black sides gleamed as their well-dressed owner reined them to a stop in front of the bakery.

"Ho, Thomas!" James Wallin heralded.

"Afternoon, Scout," his younger brother, John, said from the other side of the bench.

Thomas grinned a greeting. Though he'd been closest to the youngest Wallin brother, he'd grown up with the steady presence of all Levi's older brothers. James had hair a shade darker than Beth's but her same midnight blue eyes. His often danced with humor. John was the most scholarly of the family, though his rough work clothes might indicate otherwise to some. He favored their late mother with hair the color of cedar and eyes the color of fir.

"Good afternoon," Thomas said as John jumped down. "What brings you into town?"

"You," James said, leaning an elbow on his knee. "We've been sent on orders of the queen."

James' wife, Rina, had been raised by charlatans who claimed themselves deposed European royalty. He still called her queen on occasion. But Thomas had first known Rina as his schoolteacher. There was little he wouldn't do for her.

"What does Rina need of me?" he asked, stepping closer.

James wiggled his golden brows. "Details."

John shook his head before reaching into the back of the wagon to pull out a stack of books bound with a leather strap. "We came to pick up the mail and supplies for the mercantile, but there seems to be a great deal of curiosity about your bride, Scout."

Thomas chuckled. "From everyone, it seems. You know I will bring her to meet you all soon."

"Sunday, to be precise," James said with an arch air.

John handed the books to Thomas. "That was an invitation, in case you wondered. We thought dinner after you finish services. In the meantime, I thought she might need something to read. Cook's Voyages of Discovery for a bit on the history of the area and Culpeper's Complete

Herbal for a bit about some of the plants."

"And Everard," James put in. "Still a perennial favorite among the ladies. I trust you can still quote a line or two?"

Rina had had her older students read the work of the early century poet. "I wouldn't dare to presume," Thomas told him, taking the stack from John.

James tsked. "Faint heart never won fair lady. Then again, since she's already here…"

"We look forward to welcoming her to the family," John finished quickly, as if to keep his irrepressible brother from teasing Thomas.

"Sunday it is," Thomas promised. He couldn't help his grin as John jumped back onto the bench and James drove them down the street. The Wallins had been the family he'd always wanted. Hearing himself included made his chest swell, as if his heart had grown.

It deflated a little when he reached Beth's home and no one answered his knock. He stepped back from the door and glanced around the wide porch out onto the yard. Where were they? Surely if something had happened, someone would have sent word.

A footstep had him turning just as Beth's husband, Hart McCormick, came round the side of the clapboard house, leading his horse, Arno.

Thomas inclined his head. "Deputy. Don't suppose you know where Beth and Ada might be?"

"Beth had a meeting with the Denny ladies on a women's suffrage rally they're planning for later this summer. But I'm glad you stopped by. I wanted a word with you."

Thomas willed himself not to bristle. A year and a half ago, when Thomas had returned to Seattle, Hart had kept a sharp eye on him. The rangy lawman remembered too well the role Thomas' father had forced his son to play—first lookout over the moonshine still his father ran, then rouster, coming into Seattle to find men interested in his father's high-stakes card games. Only after Beth had vouched for him had the deputy sheriff been willing to give Thomas the benefit of the doubt.

"How can I help?" he asked.

Hart rubbed the back of his neck under his short-cropped black hair. "I'd like to help *you*, but I'm not sure you want to hear what I have to say. It's about Miss Williamson."

Thomas stiffened. "What about Miss Williamson?"

Hart dropped his hand. "Beth seems certain she's not the woman you sent for. So, I thought I could check with the sheriff in San Francisco."

Tempting. He knew Ada wasn't telling him the truth, but in word and deed she was so much like the sweet-natured, thoughtful woman with whom he'd corresponded that he wanted to trust her.

Or maybe he just wanted her to be that lady.

He must have hesitated too long, for Hart took a step closer, gun-metal gray eyes softening. "Let me help, Scout. I don't want you to run into a buzzsaw like the last time. I can't forget that I was the one who introduced you to Evangeline Jamison."

Odd to think of the upright deputy feeling guilty.

"You didn't know what she was," Thomas said with a shrug. "And I don't know if either of us knows who the real Ada Williamson is yet."

"She doesn't look like the picture Beth showed me," Hart pointed out.

"True," Thomas allowed. "But she's pretty enough on her own. I've seen the glances being directed her way. She could have her pick. Why choose me if she's not serious about marrying?"

"I hate to say it," Hart answered, "but maybe you're the richest of the bunch."

It hurt just to think it. He'd considered himself in love

with Evangeline Jamison, a widow who had moved to Seattle last year. She'd been older than him, but so beautiful, so cultured. He'd felt like a lad gazing up at the stars. He'd been awed she'd allowed him to court her and then had agreed to his proposal of marriage. Beth and Hart had uncovered the truth—he would have been the fourth in a line of wealthy husbands who had died under mysterious circumstances, leaving their fortunes to her, fortunes she'd blown through in a remarkably short time.

But Thomas couldn't put Ada in the same mercenary category. She hesitated to have him do anything for her, while Evangeline had accepted every gift and gesture as her due and asked for more. Unlike Evangeline, Ada had offered to pay him back for any expense. Her letters had been so sincere, so heartfelt. She'd made him begin to hope someone might love him for himself alone.

Even now, he could feel the doubts creeping closer, like a cougar who'd spotted weak prey.

"Ada's not after my money," he told Hart. "But you're right. I need to know why she came to Seattle and whether she truly wants to marry me. Send that telegram. Maybe we'll both learn something."

CHAPTER SEVEN

A DA WAITED IN her suite until after six in hopes Mr. Clancy would give up, but the stout businessman was still sitting in his plaid suit, hat on his knee, when she came down the stairs, new shawl draped around the shoulders of her gray silk evening gown. He stood as Thomas came forward to take her hand.

"Sorry to be late," Thomas told her, as if he had been the one to keep her waiting. "I decided to bring the carriage down. There's a restaurant up on Fourth that's newly renovated. I thought we might give it a try."

"That sounds lovely," Ada said, accepting his arm with relief and putting her back to her former traveling companion.

"Miss Williamson!"

Thomas paused at the call. Ada gritted her teeth as Mr. Clancy came to meet them.

"I believe you dropped this," he said, holding out a handkerchief. The initials MAW stood out on one corner.

Where had he found it? None of her handkerchiefs were embroidered, and certainly not with initials that could easily have stood for Melinda Ann Williamson. Surely Melinda would never have given him one of hers. He was too old, too sturdy, and far too poor to interest her sister.

Thomas looked to her. "A friend of yours, Ada?"

Left with no choice, she had to acknowledge the connection. "Mr. Clancy and I came up on the steamer from San Francisco together," she said, accepting the handkerchief and tucking it away in her beaded reticule. "Mr. Clancy, this is my… Mr. Rankin."

Mr. Clancy stuck out his hand, and Thomas shook it.

"I've been hoping to make your acquaintance," the fellow said as they disengaged. "I have a business matter I'd like to discuss with you."

"I wouldn't want to bore Ada," Thomas said. "Meet me at the Pastry Emporium on Second at ten on Monday, and we can talk."

"Yes, sir. You two have a good evening now."

Ada wanted to shake off his oily smile. She accompanied Thomas out to the carriage. She had to think of a way to warn him to be careful in his dealings with the fellow, without compromising her story.

Bobby waved his free hand from behind the reins as they came up to the yellow carriage. "Evening, Miss Williamson."

"Good evening, Mr. Donovan," she said as Thomas helped her up onto the rear bench. "Will you be joining us?"

He grinned over his shoulder at her. "No, ma'am. While you're eating, I get the use of the carriage."

"Say hello to Clay and Allegra for me when you pick up Gillian," Thomas told him, settling beside Ada with a flick of his gray coattails.

"Gillian?" Ada asked as Bobby directed the horses away from the hotel.

Thomas cocked his head, obviously waiting for his ward to explain, but the only sign Bobby had heard her was the fact that his ears were turning red.

"Gillian Howard is the daughter of Clay Howard, who you met the other night," Thomas answered for him.

"She's about Bobby's age." Again he waited, but Bobby's back remained stiff, his face resolutely forward.

"What did you and Beth do this morning?" Thomas asked as the carriage started up the hill.

Another difficult subject. "She showed me her favorite places to shop," Ada allowed. "And I ended up at TP Freeman's store. Oh, Thomas, what a treasure trove!"

"You'll have to take me," he encouraged. "Sorry I couldn't join you sooner. I kept getting waylaid."

"You have business you must attend to," Ada said. "I understand." Now would be the perfect time to tell him her reservations about Mr. Clancy, but Bobby reined in in front of what appeared to be one of Seattle's finer homes, and words failed her for a moment. Bric-a-brac clung to the pitched roof of the Bay View Restaurant, and shakes painted a rosy red decorated the sides. The scent of something grilling trickled out, and her stomach rumbled as if greeting an old friend.

Thomas came around and helped her down.

"I hope you and Miss Howard enjoy the carriage," she called to Bobby.

He nodded jerkily, then drove away. Odd reaction. It wasn't until she and Thomas had been greeted by the lanky owner and shown to a damask-draped table in what would once have been a parlor, with a view that indeed encompassed the bay, that she had a chance to question him.

"Bobby seemed unusually tense for a young man on his way to see a friend," Ada said. "Is there some problem between him and Miss Howard?"

Thomas turned the crystal goblet of water at his place setting by its stem. "I'm not sure. They became friends last year when Bobby first arrived in Seattle. I think he may be intimidated by the fact that both her parents come from prestigious families in Boston."

Ada stiffened as recognition hit. "*Those* Howards?"

He nodded. "Clay was the black sheep, I take it. He broke away from the family to come west, made his fortune on his own, and invested in others."

"Like you're investing," Ada realized.

He smiled. "I'm patterning myself after Clay. His first strike was in the California goldfields, while I earned my money around Omineca in the Canadian territories. But we both want to see Seattle thrive."

"And I can see you want Bobby to thrive as well," Ada said. "You told me he was your ward, and that it will be a few years yet before he's on his own, but I was never clear how he became your responsibility. Were his parents friends of yours?"

Before he could answer, the waiter came to take their orders. After checking with Ada on her preferences, Thomas requested thick steaks from cattle raised in the Nisqually Valley, potatoes from closer to home, and asparagus brought up from San Francisco, as if he had been born to such luxuries.

He leaned back as the waiter left. His gaze lingered on the tablecloth, but she didn't think he even saw the expanse of pristine white.

"I met Bobby through his older sister, Evangeline Jamison," he said. "She and I had an understanding."

Ada sucked in a breath. He'd been engaged before? Well, of course a man of his character and standing in the community had been engaged before. TP Freeman had said there were few unmarried women, but that didn't mean a handsome bachelor like Thomas lacked for attention.

"Did she pass on?" Ada asked, feeling craven for so much as asking about what was likely a painful subject.

"In a matter of speaking," he allowed. "It seems she'd made a habit of marrying wealthy men only to have them die. I would have been husband number four. She was convicted of conspiring to murder."

Her fingers knotted in her lap. "Oh, Thomas. I'm so sorry!"

He shrugged, but the tension in his lean shoulders told her he wasn't nearly so sanguine about the matter. "I'm grateful I learned the truth before we married."

Ada reached for her goblet and took a long swallow. So, the last woman he'd loved had been a fiction too. Was she any better? She'd certainly never murdered anyone! All she'd wanted was a chance to be loved for herself.

"Bobby never knew about his sister's crimes until they came to light," he continued. "With Evangeline away and his parents dead, he had nowhere to live and no one to look out for him. Growing up, I always had my friends, the Wallins. I wanted him to have a chance to find friends of his own."

Ada set down the glass. "That was very good of you, Thomas. I'm sure it's been a great help to Bobby."

He chuckled. "Some days I wonder who's helping whom. I'm glad for his company. The house always seemed too big for one person. It still feels a little big for two."

He glanced up at her, and Ada did her best to smile. Here was where she should tell him how much she'd like to be number three, how much she wanted a family. The ache for both was deep, but she couldn't offer, not when he was still getting to know her.

She busied herself arranging the napkin on her skirts. "The house felt entirely too large after Mother and Father died too, but it was home. The cabin of the ship was far cozier, but I doubt I could have been happy there for long. Too confining."

"I've camped along rivers among hundreds of miners," he replied. "At moments, it felt more like home than the cabin I was raised in. It's the people around you, not the space, that makes a house livable."

The waiter returned then with their dinners, and

Thomas said the blessing. The tenor voice was so filled with gratitude. She could feel it bubbling up inside her as well. Oh, if only this was where she truly belonged.

As they ate the savory food, he grew quiet, gaze going out over the buildings below them toward the water, silver-gray now in the shadows of the western mountains. The Olympics, he'd told her they were called. She could imagine some thinking the rugged peaks were the home of legends.

"Do you ever grow accustomed to it?" she asked him. "Mountains to the east, mountains to the west, the water between?"

"No," he admitted. "I don't remember living anywhere else, except when I left to pan for gold, and my spirits still rise every time I see Mount Rainier on the horizon." He sighed. "Now, if only we could capture that feeling for the Centennial Celebration."

"How did the meeting go?" she asked, belatedly remembering how he'd spent his morning.

"Not well," he confessed. "I'm supposed to write to the governor and convince him to come here instead of Port Townsend. And I need to do it soon so the letter has time to reach him and he has time to travel here by the Fourth."

He looked so downcast, as if the task was far too heavy.

"Letters aren't so hard," Ada said. "Look at all the ones you wrote to me."

His smile returned. "Those were easy. I just had to be myself."

That's how she'd felt too, even though she'd been writing about Melinda. She would read his letters to her sister, and they would discuss what to say in return, but Ada had done all the writing. If she hadn't, Melinda would never have found the time. And Ada had been the one to keep the letters, taking them out at night to read again in the privacy of her room.

"I'd be happy to help, if you'd like," she offered.

He seemed to grow a couple of inches, as if she had relieved a burden that had been weighing on him. "That would be a great service. Thank you."

They discussed approaches over dinner and on the walk back down the hill to the hotel. Mr. Carter, the clerk, provided stationery and a fountain pen, so they sat at an unused table in the dining room, tablecloth pulled back, and Ada wrote the letter.

"Such elegant handwriting," he said as she paused to consider a phrase.

"You've seen it before," Ada reminded him, "a number of times."

"That I have, and it still warms my heart."

One look in his eyes, and the words flew from her head like startled doves. Ada forced herself to focus on the letter. He'd done so much for her. If she could help him in any way, she would.

"Brilliant," Thomas said as he read the finished product. "You appealed to both his civic duty and his vanity. If this doesn't convince him to come, nothing will. I cannot thank you enough, Ada."

Ada felt warm through and through. "You're welcome. I hope the effort is as successful as you predict."

He waved the paper back and forth to dry the ink. "I don't see how it can fail. What a blessing."

She leaned forward. There were so many things she wanted to tell him, but perhaps only one was urgent.

"I'd like to be a blessing to you, Thomas," she murmured, "but I cannot help worrying about this meeting with Mr. Clancy. I don't know him well, and I have no idea what business he hopes to propose to you. Please don't take a chance on him on my account."

"I won't," he promised. "But I'm glad you told me. I wouldn't want to turn down a business proposal in a fit of jealousy."

Ada blinked, straightening. "Jealousy?"

He grinned. "What, you never had men fight over you before?"

"Never," she said before remembering she was supposed to be her sister. "That is, not recently."

"I told you about Evangeline Jamison," he said. "Why don't you tell me about one of your suitors?"

Thomas watched emotions flicker across Ada's pretty face. Surprise, calculation, and… fear? What did she have to be afraid of besides telling him the truth? What was she hiding?

She looked away. "Any gentleman who might have courted me couldn't hold a candle to you."

For the first time, the words rang hollow. Thomas folded the letter and tucked it into his coat, disappointment tightening his shoulders. "That's mighty nice of you to say. I'll see if I can find someone to carry this to Olympia on the morning tide. May I escort you to church tomorrow?"

She nodded, almost too eagerly. "Yes, that would be lovely. What time shall I be ready?"

"Half past nine. I'll bring the carriage, so you won't have to worry about getting your skirts muddy. I hear tell the previous minister's wife had a conniption about the amount of mud we tramped in."

"You didn't know the previous minister?" she asked.

"I never went to church in those days," he said. "Especially in town. Pa didn't hold with religion." Or anything else that suggested gambling and guzzling alcohol were unsavory pastimes.

He rose. "Ready to retire?"

"Yes, thank you." He held her chair as she stood. The

scent of lavender washed over him.

As if they were at a grand cotilion he'd only read about, he escorted her to the stairs.

"One more thing," he said before she could head up. "I saw James and John Wallin, Beth's brothers, in town today. They brought you some books, which I left with Mr. Carter, and they invited us to dinner after church at Wallin Landing."

Her eyes widened. "Where their family lives?"

It was on the tip of his tongue to correct her. After all, the Wallins were *his* family too. But she might not understand that. She had a sister and parents who'd loved her.

"Yes," he said. "Nothing fancy—just good friends and good food. Will you come with me?"

The softest of pinks suffused her cheeks. "I'd be honored."

He bid her good night then and went out into the cool summer evening. The sun had fallen behind the Olympics, the long shadows creeping across the tide flats. He felt as if the shadows reached for him.

Ada knew how to persuade. The letter in his pocket was proof of that. How easily she'd composed it, using words designed to convince the governor to agree with her proposal. Then again, writing to her had felt easy too, as if she would read his words and accept them.

Accept him.

He'd given her every opportunity to tell him the truth tonight, and still she hesitated. What more could he do, what more could he say, to make her feel free to share her heart?

Because he still wanted her heart. The handwriting on that letter—smooth and graceful—matched the handwriting on the letters sent to him. She was the woman who had written to him. She was the woman he wanted by his side through life.

Perhaps church services and a visit with family would help her see he was a man she could trust, even with her deepest secrets.

CHAPTER EIGHT

Ada tried not to grip Thomas's arm too hard as they walked from the carriage toward Trinity Parish Church on the corner of Third Avenue and Jefferson the next morning. The single-story frame building twice as deep as it was high crouched on the hillside, horses hitched beside it and wagons perched along the boardwalk. The steeple pointed bravely toward a sunny sky as ladies, gentlemen, and children, dressed in their Sunday best, entered through the wide front door.

She was glad to have dressed in her best as well. The mint green wool gown had been her sister's, but Ada had taken care to alter it for her smaller frame. Wide panels of lace ran down the fitted bodice to the hem, and the buttons were mother-of-pearl. The high neck was closed by a satin bow the exact shade as the dress, and more satin gathers festooned the graceful hem. With Thomas in a navy coat and green and gold waistcoat, she thought they looked very well together.

Inside, heavy wood pews ran on either side of the aisle up to a simple altar. As Ada entered on Thomas's arm, gazes darted her way and women whispered behind their hands to the husband or mother seated next to them. Even Thomas hesitated, as if he'd noticed the looks too.

Every face turned her way was new to her. She felt like

a wave was cresting, threatening to sweep her away. Then someone smiled in recognition and welcome.

Mr. Freeman.

He sat close to the back, a dark-skinned woman beside him, and a young black man and woman beyond her. There was room at the closest end of the pew.

"Let's sit there," Ada whispered to Thomas.

He escorted her to the seat.

Mr. Freeman's brows shot up, and his wife went so far as to frown.

"Is this seat taken?" Ada asked, concerned she might be usurping someone's place.

"No," he allowed. "Though some might say you'll pay a price for taking it."

"No price too high to make a new friend," Thomas said.

Mr. Freeman stuck out his lower lip thoughtfully, and his wife offered a shy smile as she urged her son and daughter to make room for them.

The music started then, the small organ near the front wheezing over the voices that rose to join it. The congregation stood, and Thomas held the hymn book for Ada. She kept her voice quiet, so he wouldn't notice that her voice wasn't as melodic as he might have expected. The service was easy enough to follow, though it differed a little from her church in Boston. Then the minister, who Thomas said was the Reverend Charles Bonnell, came to the pulpit.

Reverend Bonnell had a shock of graying hair and thick sideburns that stuck out from either side of his strong-jawed face.

"Rules," he pronounced, gazing around at his flock. "Rules are what keep society civilized."

Ahead of Ada, cotton bonnets and feathered hats bobbed in agreement.

"The people of Israel had any number of rules," he

went on. "How they dressed, how they washed, what they ate. They were proud of their rules. Do you know what the Lord told them?"

He leaned forward, gaze sharp. Ada felt as if he were looking right at her.

"Only two things matter—love God and love your neighbor."

Now she was nodding too. Her parents had taught her and Melinda to live by that rule: do unto others as you would have done to you. That was the essence of loving others.

Would she want Thomas to lie to her about who he was?

She glanced at him. His eyes were narrowed, his gaze fixed on the minister as if absorbing every word.

"And who is our neighbor?" Reverend Bonnell challenged. "Jesus was asked that very question. His answer was clear. Our neighbor may not believe the same things we do. He might not work at the same sort of job. She may not be able to find a job. He might be sick or poor or lame or deaf or blind. And she may not look like us."

Mr. Freeman's arm went about his wife's shoulders.

"Recently, we here in Seattle failed. We refused to follow the only rules to which our Lord holds us. You know of whom I speak." Once again he glanced around, and more than one fine wool suit shifted as if the wearer was uncomfortable with the scrutiny.

"Every miner at the coal mines in Newcastle is our neighbor," Reverend Bonnell thundered. "No matter where he was born, no matter how long he's lived in our fine country. We allowed our neighbors to be removed from their positions, driven from their homes. In doing so, we failed to love God. We must do better. I want to be able to stand before my God on Judgement Day and say I ran the race, I fought the fight, I lived by the example

He set. I hope you feel the same."

He nodded to the organist, who struck up the cords of the closing hymn.

Ada rose to sing, her heart hurting. She hadn't chased the Chinese miners out of the area, but she had failed too. Thomas was quickly becoming more than a neighbor. She owed him respect too. She had to find a way to tell him the truth.

As the service ended, Thomas turned to Mr. Freeman. "Thank you for letting us join you. I'm Thomas Rankin. You own the Pioneer Variety Store, don't you?"

"That's right," the store proprietor said, shaking the hand Thomas offered. "And I'm a Thomas too, Thomas Palmer Freeman, though most folks know me as TP. This is my wife Rosanna, and our children, Alfred and Harriett."

Alfred, who looked close to reaching his majority, nodded a cool welcome. Harriett, who favored her mother's slender physique, smiled more broadly.

Thomas inclined his head. "Ma'am, miss, sir. It's a pleasure to meet you. I hope to see you at the Centennial Celebration on the Fourth."

Mr. Freeman's eyes lit. "I have some fine bunting at the store. Come by and take a look."

"I'll do that," Thomas promised.

Mrs. Freeman spoke up, voice soft. "You're welcome to join us for dinner this afternoon."

"Thank you," Thomas said, "but I told my friends at Wallin Landing we'd join them today. Perhaps another time."

She nodded, but the set of her shoulders in the pretty pink gown told Ada she didn't believe him.

"Perhaps I could come calling on Monday," Ada suggested. "So we can become better acquainted."

Rosanna Freeman nodded again. "That would be real nice."

"Allow me to walk you to the door, Miss Williamson," Mr. Freeman said, "so I can tell you the address."

Thomas looked taken aback, but he edged out of the pew and let the shopkeeper escort Ada. Out of the corner of her eyes, Ada saw him offer Mrs. Freeman his arm.

"I appreciate you thinking of Rosanna," Mr. Freeman said as they approached the door of the church. "But if you think stopping by once will earn you a spot in Heaven, I wish you wouldn't."

"Well, no, I…" She stepped down from the stoop and met his gaze. "No, Mr. Freeman. I'm not trying to earn my way to Heaven. I'm new to Seattle, and I thought maybe I could make a friend."

He released her to wave at the rapidly dispersing congregation. "Whole lot of people who'd like to be your friend. Why us?"

"You were kind to me," Ada said. "I'm not used to people being kind to me. I just wanted to return the favor."

He eyed her a moment. "Then you stop by the house on Third near the university any time you like. Just know that by stopping by, you might make it less likely some folks will be kind to you in the future."

"Then I suppose," Ada said, "that those folks are not worth the knowing."

He chuckled. "You're something, Miss Williamson." He smiled as his wife and Thomas joined them, Alfred and Harriett clustered close behind. "Enjoy your Sunday, and come see that bunting when you get a chance."

Thomas clucked to Jack and Skip as he drove the horses out of town, having left Bobby with the Reverend Bonnell and the other church youths for the afternoon.

The last few years had seen marked progress on the road to Wallin Landing. The summer warmth had packed down the mud so the ruts were less prominent. He gave the horses their heads, and they pranced along under a cloudless blue sky, visible above the tall firs on either side.

Ada breathed in deeply, one hand clapped to the straw hat on her golden-brown hair. "Do you smell that? Salt, certainly, but what's that tang?"

"Fir and cedar," he said. "Look up at the tops of the trees. You see those with a little crook? Those are the cedars."

She leaned closer, head cocked as if trying to follow the line of his sight. All at once, it wasn't the familiar scent of home he smelled but something crisper, cleaner. Lavender.

"I see one!" She turned to him. Then her eyes widened, as if she too realized he was close enough to kiss. She hastily straightened and set about arranging her pale green skirts. Beth was going to love that outfit—all the lace and that bow at Ada's throat. The color made her eyes look almost green.

"You told me quite a bit about Wallin Landing," she said, as if determined to make polite conversation. "The school you helped build, the church where your friend Levi serves as minister, the post office and mercantile down by the lake."

"Don't forget the dispensary," Thomas said. "Or the library. And they just finished putting in a park along the lake."

Ada glanced around. "Who needs a park when they have all this?"

Who indeed? He'd traveled through any number of towns, none much bigger than Seattle, on the way to Omineca and back, but this stretch of woods, the shores of Lake Union, would always be home.

Sitting beside her, breeze warm and heart full, it was

easy to prose on. He'd already told her a little about his days prospecting, but he found himself recounting stories he'd almost forgotten and basking in her look of appreciation. He even coaxed a story or two out of her—tales of bundling up to make angels in the snow, of sitting by the fire with her family, devouring books from the lending library.

"You must miss your sister," he said as they passed the southern end of Lake Union, the waters today as midnight blue as Beth's eyes. "A shame she decided to stay behind in San Francisco."

She toyed with the lace at her cuff. "She was well received there. I don't think she expected Seattle to be able to beat that."

"And what do you think of Seattle?" he asked, concern starting to nibble at his contentment.

"Oh, yes," she said with such a satisfying sigh he could not doubt her. "Everyone has been so welcoming. I only wish…"

Thomas lay his free hand on hers. "What, Ada? What do you wish?"

Her gaze dropped to his hand, and she shook her head. "I don't know how to explain."

Her secret. He could see it weighing on her like a heavy wool cloak in summer. He had intended to go straight to Wallin Landing, about two hours north of Seattle at a decent pace. Perhaps if he showed her the weight on his own shoulders, she'd feel ready to throw off whatever troubled her.

"Let's take a little detour," he said.

She looked at him askance, but she didn't protest. Still, his skin itched as he turned the horses onto a lesser-used path toward the lake. The trees were closer to the road now, as if they hoped to reclaim what his father had taken.

He knew the feeling.

Ada peered out as the rough log cabin came into view, listing now as if intent on catching its reflection in the blue waters beside it.

"Where are we?" she asked with a frown.

Thomas drew in a breath, pulling the horses to a stop. "This is where I grew up. Pa lost the claim, and the new owner uses this for a woodshed. But this was the family cabin."

She shot him a commiserating smile. "I'm sure it looked much nicer when you lived there."

It took everything in him to tell her the truth. "No, it didn't. Pa didn't care about the cabin. He cared about the money he could make." He nodded to the copse of trees, some white as bone now. "That's where he kept the still for the moonshine he used to get his customers drunk enough that they wouldn't notice he was cheating them at cards. He caught me sampling it when I was fifteen. That's how I got my nose broken. He didn't care that I'd been drinking. He didn't want to lose the profits."

"Oh, Thomas."

He turned to find a tear slipping down her pale cheek. A tear, for him.

"I'm so sorry you had to go through that," she murmured, voice choked.

He couldn't stop now. The words poured out of him. "My father was a cruel, vicious man who only cared about himself. That didn't stop me from wanting him to love me. But it did stop me from wanting to be like him. So when you hear people in Seattle slight me, whisper about me, it's most likely because they knew him, and they think I'll follow in his footsteps."

His hand was shaking on the reins, and Jack and Skip fretted in the traces. Ada put her hand over his, steadying him.

"We are the products of our past," she said. "But we choose our future."

Simple words, said with conviction, but the air tasted sweeter, as if a rainstorm had come through and cleared the skies.

"I have to believe that," Thomas said. "And part of the reason I know I can do better is because of the examples I saw in the Wallin family. They mean everything to me, Ada. I can't wait for you to meet them."

"Thomas, I," she started, and he leaned closer, ready to hear, eager to know.

From the trees came a whoop and a holler. "Uncle Scout!"

Even without the call he would have recognized the red-faced ten-year-old with wheat-colored hair who jumped out of the nearest tree. The horses started. Thomas pulled on the reins to calm them even as he reined in his disappointment at the interruption.

"Sutter, what are you doing out here?" he asked.

"Levi asked me and Frisco to keep an eye out for you. Frisco was sure you'd come by the main road, but I knew you'd come this way." He stuck out his flannel-clad chest in pride.

Thomas jerked his head. "Hop in. I'll circle back and pick up Frisco too."

The youth clambered into the back seat and hung over the bench, lean arms swinging. "Can I drive? Frisco would be so jealous."

"You don't need another reason to fight with your twin brother," Thomas warned him. "Ada, meet Sutter's Mill Murphy. He and his twin brother, San Francisco Murphy, are kin to my friend Levi and his wife Callie."

"Very pleased to meet you, Mr. Murphy," she said.

He ogled her a moment, then laughed. "*Mr.* Murphy. Wait 'til Frisco hears."

Wait until they all met her. Secret or no, would they love her as much as Thomas was coming to?

CHAPTER NINE

A DA DIDN'T KNOW whether to be disappointed or grateful that the arrival of the Murphy twins prevented her from confessing to Thomas. Perhaps, on the heels of his story of his father's cruelty, anything she'd said would have sounded as if she was trying to compare her pain to his. She couldn't bear to see him hurt any further.

As if her lies weren't hurt enough.

Now the two boys bounced in the rear seat as the carriage rolled down the last bit of road into Wallin Landing. And then Ada was too busy to think.

The space was just as she'd imagined it from his letters. A weathered wood, two-story cabin sat on a bench overlooking the lake, the water sparkling through the trees. On the shore, the square, squat cabin with the jaunty red door would be the mercantile and post office. In the other direction, closer to the rise of the ridge, lay the one-room schoolhouse with living quarters behind for a teacher. Another cabin had been built to the south, and one was visible through the trees to the north. And in between lay pastures and a massive barn.

More children came running as the carriage pulled up near the barn, accompanied by a man in a fine tailored coat and silver-shot waistcoat, with dark blond hair and a twinkle in his eyes, the same shade of blue as Beth's.

"Welcome to Wallin Landing," he said with a charming smile to Ada. "I'd introduce myself, but you'll shortly be besieged, and I prefer to make my escape while I can."

"Ada Williamson, this is James Wallin," Thomas explained, handing the fellow his reins as Frisco and Sutter jumped down and mingled with the pack of children. "As I wrote you, he's the merchant and postmaster at Wallin Landing."

"And horse holder," James said with a wiggle of his brows. "Never forget horse holder."

"James owns some of the finest horseflesh in the territory," Thomas explained as the Wallin brother began unharnessing Jack and Skip from the traces. With more shouting and laughter, the children ran toward a rise beyond the main cabin.

James paused to clutch his chest. "*Some* of the finest!"

Thomas held up his hands. "Well, I am partial to Jack and Skip."

"Thomas!" A slender blonde with an air of authority about her came hurrying from the schoolhouse. "Welcome."

"Rina Wallin, meet Ada Williamson," Thomas offered with so much pride in his voice Ada might have been the most impressive specimen of womanhood this lady would ever meet. "Rina is the schoolteacher here."

"One of the schoolteachers," Rina corrected him, fingers brushing down her blue-striped skirts. "We're adding a second classroom to the schoolhouse this summer and hope to bring in a teacher by harvest." She offered an elegant hand to greet Ada.

She was followed by more, many more. James had been right; Ada was surrounded, and it was difficult to keep track, but the letters Thomas had written helped. Easy to pick out Drew Wallin, the leader and oldest of the Wallin family. The towering blonde had started out as a lumberman, and it showed in his broad shoulders and muscular build. He was married to Catherine, a pale-haired nurse with polished manners. She ran the dispensary. They had three children, Hans, Mary, and Davy, ranging in age from nine to six, and all varying shades of blond. Only Davy had his mother's crystal blue eyes.

Simon was next, as tall as his older brother but leaner, with a habit of narrowing his eyes. Ada liked his wife, Nora, straight away. A curvy woman with gray eyes and dark brown hair threaded with silver, she was a seamstress. They had two children, eight-year-old Lars and three-year-old Hannah, both of whom had inherited their mother's looks and gentle nature.

After James and Rina came the auburn-haired John and golden-haired Dottie. They had one son, Peter, a toddler, but Dottie's gently rounding figure spoke of a little brother or sister coming soon. Besides farming, they ran the library. Finally, a curly-haired man with a serious face and a blond woman about Ada's age wearing trousers came forward. Ada had never seen such a smile on Thomas's face.

"And this is Levi," he said. "And his wife, Callie."

His boyhood friend claimed Thomas' hand before offering it to Ada. "Thank you for coming, Miss Williamson. We've heard a great deal about you."

"And we aim to hear more." Callie linked arms with her. She had a grin impossible to refuse. "Where's Bobby, Scout? Dinner's almost ready."

"Bobby had a better offer—an afternoon with the church youths and dinner with the Howards," he told them.

James tilted his head against his wife's and gave a theatrical sigh. "Ah, young love. Makes you want to run right out and marry, doesn't it, Miss Ada?"

She was just thankful that Callie pulled her away,

surrounded by Wallin women, before she had to respond.

Skirts of cotton and wool swished across the grass as they climbed the rise for the long wood hall that stood next to a tall-steepled church and the log cabin parsonage.

"About your height," Nora said around Ada to Callie. "About your figure too."

"Well, that makes it easy," Callie said.

"Easy for what?" Ada managed to put in.

"To make your wedding dress," Nora said.

"Blue, I think," Catherine tossed back over her shoulder from in front of them. "To bring out the color in her eyes."

"And a lace veil, perhaps?" Dottie asked.

"But we haven't agreed to wed yet," Ada tried to explain.

"You leave that to Beth," Rina advised.

Beth, who had been arranging dishes on a long plank table that ran down the middle of the room, looked up as they entered. Her ruffled pink skirts looked bright against the view of the forest through the bank of windows on the far wall. "Did I hear my name?"

"Yes," Callie said. "Seems Scout needs a little help coming up to scratch."

"*Scout* needs help?" Beth's brows went up as she glanced to Ada.

The noise behind them heralded the arrival of the children and the men. Once more, Ada found herself unable to respond. Laughter skipped around the room as wives found husbands and couples collected children. Thomas drew her over to three men who were standing by the hearth as if attempting to keep their heads above the tide.

"Ada Williamson, meet Harry Yeager, Jesse Willets, and Kit Weatherly. They're the men Drew Wallin picked for his logging crew."

Though they all dwarfed her, they stood taller as if

proud of the fact they worked with Drew. Mr. Willets was the biggest, his reddish-brown head on a level with Simon's and Drew's. She wasn't sure what thoughts percolated behind his deep brown eyes. Mr. Weatherly had a neat beard and mustache, both nearly as curly as the black hair that fell to his collar. He offered her a shy grin. Mr. Yeager's smile was more confident as he ran a hand back through his wavy brown hair.

"Gentlemen," she said, and they all bowed to her. As Thomas led her toward the table, one of them muttered.

"Figures. Every gal that ends up in Wallin Landing is either engaged or married."

"It seems Beth has more than enough matchmaking work to keep her busy right here," Ada murmured to Thomas as they approached the table.

"Harry's already enlisted her help, but he seems to have high requirements for a bride," Thomas said, handing her down onto a bench.

So should he, but she would not say that aloud.

The Wallins and their employees filled the long table, with Drew at the head and Simon at the foot. The lumberman said the grace, his deep voice reverent and reverberating in the wooden hall. Soon bowls and platters were making their way down either side, and conversation focused on the food before them: trout from the lake, the flesh pearly and flaky; early peas fresh from the vine in a butter sauce; the first lettuces; and biscuits light enough to float their way down the table on their own.

Ada found herself fielding questions from Catherine on her right and Dottie beyond Thomas on her left, while trying to keep up with the conversation on the other side of the table as well. Thomas seemed to have no such difficulty. He questioned Drew about the prospect of clearing the land north of the lake, suggested a new author to John, and asked Nora how she was coming along with the quilt she had planned.

Dessert brought cherry as well as rhubarb pies with whipped cream to go on top.

"As good as yours?" Thomas murmured to her as she forked into the golden crust.

"Better," Ada assured him truthfully. Even her sister might have trouble matching this spread.

At the thought of Melinda, the room seemed to darken, the voices to chill. Ada shook herself. Melinda was hundreds of miles away. Ada didn't have to share this moment with anyone but Thomas.

He was clearly in his element. Each of the men took a moment to talk to him. So did most of the ladies. When Callie and Nora led the children to one end of the hall for games, he rose from the table.

"Care to play?" he asked Ada.

She hesitated. Any game she'd been good at, Melinda had declared insipid, and they had never played again. Would the Wallins feel she even had a right to join in?

"Maybe in a bit," she hedged. "You go ahead."

He promptly waded into a game of blindman's buff. As Ada watched, he scooped up little Hannah and swooped her out of the way as a blindfolded Frisco came within inches of tagging her. He caught Thomas instead.

Callie came back to Ada and put her hands on Ada's shoulders. "Come on, Ada. Let's show them how it's done."

They really wanted her. Joy pushed her up and off the bench to follow Callie into the group. Nora had already blindfolded Thomas, and Callie put her finger to her lips to warn the children not to say anything that might give Ada away.

The children darted around him, as Thomas stretched out his arms.

"Is that Victoria I hear?" he asked, and Rina's regal daughter ducked under his hand to avoid capture.

"No, Uncle Scout," Frisco shouted. "It's me. Nah-nah-

nah-nah-nah."

Ada pressed her lips together to keep from laughing.

She must have made a noise nonetheless, for Thomas spun in her direction. She froze.

Sutter took pity on her. "This way, Uncle Scout. Can't catch me!" He ran right in front of Thomas.

Thomas didn't drop his arms. He bore down on Ada and wrapped his arms around her.

"You're a little bigger than Victoria," he murmured in her ear. "And somehow I doubt any of my nieces or nephews smell like lavender.

He knew her perfume? She couldn't breathe, couldn't think. He was so close. If she turned her head a little, their lips might meet.

"Ah," Davy said, pulling to a stop. "He caught her."

"Poor Ada," Hannah said, little face falling. "Be nice to her, Uncle Scout."

With trembling fingers, Ada reached up and pulled off his blindfold, the rough cotton mussing his dark hair. His smile was crooked.

"Perhaps I should take the next round," Nora said, coming to retrieve the blindfold from Ada's unresisting fingers. "You two look as if you have more important things to do."

Ada flamed and stepped out of his embrace. "Perhaps Beth and Dottie need help with the dishes."

"Allow me," he said. "You're the guest."

She should have protested, but his proximity was doing the oddest things to her equilibrium. She found her way back to the table and dropped down on the bench.

Callie abandoned the game to return to Ada's side.

"My turn," she said, slinging a trouser-clad leg over the bench to perch beside Ada. "What do you think of Wallin Landing?"

"I've never seen anything like it," Ada confessed, trying to keep her gaze from lingering on the trio working at the other table along one wall. Thomas had rolled up his shirtsleeves to reveal leanly muscled arms.

"You have kin?" Callie asked, watching as Frisco took another turn at the game while his twin called him names.

"A sister," Ada said, pushing back the specter of Melinda. "She stayed in San Francisco."

"I had an older brother besides those two terrors," she said with a nod to the twins. "We lost him a couple years ago now." She sighed, then brightened. "But this? This is what family should be."

Ada sighed too. "Yes, yes it is."

How would they react when they learned she'd lied?

She understood. Thomas watched the wistful look come over Ada's face again as Catherine came to join her and Callie in conversation. She felt it too—the love, the respect. And it seemed she craved it as much as he did. Maybe that would encourage her to take a chance and tell him the truth.

"Any more polish and you'll wipe the flowers right off that plate," Beth teased him.

Thomas colored, setting the porcelain plate onto the stack with the others waiting to be ferried back to the main house. "Sorry. Woolgathering."

"I know something you should be gathering," Beth said. "Ma's quilts." She reached for a towel and raised her voice at the same time. "Kit! Would you help us, please?"

The lean logger pushed off the wall, where he'd been watching the games, and ambled over to join them. "Ready for the dishes to go back, Mrs. McCormick?"

Beth shook her head. "It's Beth, please."

He glanced to where Hart was watching from the opposite wall, arms crossed over his chest and gaze roaming, as if he expected to be arresting someone even here.

"I think calling you Mrs. McCormick might be safer," he said.

"His bark is worse than his bite," Thomas advised.

"But neither would be pleasing," Kit countered with a wink. He reached for the pile of plates. "I'll just take these along." He started for the door to the hall, neatly sidestepping Davy chasing Lars and Victoria attempting to teach Hannah how to waltz.

"Does he have a history with the law?" Thomas asked Beth.

"Not that I know of," Beth admitted. "But he's rather closed-lipped about his past. Wallin Landing's man of mystery. For now." She grinned at him. "Fetch Ada, and we'll see about those quilts."

Ada seemed ready for a break from the mad camaraderie, if the dazed expression on her face was any indication. She joined Thomas and Beth in venturing down the rise to the main house.

One step inside the big front room, and he hesitated, memories assailed him. Ada must have noticed, for she touched his arm.

"Thomas?"

He smiled at her. "I'm just thinking about this place." He pointed to the braided rug set before the hearth made of stones gathered from the lake shore. "I sounded out my first letters there, while Mrs. Wallin sat in that curved wood rocking chair encouraging me." He nodded to the open stairs set in the far wall. "I climbed those stairs dozens of times to shelter for the night with Levi and his brothers in their sleeping loft." He rested his hand on the worn wood table nearest the door. "And I devoured the Wallins' good food and greater joy right here."

"Why, Scout," Beth said, standing beside that table, which was now piled with quilts. "That was almost as good as Vaughn Everard's poetry."

High praise indeed. Small wonder his cheeks felt hot. He focused his attention on the quilts. So did Ada.

"Ma preferred patterns that told a story," Beth explained, hand stroking a square of dusky green, like the forest at twilight. "And she chose colors for each person she intended to give the quilt to. She cut her blocks with great care. But every once in a while, she just gathered her scraps and went wild."

Ada picked up the quilt Beth had indicated. Triangles, squares, and odd-shaped pieces were stitched together with pearly thread. Here and there, a patch had been embroidered with flowers or leaves. There—that fabric. Levi had had a shirt made of the same. It had eventually ended up in Thomas's trunk. And there, the dress his mother had so proudly worn to church services right here in this room.

"I like it," Ada murmured, hand reverently touching the blocks. "It looks like it doesn't care that it's different, like it revels in being one of a kind."

Thomas touched her hand. "Then it's the one we should take."

Ada's smile met his, and he would have sworn he heard Mrs. Wallin's call of approval from her rocking chair.

Of course, Beth wouldn't let them go with just one. In the end, Kit helped Thomas carry three quilts and a braided rug out to the carriage while Beth took Ada back to the hall, as if ensuring Thomas wouldn't head back to Seattle so soon.

A stream of children poured out of the hall as Thomas and Kit approached, Harry at the back, arms wide, as if he was rounding up a flock of geese.

"That's right, run!" he ordered them. "Run, or I'll catch you!"

Someone squealed in anticipation.

With a nod to Thomas and Kit, Jesse lumbered after

them.

Thomas tipped his head. "Are you needed, Kit?"

He looked after them, and Thomas recognized the longing in his eyes. The logger shoved his hands into his pockets as if afraid to reach for it.

"Harry and Jesse have matters in hand," he said. "Think I'll see if we need any more wood put in." He headed toward the massive pile of logs by the barn.

"Man of mystery," Thomas muttered to himself. Shaking his head, he returned to the hall.

CHAPTER TEN

MOST OF THE other adults were gathered at the long table as Thomas entered, and he spotted Ada watching the door, as if waiting for him. Her smile beckoned him closer, but Hart intercepted him before Thomas could join her.

The deputy leaned closer and lowered his gravelly voice. "Just wanted you to know I sent the telegram, but I haven't heard back yet."

The thought sent a shadow over his day. Thomas refused to allow it. "Thanks. I'm hoping Ada will tell me of her own accord first. Excuse me."

Hart tipped up his chin, and Thomas went to slide onto the bench with Ada.

Rina dropped onto the seat opposite with a grateful sigh. James came to stand behind her, rubbing her shoulders.

"Those children are a handful," Callie said to her sister-in-law from Ada's other side. "I don't know how you do it at school. I barely manage one at a time for music lessons."

"I'm looking forward to having a second teacher," Rina said. She glanced at Ada. "I don't suppose you'd be interested in the position, Ada."

Her shoulder brushed his as she stiffened. "Thank you

so much for thinking of me, but I have no experience with children. I'm sure you can find someone better suited to the role."

"I suppose I must," Rina said with another sigh. "It's just that Thomas told us how well you write. That's a skill worth teaching."

She started to demur, but Thomas put a hand on her arm. She looked to him in obvious surprise.

"Ada recently wrote a letter to the governor to convince him to come to our Centennial Celebration," he told them all.

Drew had wandered over to join Catherine. "Nicely done," he said, and the others nodded.

Ada blushed. "Well, he hasn't agreed yet."

"And he hasn't disagreed," John pointed out.

"Worst luck," James teased.

"You see?" Rina pressed. "Writing is a skill everyone needs, especially as so many in Seattle still lack it."

"It reminds me of when you first started teaching," Catherine said. "Scout and Levi were young men, Beth fourteen, and they were your youngest pupils."

Ada's brows went up. "Youngest?"

Thomas smiled at the memory. "Rina was the first teacher in the area," he explained, "and there was only the three of us nearby."

"So some of the men around Wallin Landing came to learn about reading and writing too," Catherine added.

"Now all the schools around Seattle are too full of children to accommodate gentlemen," Rina finished.

Beth had returned from the house. Now she hurried over. "I know just the thing. Ada can help them!"

"Oh, I couldn't," Ada started, but Catherine stepped in.

"Beth's right, Ada. Even if you don't teach, I'm certain there are men in Seattle who would pay you to correspond for them. Sending notes to families to let them know progress, for example."

"Writing to the territorial government about claims and such," Drew agreed.

"Answering mail-order brides," Beth added dreamily.

Ada glanced among them. "Really?"

"Really," Thomas assured her, taking her hand. "I'd be happy to invest in an office, supplies, and advertising fees to get you started, Ada."

Her lips trembled. "Oh, Thomas, I don't know what to say."

"That's easy," Callie maintained, rising from the bench. "Say yes."

His gaze caught Ada's. The gray looked mistier again, as if she longed for this too. He willed her to agree to the idea of work that would keep her in Seattle, work that would help men like him who had gone out on their own with only a rudimentary education. To say yes to the love that was growing between them.

"You've given me a great deal to consider," she said. "I promise to think it over and give you an answer soon."

They let it go at that and went on to talk about plans for the town, the hopes for this new teacher, the number of children coming in from around the area. Somewhere along the line, Ada's head tipped onto his shoulder, and Thomas's arm went around her waist. Just the right size, as he'd suspected. In fact, she fit so well, he hesitated to move. But the sun was getting lower, until it brushed the tops of the cedars. Time to head for home, even if he was leaving another home behind.

With Beth and Hart following in their wagon some distance behind, Ada talked with Thomas all the way back to Seattle, about the Wallins, about the town and its future, and about being parents in the wilderness.

"You mentioned you don't have much experience with children," he said as he eased the horses around a deep gash in the road. "Do you like children?"

"I like the Wallin children," Ada said, smiling just thinking about their antics. "So much energy, so much industry. Imagine sharing the world with someone like Lars or Hannah."

"Levi has his hands full with Frisco and Sutter," he said. "But he wouldn't have it any other way. I think I could be a good father. All I have to do is be the opposite of my father."

He said it light-heartedly, but she'd heard the pain in his voice when he'd talked about his father earlier. She'd seen it cross his face too, as if the hurt was as deeply etched as that scar.

"You are not your father," she told him.

He cast her a glance. "How do you know? I could have stolen this carriage, lied to you about everything."

She shook her head. "You forget. There are too many witnesses for it to be a lie."

He shrugged. "Maybe I lied to the Wallins too."

"But you're friends with the deputy sheriff's wife," Ada reminded him. "You think Deputy McCormick wouldn't notice if you stole a shiny yellow carriage?"

He cast a glance over his shoulder to where Beth and Hart were falling farther behind, as if they were in the midst of deep discussions as well. "There is that. And I doubt the Wallin family would welcome a liar and a thief."

Something pinched her stomach, and she looked away from him, out into the dusky green shadows of the forest. He couldn't know the Wallins had done just that by welcoming her. She was lying about who she was, and she was hoping to marry her sister's groom. It didn't matter that Melinda had changed her mind. Thomas had paid her passage, was expecting to make a match.

"Do you think there's any hope for redeeming a liar and a thief?" she asked the deep woods.

"Levi would say there's always hope for redemption," Thomas answered, voice soft. "I believe that too. I've done things I wasn't proud of, Ada. Fear of my father may have compelled me, but that's a reason, not an excuse. I could have refused. I could have run away from him. Fear kept me a captive, whispering that no one would want to help. That's not who I am anymore. Now I know it's more important to tell the truth."

"No matter the cost?" she murmured, throat tightening with her fingers.

"No matter the cost," he agreed.

She turned to face him. His gaze was out over the dappled grays, and he held the reins easily, but his shoulders looked as tense as hers felt.

"But what if the cost is to someone else?" she asked him. "What if telling the truth will hurt others?"

He frowned. "It's still the truth. Don't they deserve to know?"

Despair pushed her. "What about a mother with an ugly baby? Would you tell her?"

"How her baby looks is just an opinion," he protested. "Who am I to say my opinion is truer than hers?"

"And if that child was adopted and didn't know it," Ada challenged. "Would you tell him?"

"Not my place to tell him," he said, but he shifted on the bench as if it had grown harder. "Besides, family is family. Why does it matter whether you were born into it or brought into it?"

Ada swallowed. "What if someone had a secret, something about their past it hurt to remember? Should she tell the truth about it to everyone she meets?"

"Not everyone," he allowed. "But to those she trusts." He glanced her way at last. "With those she loves."

Now was the time. She felt it. The words pressed against

her lips. He'd told her about his father, shared his deepest pain. How could she keep silent?

As if he saw the struggle in her, he pulled the horses to the side of the road, reined them in, and set the brake.

"Ada," he murmured, swiveling to face her fully. "I hope you know you can tell me anything. I care about you."

Because he thought she was pretty and talented and sought after. How could she diminish the appreciation she saw shining from his eyes? She'd been waiting her whole life to see it directed her way.

Perhaps that was why it was so easy to lean closer, meet his lips with her own.

Sensation swept over her like an ocean wave—warmth, sweet pressure, delight, joy. This was what love should be, two people, becoming one in heart and mind. This was what she'd feared could never be hers, but this could be her future.

The rattle of tack announced a wagon approaching. Ada pulled back, feeling as if she'd come from a far distance even though she'd moved only a few inches.

Thomas blinked as if he was having similar trouble bringing himself back to the present. Then he trained his gaze over her shoulder.

Hart brought his wagon to a stop alongside the carriage.

"I was going to ask if everything was all right," Beth said, beaming. "But it appears to be quite fine indeed."

"Never better," Thomas said, fumbling with reins that had never troubled him before. "See you in Seattle."

With a laugh, Beth motioned to her husband to keep driving.

"Please forgive me," Ada said. "I shouldn't have…"

He reached across and put his free hand over hers. "You should have. I'm glad you did." He winked at her, his own cheeks turning a pleasant pink. "I hope you'll feel called to do it again."

Ada ducked her head, cheeks heating.

He clucked to the horses and set them after the wagon.

"You don't have to tell me your secret, Ada," he said, and her head came up. "Not until you're ready. Just know nothing you say will change my admiration for you."

If only she could believe that!

She'd kissed him. Thomas shook his head as he directed Jack and Skip back into town. The soft touch, the intake of breath as if it had shaken her as much as it had shaken him, made it impossible to keep his hopes from flying.

He reined them in as easily as he reined in the dapple grays. Evangeline Jamison had kissed him too, and she'd only cared about his money. Still, he'd seen Ada's reaction to the Wallins, felt her kindness when he'd told her the truth about his father. She touched Mrs. Wallin's quilts as if she knew the love that bathed each stitch. She was so close to telling him the truth about her arrival in Seattle. He had to stay the course.

"I'm not sure I have room for anything more to eat tonight," she said as one of the porters at the Occidental ran out to hold his horses so Thomas could come around and help her down.

Disappointment nipped. "I understand," Thomas made himself say. "Perhaps you could come with me Monday afternoon to see about that bunting."

Her smile blossomed. "I'd be delighted."

He took her hand and bowed over it. It was all he could do to let her go and watch her walk into the hotel. Even the porter gave him a commiserating look as Thomas reclaimed control of the horses and turned for home.

"Jack and Skip enjoy their run out to Wallin Landing?" Bobby asked him when Thomas came through the rear door of the house a short while later. His ward was seated in the parlor, feet up on the fender and coat off.

"As always," Thomas said, joining him. He tossed Bobby one of Mrs. Wallin's quilts, and his ward immediately burrowed under it.

"How was dinner at the Howards?" Thomas asked, setting the other quilts on the chair. He'd find a place for the rug tomorrow.

"Good," Bobby said, but he pulled down his feet and glanced out the window, hugging the quilt close.

"We expecting company?" Thomas asked.

His ward started, then shook his head. "No. But I've been wondering about something. Have you heard of any gold strikes recently?"

In the act of sitting on the other chair near the hearth, Thomas froze. "You want to pan?"

He thought Bobby shrugged under the quilt, but he was avoiding Thomas's gaze again. "Maybe. I mean, that's how you and Mr. Howard made your fortunes."

Thomas sank onto the chair. "It's not easy, and it's not a sure thing," he cautioned. "For every one miner who comes home with gold in his pocket, another dozen come home with nothing to show for their efforts, and many die from starvation, illness, or attacks by claim jumpers."

Bobby could not know Thomas had faced all three. He made a face. "There has to be some way to earn money."

"Plenty of ways to earn money," Thomas said, leaning back against the chair Beth had picked out. Not for the first time he thanked her good taste and sense of comfort.

"Name one," his ward challenged.

"Start your own business," Thomas said. "Pick something you're good at that others need doing. Do it better than anyone else, at a fair price, in a reasonable amount of time. That generally works for most people."

Bobby blew out a breath. "What if I'm not good at anything?"

"Doubtful. Everyone's good at something. Sometimes it's not something others want to pay for. That's the problem."

Bobby leaned forward, hair falling against his temples. "I want to marry Gillian, but her father will never accept me if I can't provide properly for her."

So, that was what had been eating at the lad. He was short and slight for his age. Too easy to forget he was almost a man.

"You're seventeen," Thomas pointed out. "She's fifteen. You have plenty of time."

"No, I don't." Bobby surged to his feet, tumbling the quilt to the floor, and began pacing the parlor, boots pressing down on the emerald and blue carpet. "She's beautiful and smart, and her parents would do anything for her. I hear tell, back East where they come from, a girl turns sixteen, and they start lining up the suitors."

"This isn't Boston," Thomas pointed out, bending to retrieve the quilt.

"No," Bobby said, "it's Seattle, where there's a dozen men for every girl."

"More like eight and a half," Thomas said, "according to the latest figures in the *Dispatch*."

Bobby glowered at him as if he wasn't helping.

"Look," Thomas said, "you may not know it, but territorial law says a man and a woman can't marry without their parents' permission until they're both eighteen."

He skidded to a stop on the carpet. "What!"

"Sorry," Thomas said, setting the quilt with the others. "But it's the law." And he wasn't about to tell him the story of how old Doc Maynard had tricked Reverend Daniel Bagley into marrying a couple by putting the number eighteen inside the girl's shoes so she could honestly claim she was "over eighteen." Seattle had progressed a bit since then.

A bit.

Bobby was regarding him, head cocked. "So, if you give your permission, and I can convince Mr. and Mrs. Howard to give their permission…"

"No," Thomas said. "You're both too young."

Bobby crossed his arms over his chest. "Beth Wallin fell in love with Deputy McCormick when she was fourteen. Ciara told me."

"But she didn't marry him until she was two and twenty," Thomas reminded him.

Bobby sagged, arms falling. "I have no hope. Some fellow with funds hanging out of his pockets will snatch her up long before she turns two and twenty."

Thomas stood and put a hand on his shoulder. "Miss Gillian might have something to say about that. If you want to marry her, the best thing you can do is find a vocation and build yourself a stake. A lady wants to know her husband can provide for her."

He nodded. "Guess I better figure out what I'm good at then."

"Why don't you start by helping me with this Centennial Celebration?" Thomas suggested. "There's still plenty to do, and every businessman in the city will be watching. Wouldn't hurt if they saw you in the middle of it."

He nodded again. "I'll do it. Thanks, Scout. You want me to check that the barn is closed for the night?"

"Sure," Thomas said. He watched his ward lope for the kitchen and the back door.

Maybe he really could be a good father someday, with the right wife beside him. And the only wife he wanted was Ada.

CHAPTER ELEVEN

IT WAS HARD for Thomas to meet with Mr. Clancy Monday morning when he'd rather have spent time with Ada. But he set a few things in motion with a little help from TP, called in a couple of favors, and consoled himself that he would see her that afternoon after keeping his appointment with the businessman at ten in the Pastry Emporium.

That late in the morning, the bakery tended to be quiet, so he and Clancy were the only ones at one of the six wrought-iron tables while Maddie moved between the back and the front, replenishing the treats in the glass-topped case for customers coming later.

"So, what can I do for you?" Thomas asked, leaning back as much as the chair would allow.

"It's what I can do for you," Clancy countered. He'd obviously shaved for the meeting, and his plaid suit looked pressed. "We're a lot alike, you and me. I was ten when I came west with my pa to the California goldfields. He didn't strike it rich, like you did, but what I saw there told me a man can find a lot of ways to profit."

He wasn't sure where this conversation was going. "And how do you profit?"

Clancy raised his chin as if proud of his achievements. "I see needs, and I make arrangements to meet them, taking a minor percentage of the proceeds for my troubles. Seattle's a growing town. You have lots of needs. I could find exactly the goods you're looking for."

"Seattle is growing," Thomas allowed. "But I don't generally invest in merchandise. I look at businesses that provide a service or manufacture goods here, not import them from outside the area."

Clancy took a gulp of the coffee Maddie had brought them. "But even manufacturers need supplies, like raw materials."

Thomas spread his hands. "Look around you. We're surrounded by raw materials."

He shifted on the chair. "I know Seattle brings all kinds of goods up from San Francisco. All I'm suggesting is that if you use my services, I can get them here faster and cheaper."

He wasn't willing to call the man a liar, but the steamships up the coast could only travel so fast, and there were no roads between San Francisco and Seattle. There wasn't even a bridge over the Columbia River! And if Clancy intended to take a percentage of the cost of what he brought to Seattle, either the price would increase or the quality of the goods would decrease.

"Perhaps you could give me an example," he said.

Clancy nodded eagerly. "Of course. I know you're planning a big celebration for the Fourth of July. I could get you bunting to decorate the whole town."

"I already have plans to buy bunting," Thomas told him. "TP Freeman's Pioneer Variety Store has some in stock, I understand."

Clancy snorted. "Maybe he does, but I can make sure you're not taken advantage of."

The statement hit a nerve. But Thomas had learned not to extend trust where it hadn't been earned.

"I don't allow people to take advantage of me," Thomas said.

"Ah," Clancy countered, raising a finger, "but if you use my services, you'll be working with a real American, not a darkie."

Thomas stiffened. "Word of warning, Mr. Clancy. Seattle's not like some other towns. Anyone who's willing to work hard, contribute to the common good, is welcome here."

His smile was knowing. "Like them Chinamen that got run out of the coal mines."

"That's to Newcastle's shame," Thomas told him. "Their consciences will have to stand them witness and so will mine." He pushed back from the table and rose. "I'm afraid I have no reason to do business with you, sir."

Clancy surged to his feet. "You dare to stand in judgment over me? I heard about your father. You're no saint."

"You're right," Thomas said. "I'm a forgiven sinner. And there's nothing that will make me go back."

Clancy's eyes narrowed. "Even the truth about Melinda Williamson?"

Something leaped inside him. He shoved it away. Too many people were willing to tell tales about him. No matter how he tried to ignore it, it stung. He wasn't about to listen to this man's stories about Ada.

"I know the truth about Melinda Williamson," he said. He started to turn away, but not before he saw the businessman's face reddening in anger.

"If you know what's good for you, you'll listen to me," he threatened. "Plenty of rich men regret that they lost their fortunes to a pretty face."

"Or a dishonest partner," Thomas said.

Maddie came out from the bakery just then, took one look at them, and strode forward, pushing up her sleeves. "Here, now. There will be no shenanigans in my bakery."

"None planned, Maddie," Thomas assured her. "Mr. Clancy and I are done with our discussions."

Clancy pushed past him. "We may be done, but we're not finished. When you see the light, you'll come to me." He stormed out.

Maddie drew to a stop beside Thomas. "I'm not liking the looks of that fellow, me boyo."

"Neither am I," he replied. "If you see Hart McCormick before I do, tell him to keep an eye on Mr. Clancy."

Because he would be.

Ada kept her promise and called on Rosanna Freeman on Monday while Thomas was meeting with Mr. Clancy. She could only hope he would see the truth about the fellow's character clearer than she first had and react accordingly.

The Freemans had a cozy house on Third Avenue, not too far from the tall columns of the Territorial University. The day was warm and sunny, so Rosanna invited Ada to sit on the wide front porch and brought out a couple of harp-backed chairs for their chat. Her daughter, Harriett, was off visiting friends, and her son, Albert, was working as a cobbler in the business district.

The two ladies spread their skirts—Ada's a gray poplin courtesy of her sister and Rosanna's a practical green gingham with a wide brown leather belt—and smiled at each other, fingers wrapped around the porcelain cups of lemonade Rosanna had poured.

"You have a nice place," Ada commented, wishing she had her sister's gift for striking up a conversation. Then again, all Melinda's conversations generally revolved around her, so maybe they were easier.

"It's very pretty when the sun sets," Rosanna agreed, nodding at the view over the tops of the other buildings toward the Olympics, which were standing in full glory across the Sound.

"I can imagine," Ada said. "And is that a birdfeeder?"

Rosanna turned her gaze on the stone figure with outstretched hand in the middle of the muddy yard. At the moment, a robin was perched on the fingers, pecking at something in the palm. "It is. A fellow traded it to TP for two pairs of boots. I thought it foolishness at the time, but TP and I have enjoyed watching our feathered friends. They're so industrious, and they can be so determined. You should see the number of nests they try to build along the eaves." She shook her dark head.

Here was something Ada could talk about. "I used to watch birds in Boston out the parlor window," she told her, pausing to take a sip of the tart lemonade. "We lived across the street from a park. My favorites were the black-capped chickadees in the winter, leaving forked tracks in the snow, and the blue jays in the summer, flashing through the trees."

"We get a few jays here," Rosanna allowed. "They're a little different from what I saw back East. These here have gray tufts on the top of their heads." She wiggled the fingers of her free hand over her tight curls.

"You came from back East too?" Ada asked.

"Most everyone in Seattle comes from east of here," Rosanna said with a chuckle. "Except those born here, of course. TP and I met in Pennsylvania. He was bound and determined to make his fortune, so he came out with the Forty-Niners."

"So he made his fortune in gold, like Thomas and Mr. Howard," Ada marveled.

Rosanna made a face. "He didn't make much of a fortune, but he made enough to get us up to Victoria and then Seattle, with a house and a store to support us."

"A wonderful store," Ada agreed. "I've already bought a few things there, and I know Thomas plans to purchase that bunting."

"It's a lot of bunting," Rosanna said. "What's he going to do with it all?"

"I didn't think to ask," Ada confessed. "I suppose he's going to decorate the town, especially if the governor ends up coming."

Rosanna's brows rose. "You think the governor will come?"

"Thomas hopes so," Ada told her.

"You going to help him put up all that bunting?" she asked.

"Absolutely," Ada said, then she grimaced, remembering what she must do. "That is, if Thomas wants my help."

Rosanna cocked her head. "So, you and Mr. Rankin intend to marry?"

Ada peered down into the depths of the lemonade. "It's my fondest wish."

"Leading you a merry dance, is he?" She tsked.

"No, I'm the one hesitating," Ada said. "He's a fine gentleman. I wonder whether he'll be happy with me."

"That's for him to say," Rosanna replied, chin coming up. "You need work in the meantime?"

Ada smiled at her. "Yes, but I've been encouraged to start my own business, writing letters for those who find it hard."

Rosanna nodded her approval. "Well, that's a noble calling. I know several fellows who'd love to have someone write to their families or sweethearts for them."

Families she could manage. Sweethearts might prove difficult. How could she share another man's love for his gal when she couldn't bring herself to tell Thomas the truth?

She had come so close yesterday, and then they'd shared that kiss, and every other thought had flown from her mind. She'd never kissed or been kissed by a man before, certainly not a gentleman who made her dream of a future together. The touch of his lips—firm, yet tender—the feel of his arms around her—oh, but she could wish those would be hers forever.

CHAPTER TWELVE

A DA HADN'T GATHERED sufficient courage to tell him the truth by the time she met Thomas for tea at the hotel later that day. Roy was working again. He led them to a different table this time, one that overlooked the busy street. Through the polished glass she could make out the curve that ran down to the harbor, the sparkle of the Sound, and the masts of sailing ships riding at anchor. Wagons trundled past, carrying goods to and from the wharves, and men in wool and rough homespun strode back and forth as if intent on keeping the city flourishing.

Thomas watched them for a moment too before turning his attention back to her with a smile that lit his warm brown eyes. "And how did your visit with Mrs. Freeman go?"

"Very well," Ada told him. "We discovered we both love to watch birds."

A slight frown gathered. "Why would you watch birds?"

He sounded so puzzled she had to explain.

"They're beautiful. And so busy. Why, they seldom stop working to feed themselves and their families. And still, they sing."

"Well, not all of them sing," he said, brow clearing. "Ravens caw, geese honk, seagulls screech. But I will agree they're beautiful. There's something about the way they soar that lifts a body's spirits."

"Exactly," Ada said.

Roy brought a pot of tea and began pouring it into their cups. Thomas thanked him, then reached for the silver sugar bowl. Ada watched as he dropped six teaspoons into his cup.

"Someone has a sweet tooth," she realized.

Pink climbed in his lean cheeks. "Since I was a boy. Ah, and that will satisfy it nicely." He nodded to Roy, who had set a plate of little frosted cakes in front of them as well.

"Spice cake," the waiter said. Then he leaned closer. "From the Pastry Emporium, but don't tell anyone we had to buy from the competition."

"I'd offer to fund a baker," Thomas said, "but why would anyone need one with Maddie Haggerty in town?"

Roy grinned. "Or Ciara O'Rourke. I hear she wants to start her own restaurant. That's going to put a dent in our profits." He bowed and went to help another couple of businessmen who had come in. The sight of their plaid jackets reminded Ada of something else that had happened that morning.

"How did your meeting with Mr. Clancy go?" she asked, stirring a teaspoon of sugar into her own cup and trying to keep her fingers from trembling in the process.

He shook his head around a bite of the spice cake he'd piled on his plate. "You were right to warn me, Ada. He isn't a fellow I want to do business with."

She let out a breath. "Well, that's settled then."

"I hope so." He glanced out the window again. "When I refused him, he was angry enough to imply a threat. I don't think he understands who he's dealing with."

She felt as if a cloud had crossed the sun. "What do you mean?"

He brought his gaze back to hers, but it lacked some of its previous warmth. "I'm well known in Seattle, I have sufficient funds to do as I like, and I'm enough my father's son that I know how to spot a criminal. He won't find me an easy target."

Fear tiptoed up to the table. Ada put her hand over his on the cloth. "It doesn't hurt to be careful. I should hate to have anything happen to you."

He set down his fork and laid his free hand over hers, surrounding her fingers in warmth. "Thank you, Ada. I'll be careful. I promise. But please believe me when I say that Clancy has more to fear from me than the other way around."

He'd meant it as a comfort. He wasn't the tallest man in town, nor the most muscular. He couldn't claim that he was the smartest, either, or he wouldn't have stayed with his father so long or been taken in by Evangeline Jamison's guile. But he'd seen enough of the world to know how it worked and where he stood in it. Seattle was his home. No one would take that from him.

She pulled back her fingers and dropped her gaze. "I'm just glad we don't have to deal with his unpleasantness any longer."

Thomas watched her select a slice of the cake and place it precisely in the center of her plate. "Did he trouble you, Ada?"

His voice must have betrayed the anger that thought stoked, for her head came up, eyes wide.

"Why would you ask? I barely know the man."

It was a quick, firm acknowledgment, but he couldn't help thinking there was more to the story.

"You must tell me if he approaches you again," he said. "I won't stand for my girl to be bothered."

Her lashes fluttered like golden butterflies against her

cheek. "I rather like being called *your girl*."

Thomas grinned. "I rather like *calling* you my girl."

She cut a bite of her cake, and he went back to his.

"Do we have plans for this afternoon?" she asked.

We. How he loved that she'd used the word. "We're going to the Pioneer Variety Store to buy that bunting, and then there's something I'd like to show you."

Her gray eyes twinkled in the sunlight coming through the window. "And here I'd thought I'd seen all of Seattle."

"This is something new," he promised her.

They finished their tea, and he made sure to tip Roy well, then he led her up the street to TP Freeman's store.

The bell jingled as they entered, and Thomas glanced around. He'd had no trouble spotting the proprietor among so many riches when he'd stopped by earlier. There didn't appear to be any other customers in the store at the moment. Where was TP?

Ada had wandered to an empty spot on the floor. "Someone must have bought the table from China. It was here last time I was in." She spread her hands and turned from side to side. "But then, who could resist the treasures?"

He chuckled. "You sound like Beth."

"There, now," TP said, threading his way through the furniture from the back of the store. "Sorry to have kept you folks waiting. I was settling a new tenant. How can I help you?"

"Still have that bunting?" Thomas asked.

"Sure do." He nodded toward a long table set for eight. "But a courting man likely needs new furniture as well, besides what you bought this morning. Why don't you have a look while I find that bunting."

He was quite satisfied with the furniture Beth had helped him pick out, but he turned to Ada as the proprietor bustled off again.

"Was there something else you liked in the store, Ada?"

She glanced around again. "It's all lovely, or at least useful. But I suspect you have all the furniture you'll need. What did you buy this morning?"

"I'll show you later," he promised. "But it's nothing that can't be replaced if you find something you like better."

"Well, I bought a lamp last time I was in," she admitted. "It might look good on your mantel."

The very idea that she was ready to move her things into his house made him stand taller. "We'll have to put it there, then."

TP thumped the bolt down on the counter he must use to tally receipts. "Plenty more where this came from. How much do you want?"

Thomas grinned. "All of it."

He raised his brows. "You're going to need someone more than Miss Ada to help you carry it."

"I'll pay to have it delivered to Trinity Church," Thomas told him. "Mr. Bonnell is allowing us to store some things in the back for the Centennial Celebration. It will only be there a little while. I'm hoping we can put it up soon."

"Rosanna might be willing to help," Ada put in.

TP thumped another bolt down beside the first one. "So would I."

He finished bringing out the bolts of red, white, and blue striped bunting, and Thomas paid him for it, adding what he requested for delivery. TP promised to have it at the church by dinner.

"He was right," Ada said as she and Thomas stepped back out onto the boardwalk. "That *is* a lot of bunting."

"We have a lot of town to decorate," Thomas said. He offered her his arm, and she took it. He led her farther up the hill. There was something fine about walking with his lady on his arm. Other men stopped to stare. Many doffed hats with respect. One went so far as to whistle, but a look from Thomas put an end to that.

He stopped before the building holding the

haberdashery, the front window crowded with tall-crowned beavers and rounded wool caps. Pulling the key from his trouser pocket, he unlocked the door that gave access to the second story.

Ada glanced at the store, then up the stairs as Thomas opened the door. "Who lives here?"

"No one," he told her. "But there's a little office space above the store. Follow me."

He could see the confusion on her face, but she fell in behind him as he started up. At the top of the stairs, he stepped to one side and let her go in front of him into the office.

She stopped and stared. "Oh, Thomas."

He motioned her forward. "Go ahead. See if it suits you."

She wandered across the thick carpet to the polished wood desk in the center of the room, then ran her hand over the scroll-backed chair behind it. She picked up the piece of paper he'd left in the center of the desk.

"Ada Williamson," she read. "Professional Correspondent." Her voice cracked on the last word.

Thomas nodded toward the desk. "There are fountain pens, pencils, and different kinds of paper. I can have Michael Haggerty, Maddie's husband, make you a sign for the door. If you want anything else, you have only to let me know."

She set down the paper with trembling fingers. "How could I possibly want anything else? This is perfect." She met his gaze, her own shining with tears. "You're perfect."

"No, I'm not," he said, crossing the space to her side. "But for you, I'll do my best."

She stood on tiptoe and pressed a kiss against his cheek. "Your best is more than I could have ever dreamed."

Gazing down into her eyes, it didn't matter who she

was or how she'd come here. She was his, to love, to honor, to protect. He felt it.

Now he could only pray she felt it too.

CHAPTER THIRTEEN

ADA TOOK ONE more look around the little office. She could see herself sitting at the walnut desk, pen tapping her chin as she listened to what a client wanted her to write. She'd suggest a more congenial wording, perhaps, or encourage them to share what they really hoped for so she could craft the perfect letter. Who would have thought such a skill could be of service to others?

"This was so kind of you," she told Thomas as she followed him down the stairs to the door. "You must allow me to repay you."

"No need," he said, stepping out into the sunlight. As Ada came through, he shut the door behind her and locked it. "TP gave me a very good price for the furnishings, Mr. Ashart, the haberdasher, gave me a good price for a three-month lease, and I wanted to help." He handed over the key with a little bow.

Ada clutched it closer, hardly daring to believe it belonged to her. But it didn't, not really. She owed him so much.

"You helped the hotel," she pointed out as they started down the street. "You've helped others. I'd like my business to be the same sort of investment."

"It's really not necessary," he told her, his bootheels clumping against the boardwalk. "But if you insist…"

"I insist," Ada assured him, determined not to take advantage of his generosity the way her sister took advantage of her beaus. "I also need your advice. How will people know to find me?"

"We'll put an ad in the Saturday *Dispatch*. We could also advertise in the business directory. But we can also speak to Beth. She'll make sure the word gets out."

She might at that. "And what would people be willing to pay for the service?" Ada pressed. "I wouldn't want to overcharge."

He took her hand to help her across the side street. "People are used to having to pay for things on the frontier, either with cash or by trading. It's often more a question as to whether they can find anyone willing to sell or trade the product or service. Why don't you start with twenty-five cents a page? You can always raise or lower it once you see if it seems fair, to the customer and to you."

"Very reasonable," Ada said. Her mind brimmed with ideas, possibilities. Her lie floated to the top, but she shoved it back down. Now was no time to confess, not when he'd been so kind. She hardly wanted to spoil his efforts.

"I promised Bobby we'd have dinner at the house tonight," he told her as they reached Commercial Street. "Will you join us?"

She glanced up the street toward his beautiful house on the hill. "I'd be honored. Should I change?"

"Not in any way," Thomas said, linking his arm with hers. "You're perfect just as you are."

Guilt was nearly as firm as his arm under hers. "I'm hardly perfect, Thomas," she said as they started up the hill.

"To me, you are," he said.

He sounded so sure of the fact, a laugh bubbled up inside her. "I'll have you know I chewed my nails as a child."

"I used to trip over my own feet," he countered.

Ada put her nose in the air. "My embroidery looks like knotted fishing line."

"Levi says my biscuits could be used as the lead weights to sink your line."

She slanted a glance his way. "So, who's cooking dinner tonight?"

He grinned. "I am, with Bobby's assistance. I never developed Levi's light hand with biscuits, but I learned a few tricks in the gold camps."

That proved to be true. For, when Ada, Bobby, Thomas, and Beth and her husband sat down to dinner two hours later, Ada found the salmon succulent and the greens fresh and spiced with a lovely dressing.

"Your garden is coming along, I see," Beth said, twirling a bit of spinach on her fork. "But is that watercress?"

"Sutter and Frisco taught me where to look for it last time we were out to Wallin Landing," Bobby admitted.

"It grows wild along the lakes and streams," Thomas explained to Ada, who was seated on his right.

"Like huckleberries," she remembered with a smile.

"Another month," Beth said with a happy sigh. "Then we'll be baking pies and putting up preserves. I'll need your help if we have as good a crop as we expect, Ada."

Her mother had never let her anywhere near the canning. "I'd be happy to help," Ada said. "But I understand Western huckleberries are different from what grows back East, so I'll have to rely on your expertise on how to cook and preserve them."

"And I'll have to rely on my expertise on how to eat them," Bobby said before helping himself to another portion of fish.

Ada offered to help with the dishes, but Beth shooed her and Thomas out onto the front porch. "Hart can help. He's very handy around the house."

Her husband cocked a brow as if he was surprised to hear that, but he didn't argue.

"He doesn't say much, does he?" Ada observed as she and Thomas sat on the steps and watched the sun go down behind the Olympics. The sky above the rugged range was a deep purple, casting the waters in shadow.

"No," Thomas said, clasping his knee with one hand. "But he certainly knows how to get his point across. Levi and I lived in terror of him growing up, for all he's less than ten years our senior. We were certain any misstep, and he'd be there to throw us in jail. And he'd likely forget where he put the keys to let us out."

Ada laughed. "Did you ever see the inside of a jail cell?"

His hands tugged his knee closer. "No. But it wasn't for lack of trying."

"Well, you seem a model citizen to me," Ada told him. "Upright, honest."

"Humble to a fault."

"Very humble," she insisted. "And a good cook too."

"An adequate cook," he said. "Nothing you can't eclipse once you're in that kitchen."

Ada smoothed down her skirts. "I may have overstated my cooking abilities, Thomas. The truth is, I struggle in the kitchen. I'm not sure I could begin to come close to what you served tonight."

He shrugged. "Guess we'll be hiring a cook, then."

She stared at him. "That's it? You just hire someone?"

He dropped his knee. "I told you, Ada. I have money to spare. If we need something done, we can get it done. So don't worry."

He wouldn't say that if he knew the truth. Now might be the time. They might have been alone in the world. The night air was cool and scented with brine. Somewhere behind the house an owl hooted. Lights flickered to life in the buildings below.

She drew in a breath, but the words that came out were,

"What are we doing tomorrow?"

He sagged, and for a moment she feared she'd actually confessed instead.

"I have another meeting of the Centennial Celebration Committee in the morning," he said, "but I'll head to the hotel as soon as it's over."

Ada glanced his way, the truth she'd wanted to speak fading with the light. "Has the governor answered the letter?"

"Not so far," he acknowledged. "I'm not even sure if he's received it yet. I'm glad you suggested he respond by telegram. Otherwise it might be the day of the celebration before we knew whether he was coming."

"What will you do if he doesn't come?"

His shadow shortened, as if his body had tightened. "Pray we can find someone as impressive."

"I'm sure Washington Territory has many impressive citizens," she assured him.

He snorted. "Not according to Walt Kellogg." He shook himself. "We'll come out all right in the end, Ada. Everyone will have a good time, and the country will be celebrated. I'm just sorry I have to be away from you to make that happen."

"I'll be fine," she told him. "In fact, I'll spend the morning thinking about what I want to put in that ad in the *Dispatch* so I can find my first client."

In the end, her first client walked in the door of the hotel before she'd even considered the ad.

She had come downstairs for breakfast and had just stepped into the lobby when Bobby shot to his feet from one of the crimson chairs. Fear shoved her to his side. "Has something happened to Thomas?"

His eyes widened, and he pushed a lock of coal-black hair off his forehead. "No, ma'am. Sorry to have frightened you. I just wanted a private word." He dropped his gaze and shuffled his booted feet. "Maybe I shouldn't have come."

Ada's heart went out to him. She put a hand on his arm, and his gaze rose to hers again in question.

"Have you had breakfast yet?" she asked.

His mouth broadened in a grin. "Yes, ma'am, but I can always eat some more."

After seeing the amount he'd consumed last night, she could believe that.

"Join me, then," she said, giving his arm a squeeze before releasing him. "We'll talk."

A different waiter was on duty that morning, but he was just as courteous about seating them at a table and taking their orders. As soon as he had gone, Bobby leaned back in his chair, fingers drumming on the white cloth.

"How might I be of assistance, Mr. Donovan?" she asked.

That grin popped back into view. "Scout said you were smart. You can tell what's bothering me, can't you? That's why you called me Mr. Donovan."

She was only being polite, but she did begin to catch a glimmer of the problem. "You're growing up," she said.

He nodded. "And some folks are having a hard time seeing that I'm a man."

Well, not entirely a man, if the boney wrists sticking out of his calico shirt were any indication. Thomas must have sufficient funds to keep Bobby well clothed. That he was growing out of the ones he had said he was still shooting up quickly.

"The first steps are always the most difficult," she commiserated.

"That's just it," he said. "There are steps I want to take, but I don't know how well they'll be received. Scout told me you understand how to phrase things, especially between a fellow and his gal."

She would never make that claim. Neither would Thomas if he knew the secret she couldn't bear to share with him.

"This is about Gillian Howard, then," Ada guessed.

He edged forward until his stomach bumped the table, setting the sugar bowl chiming against the cream pitcher. "I know her parents think she's too young for courting, but I'd like to change their minds. First, though, I need to change *her* mind. So, I was wondering. You're a smart and cultured lady. What made you take a chance on Scout?"

Ada smiled, remembering. "So many things. He wrote with such refinement of spirit. He felt the same way about life and faith that I did. And he made Seattle sound so wonderful."

His face was falling with each word, and a sigh hissed out of him as she finished. "I don't see anyone saying I have refinement of spirit. And I'm not sure what I think about life and faith."

"Then perhaps," Ada said gently, "you should wait to court until you do."

That didn't sit well with him by the frown that clouded his face, but the waiter returned with the food just then. Ada said the grace, and they both tucked in.

"I need to do something," he burst out at last, sopping a biscuit into the gravy on his plate. "She's so pretty! Every boy in town will be out to marry her."

"And you don't trust Miss Howard to make the right decision for her?" Ada prompted.

The biscuit crumbled under his fingers. "Yes. That's what worries me. What if I'm not the right decision for her?"

Ada regarded him.

He swallowed, though he hadn't taken another bite. "I see. I need to let Gillian decide."

"Exactly," Ada said with a nod. "But it wouldn't hurt to let her know you have some feelings."

He picked up his fork again and attacked the last of his food. "I will. And I know just how, if I can get up the courage. I'll ask her to the dance at the Centennial Celebration. Scout's been having me work with Mr. Kellogg and Mr. Haggerty on the preparations, but everything will be done by then."

The Centennial Celebration, of course! She couldn't tell Thomas the truth before then and take the chance her announcement would ruin his big day. It was only one more week.

***

One week. One week, and so much to do. Thomas left the meeting with a list that seemed longer than when he'd started, despite having Bobby's help. The other members of the committee had been pleased about the bunting, and plans were in place to put it up all over town. They'd been less pleased about the governor's silence. He'd placated them with the same thing he'd told Ada: Messages took time to travel between locations on the frontier. A shame he couldn't make himself believe that was the only problem.

And he had other matters to concern him. He'd put out the word to the various organizations in which he had invested or donated to be wary of working with Clancy. Two had reported being approached, only to turn the businessman away. Thomas could only hope Clancy would realize he wasn't welcome and leave town of his own accord.

He started toward the hotel, the thought of spending time with Ada quickening his steps.

"Rankin!"

He stopped on the corner of Mill Street as Hart rode up to him. The deputy sheriff swung down onto the boardwalk but kept the reins in one hand as if prepared to remount and gallop off any moment.

"Something wrong?" Thomas asked.

"Just wanted to let you know about a couple of things," the deputy said, gray gaze sweeping the street as if he expected to find highwaymen in every doorway. "Maddie told me about this Clancy character. I haven't been able to run him to ground."

That said a lot about Clancy that he could evade notice from Seattle's finest. "He was staying at the Occidental."

"Not anymore," Hart reported. "But I haven't heard of him causing any trouble. Still, I'll be watching."

"Appreciate it," Thomas said.

Hart rubbed a bootheel against the edge of the boardwalk. "I also heard from the sheriff in San Francisco."

His stomach sank toward his own boots. "And?"

"He reports that Miss Melinda Williamson caused quite a stir there. Had three fellows all set to propose. Accepted gifts as if she intended to agree. Then took ship for Seattle." He shook his head. "I'm not sure whether to be glad or sorry she isn't a fraud."

"And I'm not sure whether to thank you for your trouble or thank you to stay out of my business," Thomas admitted. "The report makes no sense. I haven't seen Ada flirt with anyone while she was here, aside from a few kind words to someone who'd done her a service."

Hart's gaze went off toward the wharves. "Well, you haven't been with her every moment."

He stiffened. "Careful. You're talking about the woman I intend to marry."

Hart held up both hands, raising the reins enough that his horse, Arno, shot him a look.

"I haven't heard anything either," he told Thomas. "And you know how gossip tends to fly in this town. Far as I can tell, she's the perfect lady. But the sheriff in San Francisco has no reason to lie. I'm not sure either of us knows the real Melinda Williamson."

He'd thought he'd known. Melinda Ada Williamson

was kind, gentle, supportive. Ready to make a friend and be a friend wherever she went. She brightened when she saw him coming. She made his life feel worth living.

He wasn't ready to let that vision go.

Even as he feared she might be only a dream after all.

CHAPTER FOURTEEN

THOMAS DIDN'T JOIN Ada until dinner that night, and then he was quiet. She had spent the afternoon planning what to say in the ad, what else she might need in the little office, and how she should dress for her new profession. She'd taken a brief jaunt up to the Pioneer Variety Store to thank TP for her office furnishings. Rosanna had been there, and the two had ended up commiserating about the difficulty of cooking on the frontier.

"I got a stove," TP had assured Ada. "Makes the food almost cook itself."

"Maybe you ought to bring that stove home, then," Rosanna teased him. "If it makes cooking all that easy."

"Why, I wouldn't want to deprive Miss Ada," TP protested.

"Thomas has a fine stove," Ada told them both. "It remains to be seen whether I can make it work its magic."

"I got pots and pans too," TP had offered, and she and Rosanna had laughed.

Ada also wanted to talk to Thomas about Bobby and the Centennial Celebration. In fact, a dozen things crowded her mind. But she understood the need for stillness sometimes.

"Penny for your thoughts," she finally said as Roy

brought them slices of rhubarb pie.

Thomas paused until the waiter had left, then offered her a wan smile. "They probably aren't worth that much."

"Did the meeting not go well?" Ada asked, watching as he flaked at the crust of the pie with his fork.

"Well enough," he said. "We're going to help spread TP's bunting all over town. Reverend Bonnell volunteered the church youth for Saturday. I offered to chaperone. Will you join us?"

Ada beamed. "I'd love to!" She forked up a mouthful of pie and used the time it took to eat the tart treat to think about how she'd phrase the next question. "Will Bobby and Miss Howard be among the group?"

"Bobby will be," he said. "Very likely Allegra and Clay will send Gillian as well."

"Good," Ada told him. "Bobby came to see me today. It seems he would like to marry Miss Howard."

His fork froze over the pie. "What did you tell him?"

Ada blinked at the wary tone. "I didn't think it my place to *tell* him anything. But he asked for my advice, and I suggested that the two of them might be too young to consider marriage. He wisely decided that asking her to the dance for the Centennial Celebration might be a good start for now."

He blew out his breath. "Forgive me, Ada. I should have known you'd respond with your usual good sense. I tried to tell him something similar, but I suppose I'm too new at being a guardian to say and do the right things."

"I suspect many guardians struggle to say and do the right things," Ada told him. "Parents too. But I'm glad you and I are in agreement over this."

"Complete agreement," he assured her.

The pie was vanishing much faster now. She might only have a few more minutes of his time. It felt as precious as gold nuggets.

"I was thinking about the ad, in the newspaper," she

said. "I'd love for you to look over the wording, if you have a moment."

He leaned back from his now clean plate. "For you, I always have a moment, and more."

Ada slipped the sheet of paper from her reticule and handed it to him across the table. They spent the next little while debating wording. Finally, he put the hatch-marked paper in his pocket.

"I'll copy this out properly and deliver it to the *Dispatch* tomorrow, and I'll have a word with Beth as well." He cocked his head as he watched her across the table. "Are you certain you want to take my help as a loan, Ada?"

"Absolutely," she said. "I want to pay my own way, as much as possible."

"Why?" he asked.

She could have told him straight out. But the reasons had more to do with Ada Williamson than her sister Melinda. She had to be careful, or the story wouldn't ring true.

"Sometimes, it feels as if I've never had anything of my own," she said, hand pleating her skirt under the table. "I know most children receive what they need from their parents, but in my case there were moments it felt as if they were gifts grudgingly given. This work, this would be mine. Its success or failure would be on my shoulders. There's something satisfying in that."

He nodded slowly. "I felt the same way about gold panning. How hard I worked was up to me. But the success belongs to the Lord. I didn't put that gold in the stream. I just took it out."

"And I don't know who the Lord will send me for clients," Ada said. "But I'll help however many I can."

Ada and Thomas had parted on good terms that night, but he had business to attend to in the morning. Ada thought about going up to see TP, but she'd feel guilty taking more of his time without buying anything. She certainly didn't want to put it on Thomas's credit, and her own funds were running perilously low.

Thomas had brought her the books John Wallin had lent her, so she dived into the volume of poetry. My, but Vaughn Everard was a passionate fellow! She only managed to pull herself away from his words when someone rapped on the door mid-morning.

"Gentleman downstairs to see you, Miss Williamson," the porter offered when she answered the knock.

Her first thought was Mr. Clancy, and the words dried up in her throat.

"Did the gentleman offer his name?" she managed.

"Mr. Harry Yeager, ma'am," the porter said, with a nod. "He seemed to think you'd know him."

She did. Mr. Yeager was the overly confident, wavy-haired fellow on Drew Wallin's logging crew. What could he possibly want with her?

She thanked the porter and promised to be down shortly.

Mr. Yeager was pacing the floor, thick-soled boots thudding against the polished wood, as she stepped into the lobby. She crossed to meet him. "Mr. Yeager. How nice of you to call."

He had taken off his derby hat and now turned the brown brim in his strong hands. "Thank you for seeing me, Miss Williamson. Mrs. McCormick suggested I speak with you." He leaned forward and lowered his voice. "It's personal."

Ada frowned at him, mystified. "And you're certain Mrs. McCormick thought you should discuss it with me?"

He straightened with a nod. "On account of your

writing."

Ah. Apparently, Mr. Yeager needed a letter written on a sensitive matter. She wasn't willing to bring him to her new office alone. She didn't know him that well. But that would be true of any of her clients! A lady did not meet with a fellow unaccompanied. What was she to do about her reputation? Was her business doomed before it started?

No! She nearly stomped her foot at the thought. There had to be a way for her to meet with him, somewhere private, but public. She reviewed all the many places Thomas had pointed out on their tours. Then she cocked her head.

"Do you care for lemon drop cookies, Mr. Yeager?" she asked.

One side of his mouth hitched up. "If you're talking about the ones at the Pastry Emporium, yes, ma'am."

"Then perhaps we could stroll up there together and chat," Ada said.

He was agreeable, and so a short time later, they were seated at the table farthest from the counter in the little bakery. Ciara was working again. She brought them the cookies and tea. Ada caught her eyeing Harry, but the look seemed to stem more from curiosity than interest in the logger. Over Harry's head, Ciara met Ada's gaze and spread her hands, brows up in question.

Ada shook her head. With a sigh, Ciara returned to the counter to wait on the next customers, who had just come in the door to the sound of the bell.

"Private enough?" Ada asked, after Harry had consumed three of the dainty yellow cookies and slugged back a mouthful of tea.

"Private enough," he acknowledged. He braced his elbows on the table. "I'm aiming to wed, Miss Williamson. But most of the gals in the area are married or spoken for."

Perhaps he had been the one to complain as much at Wallin Landing on Sunday.

"So I was given to understand," Ada agreed, selecting a cookie of her own.

"Mrs. McCormick helped Scout Rankin place an ad for a mail-order bride. And that brought you here. So, I was thinking, maybe I should place an ad for a bride too."

Ada set down her cookie and held up one hand. "Mr. Rankin may have placed an ad, but he answered an ad I placed. I'm not entirely sure what I said to catch his eye. You'd have to ask him."

He deflated. "So you don't know how to write an ad for a fellow?"

"I do," Ada assured him. "That is, I'm sure I could craft such an ad. But I think it only fair to tell you, Mr. Yeager, that I'm about to open a business. If I agreed to help you write your ad, I would expect payment."

He nodded. "Whatever you like."

She raised a brow. "Twenty-five cents."

He snorted. "For the perfect bride? That's nothing."

"Very well." Ada sat back. "What will you tell your prospective bride you have to offer?"

He ticked the qualities off on his fingers. "One hundred and sixty acres abutting Lake Union. Two-room cabin with stone chimney. Floor's still dirt, but I'll have planks in before winter. I have steady work, for good pay."

Melinda would not have given his ad a second glance. But that didn't mean other women wouldn't be attracted to a home and a good provider. "And what about you, Mr. Yeager? What sort of husband will the lady be getting?"

He frowned. "I just told you."

"You told me the material things she gains. What sort of man will she be sharing her life with?"

"I don't chaw, don't smoke, and only drink when it's a celebration," he said.

"Well," Ada said, "there's something to be said for that."

"You bet there is." He reached for the last cookie, then hesitated, glancing her way. Not entirely selfish, then.

She nodded for him to take it, and he swallowed it in one bite.

"And what sort of bride would you like to attract?" she asked.

Once more his smile tilted up. "Pretty as a sunrise. Smart, but not so smart she'll think she's better than me. Strong. If I prove up my land the way I hope, I'll want to have a dairy someday. She'll need to help with the milking. And the hoeing in the garden. And she'll need to be a good cook. I eat a lot."

Ciara marched up to the table and slammed down a plate of cookies so hard Ada thought the porcelain might crack. "Good cooks aren't hard to find, Harry. Good husbands are." She snatched up the empty plate and stomped back to the counter.

Harry was frowning again as he glanced after her. "What'd she mean by that?"

"I believe Miss O'Rourke was referring to your list of requirements for a bride," Ada told him, hiding a smile. "Some might consider it a little high."

Harry leaned back in his chair and crossed his arms over his broad chest. "A lady's allowed to dream of the husband she wants. Why can't a fellow dream as well?"

Why indeed? She hadn't allowed herself to dream before she'd read Thomas's first letter. Now she feared she would lose that dream all too soon.

Thomas was crossing Second Avenue, on his way to an appointment with his accountant, when a movement inside the Pastry Emporium caught his eye. Ciara O'Rourke, face livid, had nearly thrown a plate of cookies at a customer.

A customer who was having tea with Ada.

He stopped, took a breath, shook his head. But the picture didn't change. Ada was sitting across the table, smiling her sweet smile at Harry Yeager.

He barreled into the bakery and strode up to the table.

"Thomas!" Ada beamed up at him. "Done with business so soon?"

She didn't look the least guilty. He glanced at Harry, who was turning redder by the moment.

"Nearly," he said, gaze meeting the logger's. "What brings you to town, Harry?"

"Business," he said. He gulped the last of his tea and stood. "Thank you for your help, Miss Williamson. I think I know how to take things from here." He dug into his pocket and placed a two-bit coin on the table. Then he lit out of the bakery as if he thought Ciara would chase after him with a cast iron fry pan aimed at his head.

By the way Ciara's eyes were narrowed, she might at that.

Ada grabbed the coin and held it up, eyes shining. "Look, Thomas! My first commission!"

Her commission. She'd been helping Harry write something.

He dropped onto the chair, calling himself six times a fool. "Good for you," he told her. "What did Harry need help with?"

She blushed. "I probably shouldn't say."

"I'll say," Ciara declared, bringing a fresh plate of gingersnaps to the table. "The big galoot wants to write for a mail-order bride. As if courting and marrying were as easy as writing a letter." She shook her head.

"Sometimes it *is* that easy," Thomas said. He looked to Ada. "If you find the right lady."

Her blush deepened. "And the right gentleman answers your ad."

Ciara glanced between them, and a smile brightened her face. "Well, that's just lovely. Cup of tea, Scout?"

"I should be going," he said. That didn't stop him from taking a gingersnap first.

Chuckling, she wandered back to the counter, wiping a crumb off another table along the way.

"Is there anything I can do to help with your work?" Ada asked, slipping the coin into her reticule. "Apparently, it's becoming known I have a way with words."

She certainly had with him. But Hart's story had sat on his gut all night like a bad batch of clams. He'd seen no indication that Ada was a shameless flirt, yet one glimpse of her in the company of another man had raised his suspicions. What was wrong with him? He wanted her to trust him. He had to be willing to extend the same trust.

"At the moment, I'm heading to see my accountant, then I'm scheduled to inspect a mill that wants funding to add another saw," he told her. "But later this afternoon, I'm supposed to sit in on a practice of the Seattle Brass and String Band."

"The ones who played when I arrived?" she asked. The delight in her voice made the expense worth every cent.

"The very ones," he agreed. "They'll be leading the parade for the Centennial Celebration and playing for the dance. Would you like to join me?"

"I'd be delighted," she said.

And so, a little after four, he and Ada strolled down to Yesler's Hall. The cavernous space had been used for a cookhouse and theater during its busy life. Now the members of the band, dressed in their rough work clothes, clustered around the leader, William Striet, tooting horns and plucking strings. Thomas led Ada to chairs that had been set up to one side.

But he found it difficult to listen as the band went through its repertoire with Ada next to him. Her eyes were wide, and she swayed with the music as if every song was played by a fancy orchestra.

The band members had probably never had such a receptive audience. Most of the men had learned to play their instruments from friends or family, not prestigious music tutors. Besides the fifes, drums, bugles, and fiddles, they'd added a set of cymbals recently. They were played by Rif Hoolan, a logger with a fiery red beard down the middle of his flannel-clad chest. Every time he played his part, he grinned as broadly as the great brass disks.

Ada applauded after every song, until the musicians' heads were high and chests puffed with pride. It might even have helped their playing. She seemed to have that effect on people—encouraging them to do their best.

Why did some part of him persist in wondering whether she was someone else entirely?

CHAPTER FIFTEEN

BETH MUST HAVE passed the word all over town, because people kept showing up at the hotel requesting Ada's help over the next couple of days. That was all to the good, for Thomas had his business and the Centennial Celebration to attend to. They still met for dinner every evening, sharing the triumphs and frustrations of their days. If she missed him overly much, she took a peek at the letters he'd written, and her heart swelled anew. The biggest issue was society's strictures.

"If I were a man, there'd be no question I could meet in private with my customers to write the letters," she told Thomas Friday evening over a dinner of venison steak at the hotel restaurant. "But I keep thinking there will be those who question my reputation if I do so as a woman."

He nodded. "And there's your safety to consider. Most folks in Seattle are as nice as they come, but there are a few harder characters. I don't like the idea of you getting caught all alone with one. I guess I should have thought of that before I leased the office."

Ada puffed out a sigh. "There has to be a solution! I made three dollars this week, Thomas. Three dollars! I know that's not a lot compared to what you must make on your investments, but it's more than I ever dreamed."

"More than some of the workers at Yesler's Mill bring

home in a week," he allowed. "And you're helping folks. Since you earned three dollars with only Beth for advertising, you should be able to bring in more once your ad starts running. Let's look for an older lady who can serve as your assistant and sit with you and your customers when you have to use the office."

"Maybe Beth knows someone," Ada said, thinking. "Thank you, Thomas. It's so comforting having someone to share ideas with."

"Any time," he said, smile pleased.

Saturday morning, Ada hurried downstairs and snatched up a copy of the *Dispatch* before breakfast. There it was! On the third page, in a nice clean block: "Lady available to compose letters for businesses and personal interests. No task too big or too small. Twenty-five cents a sheet of finished letter. Inquire above the haberdashery on Third Avenue."

She shivered in excitement.

"Sale at Kellogg's?" the hotel clerk asked.

She shook her head as she carefully folded the paper. "Important business dealings, Mr. Carter. I'm going to be a professional correspondent, helping people write letters."

"There's a need for that," he acknowledged. "Can I help you with anything else today?"

"Only information," she told him. "Mr. Rankin will be helping deck the town for the Centennial Celebration. Do you know when the proprietors will be decorating the hotel? I'm sure they'll want to show their civic pride."

"Yes, ma'am," he said. "The bunting's going up this afternoon."

All over town, it seemed, as Bobby drove her and Thomas to the church later that morning. Red, white, and blue material draped from windows and balconies, hung over doorways, and wreathed signs. A few industrious folks were out with cans of paint, offering to cover doors in a fresh coat of one of the three colors. Flags flew from every pole.

The young people and chaperones that Reverend Bonnell had gathered were ready to lend a hand. Besides Bobby, Thomas, and Ada, the band of twenty included Beth, Albert and Harriett Freeman, Gillian Howard and her parents, and Ciara O'Rourke and her brother Aiden, a dark-haired joker who soon had them all laughing as they waited for the minister to assign them to teams.

Ada found herself working beside Bobby, Gillian, Beth, and Ciara. Thomas and his team were next door. She could see him pointing them to their tasks and helping them tack up the bunting around the side of the minister's house. At least both the church and the parsonage faced west, so they were shaded from the glorious summer sun that had parted the clouds that morning.

"I hear business is going well, Ada," Beth said as she held the ends of the bunting Ada was affixing to the church front. "Lots of customers?"

"More than I expected," Ada agreed, stretching to secure the fabric to the window ledge. "Thank you so much for sending them my way!"

"I saw that ad in the *Dispatch*," Ciara said from where she, Bobby, and Gillian were working on the other window. "Good for you, Ada."

"Thank you," Ada told her. "I can't wait to see who else walks through the door. Which reminds me."

She went on to explain to Beth about the need for a chaperone.

"I'll give it some thought," her friend promised. "Seems like everyone is working these days, if not at a business than keeping the home." She called over to Ciara. "And when are you starting your restaurant?"

Ciara must have rapped her thumb with the hammer, for she jerked back and spent a moment sucking on the digit.

"I can't, Beth," she admitted at last. "There are plenty of good restaurants in Seattle these days, and I hardly want to compete with Maddie and open another bakery."

Ada tacked the last of her bunting around the window. "Why not open a restaurant at Wallin Landing? Thomas says it's always growing."

Beth clapped her hands. "Ada, you're brilliant! Ever since I left, Drew's been having trouble finding someone to cook for his logging crew. And I know Dottie and the others would love having someone there to bake bread and pies and such, not to mention a special place to eat besides always having to cook the meals themselves."

Ciara climbed down from the step stool she'd been using. "Really? You think there'd be enough work?"

"I'll be staying in town this Sunday," Beth said, "but Drew and the others are coming in for the Centennial Celebration on Tuesday. You could talk to him then."

"I will," Ciara agreed, grinning. Then she glanced around. "Where did my helpers go?"

Ada glanced around as well. "Oh, dear. Some chaperones we are."

Beth nodded toward a tree at the edge of the churchyard. "There they are."

Bobby and Gillian stood, heads close together. Even as Ada watched, the girl stepped back and gave a tremulous nod. Bobby's shout of joy echoed across the yard.

"What was that all about?" Ciara asked as Gillian ran to where her parents were helping decorate the shops across the street.

Bobby strolled back to them, hands shoved into his pockets and face red. "Gillian said she'd go to the Centennial Celebration dance with me. If her parents allow, of course."

"They'll allow," Beth said. "I'll make sure of it." She too headed across the street.

Bobby watched her go. "You think they'll need that

much convincing?"

Ada put a hand on his shoulder. "No, I don't. I think they'll be delighted Gillian has such a thoughtful young man beside her."

He nodded, but his color was fading, and so, she thought, were his hopes.

"Go ahead and start on the next building," Thomas told his crew, eyeing Ada and Bobby near the church. "I'll be right back."

He'd heard his ward's shout, and he couldn't tell if it was delight or defeat. He strode back to join the two people he most cared about in all the world.

"Everything all right?" he asked, glancing between them.

He wasn't sure Bobby even noticed he'd come up. The lad was staring across the street to where Clay, Allegra, Gillian, and Beth were in deep discussion.

"Bobby asked Gillian to the dance," Ada said, as if she too realized Bobby was incapable of speech at the moment. "Now he's waiting for her parents to agree. Beth's attempting to help."

Thomas frowned at the group across the street. "Why does Beth need to help?"

Bobby roused himself. "That's what I asked. I told you, Scout. They want someone better than an orphan for Gillian."

Thomas laid a hand on his shoulder. "As far as I'm concerned, there is no one better. But you have plenty of time."

His ward's body was as taut as a bowstring. "You don't know what it's like, waiting."

Oh, but he did. He felt as if he'd been waiting his

whole life for something he couldn't even name. Beth, her brothers, and their mother had begun to fill the hole in his heart. But he was beginning to think only Ada held the final piece.

Gillian came hurrying back, ruffled skirts rustling and blue eyes sparkling. He could understand Bobby's fixation. She had golden curls clustered around a heart-shaped face and a figure that was just beginning to make itself evident in the fashionable gowns her mother chose for her.

"They said yes," she told Bobby, seizing his hand and giving it a squeeze. "Oh, Bobby, I can't wait!"

Bobby visibly swallowed. "Me either."

"And what time should Bobby come for you, Gillian?" Ada asked after they'd stared into each other's eyes a few moments.

The girl blinked. "Maybe you could sit with us for the fireworks. Then we could just walk up the hill to the dance."

"I'll be there," he promised. "And I bet you'll be the prettiest girl at the dance."

"No," Thomas said, slipping his hand over Ada's. "I can think of at least one other prettier."

Ada dropped her gaze, blushing.

Bobby nudged him with his shoulder. "Then maybe you ought to ask her, Scout."

"Oh, there's no need," Ada started.

Thomas turned to face her fully, taking up her other hand as well. "No, Bobby's right. A gentleman should never take his lady for granted. Would you do me the honor of attending the Centennial Celebration dance with me, Ada?"

"I'd be delighted," Ada said.

"And she doesn't have to ask her parents' permission," Gillian whispered to Bobby.

She didn't have to ask anyone's permission. She knew

her own mind. He could see the conviction shining from her misty gray eyes. He could hardly wait for the dance.

They finished putting up the last of the bunting, then he treated everyone to dinner at the Occidental. They made a merry crew, keeping Roy and two other waiters busy. He could imagine many more days like this, working together on projects for the community, spending time with friends.

Starting a family.

"What a fine day," Ada said as the others headed for home. "The bunting up and my ad in the paper. Thank you so much for placing it, Thomas. It was a thrill to see."

"And it's a thrill to watch your business blossom," he told her as they stood in the lobby. Most of the other guests were either in the dining room or had retired for the afternoon, leaving the space quiet. Even Carter, at his stand, looked ready to doze off.

Ada seemed to have no interest in leaving for her suite. "That's one of the reasons you invest, isn't it?" she asked him. "You like seeing others achieve their dreams."

She made him sound almost noble. "It's an honor to help," he assured her. "Why else was I given all this money?" He glanced toward the stairs, then leaned closer. "I'm not ready to let the day end. Care for a walk?" He offered her his arm.

She latched on. "Wherever you like."

Feeling as if he owned the territory, Thomas led her out onto the boardwalk.

Henry Yesler expected the Centennial Celebration to attract people from all over the territory, so he was having an open-air pavilion erected next to his hall to allow more room for the dance. The workers were putting away their tools as Thomas and Ada strolled past. Two nodded respectfully. Thomas nodded back. He could only hope the wily old pioneer was right about the number of people coming.

They started up the hill to Second, waving through the window at TP as they passed the Pioneer Variety Store. Two couples and a matron were inside, perusing the wares, but TP managed a moment to wave back. Above the store tops, clouds were spilling up the Sound, and he could smell rain in the air. He tucked Ada a little closer, praying it would hold off until they were done with their walk.

"It all looks so festive," Ada said, nodding to the bunting draped along Second Avenue as they started toward Kellogg's. "Everyone is getting into the spirit."

"It's nice to see the town coming together," Thomas agreed.

He glanced in the window of the mercantile, only to find a white-lacquered crib and some kind of contraption with wheels with a doll propped up inside it. Apparently someone in the store thought the mostly bachelor population should be considering starting a family. That only reminded him of his earlier thoughts.

"We never discussed having children in our letters," he ventured, pausing before the window. "You told Rina you had no experience, but you seem to know how to deal with Bobby."

Her gaze lingered on the display as well. "Bobby's on the cusp of becoming an adult. I remember those feelings of wondering where I belonged, what my future held. I've never had much call to spend time with little ones, but if the Wallin children are any indication, I think I could be a good mother." She glanced up to meet his gaze. "As you said, at least I know some of the things *not* to do."

Thomas nodded. She had a way with words and people, and he knew things she'd never experienced. Together, they likely could manage a family.

A family. The dim reflection in the glass showed a huge grin on his face. It faltered as he spotted Hart riding up to them.

The lawman reined in as Ada turned to him as well. He tipped his hat. "Miss Williamson, Scout. Either of you seen Mr. Clancy recently?"

Ada shook her head, but she paled.

Thomas tensed. "Is he causing trouble?"

"Nothing tangible," Hart admitted. "Had a complaint from Jackson, the foreman at Yesler's Mill. Seems this Clancy tried to interest him in importing equipment, and Jackson refused, saying he'd heard nothing good about the fellow. Clancy railed about how you were out to get him and vowed to show you up for the skunk you are." Hart held up one hand. "His words, according to Jackson, not mine."

Ada glanced between the two of them. "Do you think he's dangerous?"

"Someone to watch," Hart allowed, eyes sharper than a hawk's. "Just be sure you do the same, Scout."

"I will," Thomas promised. "But if it's a fight he wants, I'm ready. Seattle knows all my secrets. There's not much he can say that hasn't been heard before."

Hart cast a glance at Ada, who stepped closer to Thomas as if for protection. But the deputy touched the brim of his hat in salute and continued his patrol.

"Don't worry," Thomas told her, resting his free hand over hers on his arm. "Clancy can't hurt me."

She pressed her other hand to the neck of her gown as they started forward again. "I hope you're right. If I've said something, done something, that would give him any advantage, I will never forgive myself."

This was it. She was finally going to tell him the truth. He stopped as they came to a side street and met her gaze, trying to put every ounce of compassion into his words. "Is there something you'd like me to know, Ada?"

Her lower lip trembled, and her eyes dipped down at the corners as she looked up at him. "Thomas, I..."

"Rankin!"

Thomas could have cheerfully dumped Walt Kellogg into the deepest part of Elliott Bay. The shop owner bustled up to them, even as Ada dropped her hold on Thomas' arm.

"Evening," Thomas greeted him. "Ada Williamson, this is Walt Kellogg, co-owner with his brother of the mercantile we just passed."

"Mr. Kellogg," Ada acknowledged. "You have a fine store."

He nodded. "That we do." He turned to Thomas. "Weinclef said he saw you stop by the front window. Were you looking for me? Have you heard from the governor?"

"Nothing yet," Thomas said, hoping he sounded reassuring. "There's still time."

"Less every day," Kellogg informed him, as if that weren't obvious.

"The town certainly looks prepared to greet him," Ada put in. "Your store is one of the most patriotic, Mr. Kellogg. I'm sure Governor Ferry will notice."

Her praise finally penetrated his panic, and Kellogg puffed out his chest, swelling his paisley waistcoat. "We aim to please at Kellogg's." He glanced at Thomas again. "You'll be sure to let me know as soon as you hear?"

"Of course," he said. He waited only until the man had returned to his store before looking to Ada. "Sorry for the intrusion. You were saying?"

Her smile was fainter than Mount Rainier on a cloudy day. "Nothing that can't wait until after the Centennial Celebration. You deserve your moment to shine."

CHAPTER SIXTEEN

THEY FINISHED THEIR walk, and Thomas saw her back to the hotel, but some of the sparkle had rubbed off the day. Ada knew it was her fault. He'd looked so ready to listen, ready to forgive, there on the boardwalk, that she'd almost told him everything. Now, she could only be glad for the interruption from Mr. Kellogg. She couldn't bring herself to end what she and Thomas were beginning. And he did deserve the perfect day for the Centennial Celebration.

The governor, unfortunately, thought otherwise.

Thomas had escorted Ada to church Sunday morning with Bobby. They'd returned to his house for luncheon with Beth and Hart, Beth providing the victuals. They had been sitting in the parlor, discussing the possibility of Ciara's restaurant at Wallin Landing, when someone rapped at the door.

Bobby, who was seated on a chair beside the sofa, twisted to see out the front window. "That looks like Mr. Hennessy."

"I thought you were done working for him," Hart, sitting with Beth across from them, commented with a frown.

"I am," Bobby promised, rising as the rap came again. "Running telegrams all over town was my sister's idea.

Excuse me."

"Mr. Hennessy is the telegraph operator," Beth explained to Ada as if she had seen her puzzled look. "But who could be sending Scout a message?"

Ada was afraid she knew. She couldn't take her eyes off Thomas as Bobby returned to them and held out a note so fast he might have thought it would rear up and attack him.

Thomas reached for it more slowly, then cracked the seal and spread open the telegram. Ada craned her neck to read over his arm. The words struck her as hard as a fist.

"Not coming!" she cried, head jerking up. She met his gaze, which was darkening. "Neither Governor Ferry nor his lieutenant. Oh, Thomas! I was so sure. I'm sorry."

"It's not your fault," he told her, though he held the telegram so tightly she feared it might crumple in his fist. "Since the Northern Pacific Railroad announced Tacoma as its terminus, Seattle isn't as important to the territory."

Hart snorted. "That's true enough."

"We're fortunate they allowed us to keep the Territorial University," Beth agreed, face puckered. "Still, I'm sorry too. I know how hard you and Ada worked to persuade him. What will you do now? It's only forty-eight hours until the orations."

Ada put her hand on his arm in support.

He raised his head as if her touch had comforted him. "Seattle's full of brilliant people. Surely one of them wants to speak. We've all worked too hard to see the day come to fruition. I intend to make sure it's perfect."

Ada wasn't sure what Thomas intended, but it seemed

to require all his efforts on Monday. It rained that day, a mist that enveloped the town and the harbor, until the horizon was a slash of gray and the streets a wash of mud. Thomas was grim over dinner, and he declined dessert. Ada hurt for him.

Tuesday morning dawned bright and clear. Ada was witness to it. She hadn't been able to sleep much that night and had watched the sky brighten from her window. She sent up a prayer for Thomas, that his hard work would pay off.

And that he would forgive her when she told him the truth tomorrow.

As if Seattle doubted that, a boom sounded from up the hill, then another and another, until the waters echoed the noise. Ada shivered. Thomas had told her the barrage would come from Seattle's few cannons, offering their salute to the day, but she couldn't help feeling as if their smoke would hover over her until she confessed. She shook off the feeling. Today was about celebrations, and she fully intended to enjoy it.

She was waiting in the lobby, dressed in her white sprigged muslin gown with the ruffles on the overskirt—hair coiled up under a straw hat trimmed in red, white, and blue ribbon, when Thomas arrived just after seven that morning. He wore a jaunty blue jacket with a white shirt and red neckerchief.

He bowed to her. "You look perfect."

Ada curtsied. "Thank you, kind sir. I just want to do you proud."

"You'd do me proud wearing an old flour sack," he said, which only made her cheeks feel hot. He offered her his arm, and together they started out of the hotel.

The streets were already crowded. Men, women, and children, dressed in patriotic colors and some waving little flags, filled the boardwalk, and everyone seemed to be heading toward the docks.

"I thought the festivities were up on the university grounds," Ada said as Thomas turned in that direction as well.

"They are," he promised, "or they will be this afternoon. This morning, we have the regatta. But first, I want to see who else might be coming. The governor may not be on the morning steamer from Port Townsend or Olympia, but others could be."

Like the buildings and homes of the city, many of the ships at anchor had decorated their hulls for the day, with flags flying in the sea breeze and flowers and evergreen boughs draped along the bulwarks. Ada and Thomas stood on one of the docks, not far from where he had waited for her to come in nearly two weeks ago now. How much dearer he had become to her since then.

She clutched his arm, then trained her gaze out over the waters as a white-sided steamer slid to a stop on Puget Sound with a blast of her whistle. Gulls leaped off the pilings to launch themselves into the air like confetti.

The sailors began lowering the boats, all the boats, each filled to capacity and beyond. Soon dozens of heads bobbed as the small boats crossed the waves. There were easily three times the number of passengers as when Ada had arrived.

"Oh, Thomas," she said, and his smile lifted higher.

More steamers pulled into port, filling the bay. Soon the dock teemed with so many visitors Ada could no longer see the water. Thomas shook hands, pointed folks to good vantage points for the regatta, and thanked them for coming. Ada waved a welcome, encouraged mothers with little ones, and fended off more than one suggestion to join a gentleman to view the festivities.

"Let's find a place to watch," Thomas said, tucking her arm closer as the last passengers streamed up the planks for the shore.

A number of families had parked their wagons along

the water. Thomas led her to where the Howards were seated on theirs, Allegra on the bench with her son, Georgie. The nine-year-old had his father's fair hair and his mother's delicate features. Gillian and Bobby sat in the bed.

"Allow me," Clay said, offering Ada his hand.

"That's my duty," Thomas told him before she could answer. He put his hands on her waist and boosted her up onto the bed, then jumped up beside her. Once more, Ada felt entirely too warm for the summer's day.

"Sit here, Miss Williamson," Gillian said, patting the spot beside her. She too wore sprigged muslin, with far more gathers and bows. Melinda would have loved that gown.

Ada shoved back any thoughts of her sister. Smiling, she lowered herself beside the girl. Bobby sat on Gillian's other side, and Thomas settled next to Ada, legs drawn up.

About a dozen ships were anchored off one of the wharfs jutting into the bay, long sleek sloops of various sizes, sails already in place; and their smaller cousins, rising and falling with the waves.

"Who do you favor?" Ada asked Thomas.

"The *Minnie*, under Captain Hanson," he answered with a nod toward the longest boat in the group. "He likes to crowd on the sail."

"The *Jolly Times* for me," Bobby put in, leaning around Gillian, likely as an excuse to move a little closer. "Captain Diggs was always good about tipping if I brought him telegrams when he was in port."

"I'm hoping for good things from the *Centennial*," Gillian said, blue eyes shining. "Father helped with her funding. And the name is perfect for today."

"Indeed it is," Ada said. "I'll cheer for that one too."

"Me too," Georgie put in, leaning precariously around his mother.

Clay offered his wife a wink. "What about a wager? Whoever boat wins a prize in its class is allowed a kiss from the person of their choosing."

Georgie gagged.

Gillian exchanged looks with Bobby. Ada glanced at Thomas, and her stomach fluttered at the look in his eyes.

A raven-haired beauty with a heart-shaped face, Allegra nodded to her husband. "Done. I'll join the ladies and Georgie in cheering for the *Centennial*."

"And I'll take the *Tibbals*," Clay said, turning his gaze once more out onto the waves.

As one of the churches rang the ten o'clock hour, the captains positioned their boats along a buoy, with the *Minnie*, as the largest boat, at the leeward position. A bang from a pistol echoed across the water, and the ships moved out.

"There's the *Sappho*," Bobby called, setting up on his knees as if to see around Gillian's flowered hat. "She's the only one heading for the next buoy at Freeport Point."

Thomas shaded his eyes with his hand. "The others look like they're heading for the Duwamish to come around."

Having seen a few races with her family, Ada thought she knew why. She pulled off a glove, licked one finger, and held it up. "There doesn't seem to be enough wind."

There wasn't. The boats slowly made their way around the buoy, tacking as needed, then turned to head across the water to Eagle Harbor. The *Lillie Bell* was soon becalmed, floating aimlessly with the tide. Likewise the *Isabel* fell out of the line and drifted back into Elliott Bay. Around them, people muttered, shifted on their seats. A few went for better sport in town.

Then Bobby surged to his feet, rocking the wagon. "Look! The *Tibbals* has caught the wind!"

Across the Sound, the sloop's sails belled white as she flew toward Five-Mile Rocks to the north of Elliott Bay.

"And the *Minnie* is right behind!" Ada cried, recognizing the smaller ship.

The *Sappho* was not to be outdone. The three boats vied for position, first one ahead, then another, before swooping into Elliott Bay to the cheers of the remaining crowd.

In the end, the *Tibbals* took first in its class, with the *Minnie* second, and the *Centennial* took second among the smaller boats.

Thomas met Ada's gaze. "Looks like we both won."

She licked her lips. "It does. You go first. Who do you want to kiss?"

He smiled as he bent closer, brushing his lips against hers, as soft as a feather. The touch still made her tremble.

"Your turn," he said.

She swallowed, then leaned in to press her lips to his. The very air seemed to sparkle.

"Whatever the rest of the day brings," he murmured as she pulled back, "it can't be better than that."

She could only agree.

"You won," Bobby said beside them to Gillian.

Gillian rose with a swish of her skirts. "I did. I wonder who I should kiss."

Bobby stood to meet her, a good head taller, but he didn't answer. Ada could almost feel his hope.

"Hurry up!" Georgie urged, squirming down from the bench. "I don't want to miss the parade."

Already people were strolling past, on their way to the square by Yesler's Hall for the procession up Mill Street.

Gillian cast them a glance, then sighed. "Oh, very well." She stood on tiptoe and pecked Bobby on the cheek. It was the most cursory of touches, and Gillian turned away before Bobby could respond. But Thomas' ward touched his cheek as if he never intended to wash it again.

Thomas jumped down onto the ground and raised his arms for Ada. "We should go. I promised we'd walk with

Michael and Maddie Haggerty and the Irish Brigade."

She hadn't met Mr. Haggerty yet, but Thomas weaved his way unerringly through the hundreds who now thronged the square, and she realized why. Mr. Haggerty's height would have made him visible even if the flame-haired Maddie hadn't been at his side. His trousers boasted a band of red, white, and blue material at the cuffs and waist, and Maddie wore a sash across her blue gown with the same colors.

"And are you ready for the walk, me darling girls?" she asked Ada and Gillian, linking arms with each of them.

"Absolutely!" Gillian said, and Ada nodded.

Clay grabbed Georgie and slung him up on his shoulders, to a whoop of delight from the boy.

The rest of the Irish Brigade formed around them. Others fell in as well, until a broad stream filled Mill Street and flowed up the hill, hats and bonnets swaying, flags waving.

Thomas's head was high, his smile wide, as he walked beside Ada. People came out of the businesses to flap flags as they passed. The Seattle Band marched out of First Avenue, music rolling across the crowd. Her feet began to move with the tune.

"My country tis of thee, sweet land of liberty, of thee I sing."

They crested Mill Street and turned onto Third to follow it to where a clearing opened before the main building of the university. Only this June, Rosanna had told her, the first student had graduated with a college degree. That student had been a woman. It seemed anything was possible.

Some chairs and a podium had been placed on the porch of the white-columned building for the dignitaries, but Thomas led her to an open spot on the grass even as Bobby trailed after Gillian and her family to a spot closer to the front. Ada pooled her skirts to sit. Around them, others did the same, conversations rising and falling like the ships they'd just watched in the regatta. She spotted Rosanna, TP, Alfred, and Harriett on one of the wagons near the back of the clearing. Her friends returned Ada's wave.

A church bell chimed two by the time everyone was settled. Mothers rocked babies in their arms; fathers kept an eye on their progeny. Bachelors bumped shoulders for a better view. Sweethearts sat close together, holding hands. She slipped her hand over Thomas' and held on.

The band finished with a clash of cymbals and a grin from their player, then went to find seats amidst a round of applause. An older man, graying hair sticking out around his head, beard sticking out from his chin, stepped up to the podium and raised his hands. Voices ebbed away until Ada could hear a gull call overhead.

"Henry Yesler," Thomas murmured to her. "One of the founding fathers. And that's Reverend Daniel Bagley coming up beside him."

The white-haired minister led them in a prayer of thanks for the nation, the territory, and the city. Next a professor from the university read the Declaration of Independence, then another professor read his own poem composed for the day. As the sun beat down and the air grew warmer, two lawyers took turns, the former telling a number of stories from Seattle's early years and the latter speaking with such fervor and eloquence that everyone perked up. They must have been the ones Thomas had found to replace the governor.

"Thank you, Mr. White," Mr. Yesler said as the lawyer retired to his seat amidst a decent level of applause. "Our next speaker is a self-made man, who was raised in Seattle and chose to return to it after seeking his fortune. Mr. Thomas Rankin."

Ada stared at him. Thomas squeezed her hand and rose. He hadn't been sure about speaking, but the other men on the committee had encouraged him. Perhaps they were still seeking that scapegoat. At least Ada would be proud of him.

As his name echoed across the clearing, someone booed.

He stiffened, but he didn't look to spy the culprit. Why give the miscreant any attention? He started for the podium, and other voices sounded.

"You tell 'em, Scout!"

He tried not to smile. Beth ever had his back.

"Preach the truth!" So did Levi.

But still more voices shot out.

"You know Seattle better than anyone," Michael Haggerty called.

"The perfect candidate," Simon Wallin shouted.

"The next best choice after me." Ah, James.

By the time he reached the podium, the shouts and calls had grown so loud he had to hold up his hands for quiet. It was slow in coming, giving him time to look around. Faces he'd known all his life beamed up at him, friends, the family he'd been adopted into. Towering over the others, Drew gave him a nod.

But the smile that buoyed him the most came from Ada. She had her hands clasped before her pretty white gown, and her gaze met his, as if she thought he would tell her something no one else ever had.

He forced himself to look over the crowd again.

"Many of you know me," he started, setting the speech he had prepared on the polished surface of the podium. "I grew up on the shores of Lake Union. I watched Seattle grow right along with me. Ten years ago, we had three mercantiles. Now we have more than double that. It was a while before we had our first church. Now we have five. For a long time, we had barely enough children to fill a one-room school. Now we have twenty buildings, with multiple rooms, and the Territorial University is graduating students. Asa Mercer had to go all the way back East to find brides for the early settlers. Now, we have some of the finest ladies right here in Seattle."

Several men hooted and whistled at that. Drew, Simon, and James were smiling at their wives, all of whom had come with Mercer, as had Maddie Haggerty and Allegra Howard.

"We've all heard stories of how America was founded," Thomas continued as the voices quieted again. "The battles fought, the wars won. The names of Washington, Jefferson, and Adams are famous to us. But I tell you, someday, perhaps one hundred years from now, people in Seattle will look back and tell stories of Denny, Mercer, Yesler, and Wallin."

A cheer went up. He waited for it to die down. "Like those men and women who fought for a new country, we're fighting for a new territory. We're building homes and businesses in the hope of a prosperous future. But just as one colony standing alone could not survive, one family alone cannot thrive in the wilderness. We need each other—no matter our background, no matter our pasts. Together, we will make sure America, and Seattle, continues to grow, another one hundred years and beyond. Thank you."

The applause was so thunderous, he took a step back. Yesler nodded, grin raising one side of his mouth. The other members of the committee exchanged glances as if trying to decide who would take the credit for asking him to speak.

His face felt hot and his heart full as he started toward his seat. Men stood to shake his hand or pat his shoulder. Ladies smiled at him. Children waved. He wasn't sure how he made it back to Ada's side.

"Well done," she mouthed over the noise.

He didn't hear much after that. He'd done it—spoken before the entire city and visitors from far beyond it. With Ada beside him, who knew what wonders the future held?

CHAPTER SEVENTEEN

SHE WAS IN love with the most amazing man. Might as well admit her feelings, if only to herself. Ada couldn't imagine finding the courage to speak like he had in front of so many people and speaking so well, especially when some had seemed determined to belittle him. Yet Thomas didn't puff himself up, didn't pretend he was the focal point of the day. His hand warm around hers, he walked with her in the procession out of the university grounds and back down to the square in front of the Occidental.

There, everyone dispersed into homes, restaurants, and saloons for the evening meal. Bobby claimed he was too nervous to eat and headed home to change for the dance. The line for the Pastry Emporium was so long that Ada could see the last men waiting around the corner on Mill Street. The dining room at the Occidental was nearly as full, but Roy found Ada and Thomas a table in the corner.

"I suppose I should have thought ahead and asked for a picnic hamper," Thomas said after they had placed their order for fried chicken and macaroni salad.

"We were too busy preparing for the day," Ada reminded him. "And what a day! Oh, Thomas, everything went so well!"

"Well enough," he allowed.

What was troubling him? The regatta had been a little slow, but he could hardly be responsible for the wind. Or was it the few men who had heckled him that had made the day less than a full success?

"It went *very* well," she insisted. "The race ended in a splendid fashion, the parade was invigorating, and the orations were informative and educational. Yours was particularly inspiring."

He eyed her as he leaned back in his chair. "You know what they say about pride, Miss Williamson."

"Self-pride," she corrected him. "And I know no reason why I cannot be proud of the man I admire."

"So long as I can be proud of the woman I admire."

The warmth in his gaze made her want to sink into it like a favorite chair near the fire. Once more, her conscience poked at her. Soon, she promised herself. Right now he deserved to bask in his own achievements.

He had every opportunity over a leisurely dinner, with ice cream for dessert. People came up to him, shook his hand, shared stories of the earlier days of the city. None brought up his father, for which Ada was grateful. Today was all about Thomas, the man he had become, not the child he had been.

The sun had just set beyond the Olympics when they walked down to the waterfront once more. The Howards had left their wagon, so Clay invited Ada and Thomas to join them again. He sat on the bench, arm about his wife's waist, and Gillian and Bobby sat in the bed, holding hands. Georgie, still full of energy, dashed back and forth in front. As the first fireworks burst in the twilight, oohs and aahs echoed across the waves.

The light was nothing to the joy bursting through Ada when Thomas leaned over and kissed her. Whatever happened, she would hold this day and these memories to her heart.

After the fireworks ended, everyone made their way

back to Yesler's Hall. So many people had stayed for the dance that they filled the hall to overflowing and spilled out onto the makeshift plank floor of the pavilion as well. With the hall's windows and doors open, the music flowed out too.

Thomas shouldered his way through the crowd to lead her inside, where the rough log walls had been covered in TP's bunting. Tables at one end held pitchers of lemonade and cookies of all varieties. On the floor, couples glided by in a waltz. Ada spied TP and Rosanna Freeman, Michael and Maddie Haggerty, Beth and Hart McCormick, Drew and Catherine, Simon and Nora, and James and Rina. Even Harry and Jesse had found ladies with whom to dance. Thomas had confided at dinner that John, Dottie, Levi, Callie, and Kit had returned to Wallin Landing with the children. The others were staying with family or friends for the evening. Clay and Allegra had taken Georgie home.

The tune ended, and gentlemen escorted ladies off the floor. Thomas gave Ada's hand a squeeze.

"Would you favor me with the next dance?"

She nodded eagerly. As soon as the music started again, he led her out onto the floor.

This was a line dance, so Thomas took his place with the men. James squared off next to him as Rina moved in beside Ada. Gillian and Bobby were on their other sides. Ada had danced to the lively tune once or twice in Boston when she had been accompanying her sister, so she knew the steps. She lifted her skirts to swish them back and forth with the other women before skipping forward to dance shoulder to shoulder with Thomas. His grin made her feel as if she were dancing on air.

Two dances later, and she was ready for a deep breath of that air instead. Thomas and Bobby went for refreshments, leaving her with James, Rina, and Gillian near one of the open windows. She tipped back her head and drew in the cool, brine-tinged breeze off the Sound, tonight hinting of firework smoke as well.

"Good man, our Thomas," James said. "Always *scouting* about."

Gillian giggled.

His wife gave him a look. "You can do better than that feeble joke, sir."

He tapped his chin, reminding Ada of his sister. "Well, I didn't think Ada would appreciate a pun associated with Rank-in."

Now Gillian shook her head, curls bouncing.

"Indeed, I would not," Ada told him. "Thomas worked hard for this celebration. I want him to enjoy it too."

"Even if some are enjoying it entirely too much," James said with a nod across the dance floor.

Ada followed his gaze to where Mr. Clancy and some men were elbowing each other, color high and grins sloppy. One of the men looked a great deal like the fellow who had smiled at her when she'd caught them following her that day she'd ducked into TP's store. Had Clancy put them up to it? He caught her eye and toasted her with a metal flask before downing another mouthful of the contents. She was glad when Thomas and Bobby returned with cups of lemonade bracketed in their hands.

James drank his, then lifted his brows. "Is that another waltz I hear?" He set the cup on the windowsill and bowed to his wife. "May I have the honor, your highness?"

Her smile lit the night as she too set the cup aside. "The honor is mine, king of my heart."

He swept her out onto the floor.

Bobby stood straighter. He took the cup from Gillian's hand and bowed too. "Beautiful princess, may I be your knight in shining armor?"

"Always," Gillian said, look tremulous. He took her hand and led her out.

Thomas watched them go. "Hard to top either of those,

but I must try." He took Ada's empty cup and set it with his on the sill. "I've accomplished more than I set out to in my life, but I've never danced with the prettiest girl in Seattle. May I?" He held out his arm.

And in his eyes, in his embrace, she was the prettiest girl there. She floated across the floor, the music and voices fading against the look on his face. And when he leaned closer, she met him halfway. The kiss lifted her off her feet, sent her dancing over the treetops.

Applause brought her to her senses. The music had ended, and she and Thomas were standing in the middle of the dancefloor, arms entwined. The other couples sent them amused looks as she and Thomas disengaged. His walk was decidedly cocky as he escorted her off the floor.

He led her out the door and to the edge of the hill overlooking the water, the blackness beyond broken by the glow of lamps on the ships at anchor. Holding her hand, he faced her, cheek outlined by the light from the dance.

"I've fallen in love with you, Ada," he murmured. "I asked you to let me court you to see if we might suit. I can't imagine a finer woman to call my wife."

Her heart soared, then plummeted. "And I cannot imagine a finer man to call husband. But there is something you must know, something I must tell you. I had hoped to tell you tomorrow, but…"

He squeezed her hand. "I'm here now, and I'm listening."

So was she, at a sound she'd never thought to hear again. Gossamer and enchanting, the laughter rode on the breeze, approaching from the dance.

"There he is!" Mr. Clancy proclaimed, voice thick and slurred. "The man of the hour. See here, Mr. Rankin. I've brought you your bride."

Ada's heart stuttered. At Mr. Clancy's side, Melinda batted golden lashes over big blue eyes and spread her blue silk skirts to curtsey. "Good evening, Mr. Rankin. I do hope you'll forgive my tardiness. I was delayed in San Francisco, but I'm pleased to say you won't have to content yourself with Ada's company any longer."

Thomas stared at the vision in front of him, lit from behind by the lights from the dance. He could make out the golden curls, artfully arranged, the womanly curves shown to advantage by a gown that would likely send Beth into raptures.

But the only woman that mattered was standing beside him, shrinking in on herself more every moment.

"I don't understand," he said.

Clancy sidled closer, his elbow as much a jab in the gut as Ada's reaction. "You've been hoodwinked, my lad. Bamboozled. Lied to. But then, that's nothing new, is it? I warned you not to dismiss me. And I warned little Miss Williamson what would happen if she didn't convince you to go into business with me."

"And I wouldn't," Ada cried. "Thomas, you know I didn't."

His free hand was fisting, but he kept it at his side. "Go find your friends, Clancy. You've done enough."

His laughter had an ugly ring to it. "Oh, I'm only getting started. By the time I'm done, you'll be sorry you didn't agree to my proposal. Nobody gets the better of Rupert Clancy." He sauntered back toward the dance, steps unsteady.

Melinda Williamson wrinkled her pert nose. "Unpleasant person. I'm very glad to hear you weren't taken in by him, Ada. However, I can only be grateful he pointed you out to me, Thomas. I've been trying to make your acquaintance for hours. I never imagined so many people would be in Seattle or at the dance. I was quite swept up in it all."

She didn't seem to expect a response, which was just as well, for his thoughts swirled like the waters of Puget Sound when the tide changed, currents colliding.

She glanced back at the hall, illuminated from within like a Chinese lantern. "Although, I must say, the town is everything you said it was, Thomas. I saw that the moment I disembarked." She turned back to him. "I hope you will forgive me for arriving so late. It was a case of maidenly reserve. Think of it—I came all the way to meet you, and I simply couldn't force myself to go the last little distance. I'm just glad my dear Ada agreed to come ahead and explain."

"I tried." Ada's voice trembled. "I intended to tell you, Thomas, first thing. But when I saw all those people on the dock that day, I couldn't disappoint you in front of them. Then, when you made your kind offer to court, I jumped at the chance. I know you wanted Melinda, but I had thought maybe you might like me for me."

How could he fault her for that? All his life, he'd wanted the same—first to stand out from his father's shadow and then to be sure it wasn't his wealth that eclipsed him. And yet, had she taken the chance he might like her, because he was a wealthy man?

"Now *I* don't understand," her sister put in, golden head turning as she glanced from one to the other. "Do you mean you never explained, Ada?"

Ada slumped further. "No, Melly. I never explained. I let them think I was you."

She laughed, a warm sound he thought might be utterly charming under other circumstances. "Why would anyone mistake the two of us? You look nothing like me. Surely you noticed, Thomas." Melinda put a delicate hand on his arm. "We shared so much in our letters."

They had. Or someone had.

"I suspected," he admitted, and Ada's head jerked up, starlight gleaming on eyes wide in shock. "But I hoped Ada would trust me enough to tell me the truth."

She cringed.

He wanted to gather her close, tell her none of it mattered. But it did matter. Once again, the woman he thought to marry was a phantom.

Or was she?

He turned to the beauty in front of him. "Answer me one question, Miss Williamson. Who wrote those letters to me?"

"Ada," she said. "She would read me your notes, and we'd agree on my response, but Ada penned the letters and added the proper phrasing. She has a way with words."

She did indeed—words that had filled the hole inside him, words that made him dream of a future.

But were they words he could believe?

From the hall came the sound of laughter, rough and heavy. Things could get out of hand shortly. Time to make sure Ada, and her sister, were safe.

"Thank you," he told Melinda. "Where did you intend to stay tonight?"

She shifted, setting her skirts to swinging. "I had hoped to stay with Ada, if you were willing to keep your promise about a hotel."

Ada roused herself. "There's room in the suite, if you'd allow us another night, Thomas."

"Ada," her sister scolded before Thomas could answer. "Of course Thomas will let us keep it another night. He's a gentleman."

He wanted to be a gentleman. He also wanted not to be taken for a fool. At the moment, everything he wanted seemed to be fighting inside him. What he needed was time to think.

"Please be my guests for as long as you like," he told them both. Then he offered each an arm. "Allow me to escort you back to the Occidental, ladies. Perhaps we could talk more in the morning."

Melinda accepted, tucking her hand in his elbow with a proprietary smile. Ada hesitated only a moment before placing her hand on his other arm. Like her voice, her fingers trembled. Once more, he only wanted to comfort her, but he hardly knew where to begin. All he could do was start off for the Occidental.

Funny. Many stories had been shared at the celebration about the early days of Seattle. One that hadn't been mentioned in his hearing was the time old Doc Maynard discovered that the divorce of his first wife had never been legal, even though he'd married his second wife since. The first Mrs. Maynard had come to Seattle to confront him, and he'd ended up walking down the street with a wife on each arm.

Now Seattle would have a new story to add to its collection: the night Scout Rankin escorted both of his mail-order brides back to their hotel.

CHAPTER EIGHTEEN

IT WAS ONLY a block back to the hotel, around the edges of the pavilion, but, to Ada, the walk had never felt so long. More people stopped Thomas to thank him for a wonderful celebration, to wish him a happy Independence Day. A few glanced between Ada and Melinda as if wondering why he had two ladies with him. Regardless, Melinda beamed each time, as if she had had anything to do with his success. He nodded and thanked his well-wishers for their kind words. But he moved as if his legs were weighted wood, and the arm under Ada's was just as stiff.

No use berating herself that she hadn't told him sooner. She'd let fear rule her, finding excuse after excuse to delay the inevitable.

Fearing he'd turn away from her.

Now, it seemed as if he was farther away every moment. She'd written words that had persuaded him to send for a bride, unwilling to admit she wished she was that bride. She had lost her heart after the second letter.

But he had never really been hers.

"Thank you so much for all your efforts," Melinda said as he stopped in the lobby. "It truly was a marvelous day. I only wish I had found you sooner so we could have spent it together."

His look was regretful. "Maybe next year, if you decide to stay in Seattle."

She squeezed his arm. "Why wouldn't I stay in Seattle? Everyone here is so welcoming. I look forward to our talk tomorrow." She angled her chin, offering him her cheek to kiss. Ada had to fight the urge to pull him to safety.

If Thomas noticed her sister's posturing, he ignored it, stepping back from them both. She had never felt emptier, more alone. It was as if he were on the other side of the country again.

"Good night, ladies," he said, meeting neither of their gazes. "I'll see you at ten."

"Oh, could we make it eleven?" Melinda begged. "I need my beauty sleep." Again she waited, this time likely for the protest that anyone with her looks would need extra sleep to improve them.

But Thomas merely took another step back, as if he couldn't wait to escape them. "Eleven, then." He turned and left.

Taking Ada's hopes with him.

"Perhaps not the most loquacious man," Melinda allowed. "And that scar. Positively piratical." She shuddered.

Ada pulled her thoughts together. She had so much to say to her sister, but already, men and families were coming through the doors, and she hardly wanted a witness to the conversation.

"The suite is this way," she said before leading her sister up the stairs. She was just thankful Melly said nothing more until Ada had let them in.

"Why, how nice," her sister said, turning slowly to take in the space. "Much better than I'd expected in the wilderness." She traipsed over to the settee and settled gracefully, skirts spread about her.

Ada couldn't sit, even if her sister had left her room.

"What are you doing here, Melinda? I thought you had decided to remain in San Francisco."

"I changed my mind," her sister said brightly, as if she hadn't changed her mind a dozen times since their parents had died. "There was smallpox in San Francisco. I certainly didn't want that. So, I came to see my dear sister. I missed you."

Had Ada missed her sister? She couldn't remember. Her heart felt dull, as if someone had wrapped it in one of Mrs. Wallin's quilts and tucked it away in a trunk.

"Where are your things?" she made herself ask, standing in the middle of the lovely sitting room, unable to move lest she crumble.

"With a very nice Mr. Mercer," Melly said fondly. "He promised to store my trunks and bandboxes for me until I knew where to have them delivered. Truly, everyone has been so kind. I don't know why I didn't head north sooner."

Because she was capricious and selfish and… Ada drew in a breath. It would do no good to shout at her sister, for all it might feel satisfying at the moment. If Ada had acted and told Thomas the truth, perhaps Melinda's coming would have made no difference. The fault lay with her, not her sister.

"It's been a long day," Ada said. "Let's go to bed. You're welcome to use one of the nightgowns. Many were yours anyway, and I never had the time to tack them in."

Her sister rose and followed her to the bedroom, where she went first to bounce on the feather bed, before going to rifle through the dresser and pull out the prettiest gown.

"Oh, this is going to be so much fun." Holding the gown to her chest, she spun around the room, as if she were still at the dance. "Come on, Ada. Waltz with me."

The only person she wanted to waltz with likely would never speak to her again. "No, thank you."

Melinda drew to a stop, smile wilting like day-old flowers, and she lay the gown on the bed. "What's wrong? Aren't you happy to see me?"

She should be. Melinda was her last remaining kin. Yet she struggled.

Ada sank onto the bed beside the gown. "Everything is wrong, Melly. I came here to tell Thomas you'd changed your mind…"

"Which was very nice of you," she said. She turned her back, obviously expecting Ada to act as maid and unbutton her gown.

Ada sighed, rising to begin freeing her sister of the silky blue dress. "It would have been nice, if I'd told him the truth. But I couldn't. I love him, Melly. I want to marry him."

"Oh." Melinda stilled as the last buttons came free. "Well, that does present a problem. He offered for me."

"But you don't want him." Frustration made her put her hands on her sister's shoulders and turn Melinda to face her. "You weren't even willing to write to him without my help."

Melinda waved a hand, breaking Ada's hold. "Because you're the better writer, silly. But that doesn't mean I don't want him. I watched him today. He's rather presentable."

Ada stepped back. "You watched him? I thought you couldn't find him in the crowd. When did you arrive in Seattle?"

"Mid-morning," her sister admitted, starting to wiggle herself out of the dress. "So many people wanted to come for the celebration, the steamer company had put a second ship on the run, and we made very good time from San Francisco. I came in just as the regatta was ending. I heard him speak. It was very moving."

"But you didn't introduce yourself," Ada challenged.

She made a face as she stepped out of the gown, leaving it puddled on the floor. "It was so crowded. And all the gentlemen were so kind, offering me seats in their buggies, dinner at a very fine restaurant. I couldn't disappoint them, could I?"

"Yes," Ada said, "you could. If you love Thomas, he should have been the most important person today."

"I never said I loved him." She turned her back on Ada again to give her access to the strings on her corset.

Ada spun her around once more. "If you don't love him, you have no business marrying him."

Melinda frowned. "I don't understand. You've been after me for months, trying to get me to pick a husband. Now I do, and you don't approve?"

Ada pointed to her own face. "Look at me, Melinda, and listen. I love Thomas. I love him! I want to stand by his side, help him build this city into a place where everyone is welcome. I want to nurse him when he's ill. I want to dance with him under the stars. God willing, I hope to bear his children."

Melinda wrinkled her nose as if the thought was distasteful.

Ada dropped her hand. "Let me put this in terms you'll appreciate. Thomas Rankin is mine, and if you get in the way, I will pluck every one of those golden blond hairs off your head."

Melinda reared back, blinking. "You're serious."

"Very."

Her sister's lower lip trembled. "Oh, Ada, I'm so sorry. I never wanted a man to come between us."

Ada sighed, fire ebbing. "Me either."

Melinda drew her close for a hug, arms soft and warm. "Well, never fear. Seattle is full of gentlemen. I'm sure you'll find another to marry."

Ada stared at her as her sister disengaged. "*I'll* find another?"

"Of course. Mr. Rankin offered for me, you see. It would be terribly rude to go back on my word now."

She turned away and shook her hips as if encouraging Ada to hurry in unlacing her.

"Almost as rude as staying in San Francisco," Ada agreed, "but you had no trouble doing that." She walked to the dresser for her own nightgown. She'd found ways to deal with her corset strings when she'd been alone. Melly must have too. There was no reason for Ada to play the servant.

"Oh, why must you be unpleasant?" Melinda asked with a sigh. "We always got on so well before."

Because everything had been about Melinda. Her sister had been confident in that, and Ada had been accustomed to that. In the last two weeks, she'd discovered that her feelings, her preferences, were every bit as valid. Because of Thomas, Beth, Rosanna, and Ciara, she'd learned her opinions and skills were something to be valued, not hidden away in shame.

She wouldn't allow Melinda to take that truth from her.

Oblivious to the change in Ada, her sister wandered to the wardrobe. "I hope you haven't tailored the pink poplin. It would be just the thing for tomorrow."

"Too late," Ada said, perversely glad to be able to deny her something. "The only gown I didn't take in is the lavender twill. You're welcome to it, but I won't be giving you Thomas."

Her sister's smile was sad. "Neither will I. My mind's quite made up. I don't think it will take much effort. He seemed rather put out with you."

He had, but Ada would do everything she could to change his mind. Because Thomas deserved better than her self-centered sister. For once in her life, Melinda Williamson was not getting her own way.

Thomas wasn't sure where he was walking or how long he had walked. He wasn't even sure what time it was. Everything was dark, but the darkness seemed to be inside him.

So he was surprised when he glanced up and sighted his house just ahead. It seemed his footsteps were leading him somewhere he would feel comfortable, settled.

Even if his thoughts still chased each other around his head.

He'd been duped by a pretty face—again—this time willingly. What was it about him that made people take advantage? His father, Evangeline, Clancy. Even his dearest friend, Levi, had once left him to bear the brunt of a crime Levi had committed. Was Thomas so lacking in courage, character?

Sense?

"'Bout time you showed up." Beth McCormick stood on his front porch, hands on her hips, her slim silhouette outlined by the light from a lamp in the parlor.

Thomas shook his head, in no mood for company, even from one of his best friends. "Where's your husband? Shouldn't you be with him?"

"Hart is making sure the merrymakers reach their hotels and houses with no mischief," she informed him as he climbed the steps. "I'm doing the same for Bobby."

Bobby!

Thomas groaned aloud. "That should have been my job. Sorry, Beth. I've obviously failed as a guardian as well as a groom."

She stepped aside to allow him up onto the porch next to her. "No, you haven't. Bobby's upstairs, changing for bed. I take it tonight went particularly well for him and Gillian, if that besotted grin was any indication. I only wish I could say the same for you." She lay a hand on his shoulder. "That odious Mr. Clancy told as many people as he could about Melinda Williamson. So, Ada has been pretending all along."

Pretending. The phrase sounded carefree, lighthearted. His heart felt leaden. "We knew she was lying. Now we know why."

Beth cocked her head, hand falling. "Do we? What did she hope to gain by impersonating her sister?"

"Marriage," he could barely say the word. "To me."

"So, she loved you so much she was willing to take a risk, carry out this charade, just for the chance you might love her too?"

"You see love," he countered. "How do you know it wasn't larceny, just like Evangeline Jamison?"

Beth poked him in the chest. "Because the Widow Jamison asked you for the moon and expected it immediately: tickets to see the theatrical touring company, groceries supposedly for Bobby but in reality for that gang of hers, and a honeymoon to New York, London, and Paris!"

More than he'd remembered. At the time, he'd considered it the least he could do for a woman to show him favor. Was he so pathetic he'd learned nothing from the encounter?

"What has Ada asked of you?" Beth pressed.

That was an easy answer. "Nothing. She even refused my money to start her writing business. She's promised to pay me back what I invested."

"You see?" Beth asked. "If she was after your money, she would have asked for something. Instead, she's done everything she could to support you. She wrote the governor for you. She helped decorate half the town. She put up with our antics. I was certain she intended to explain herself to you. I don't know why she didn't get around to it, Scout, but I think you should listen now that her sister's arrival forced her hand."

He stiffened, feelings of betrayal wrapping their arms around him anew. "You knew?"

Beth dropped her gaze. "No, not really. I told you she wasn't what we'd expected, but I certainly never guessed the real Melinda Williamson would show up. I like the one that has been trying to make Seattle her home. And I know she cares about you."

Hope was dimmer than the farthest star. "I suppose we'll see. I plan to talk to her and her sister tomorrow."

"But you don't like the idea," Beth surmised.

He sighed. "I thought I was in love, Beth. I was ready to propose. Now I wonder whether I can be any sort of husband, as easily as I'm taken in."

Beth stomped her foot, shaking the pink of her skirts. "Thomas Rankin, don't you dare say something like that about a man I admire! Your father was abominable, but you managed to raise yourself. Some in Seattle weren't willing to give you a chance, so you went and made money on your own. Now you're helping any number of people. If you can't see that as heroic, then maybe you need a good talking to!"

Thomas slanted her a glance. "I think I just got one."

"Yes, you did," she said primly. "And what are you going to do about it?"

He blew out a breath. "I'd like to see myself as you do, Beth, but there's evidence to the contrary."

"Piffle," she said with an airy wave. "None that I can see. And none that Ada can see either, I warrant." She dropped her hand to his arm. "I'm a matchmaker, remember? I know when a woman is in love. Talk to her, and if you can live with her explanation, propose."

His neck felt tight, and he rubbed a hand inside his collar. "It's not so simple. Her sister agreed to come here with an expectation of marriage. I owe her an obligation."

Beth's teeth flashed white in the moonlight as she

smiled. "Oh, I wouldn't worry about marrying off Melinda Williamson. There are still eight and a half men to every female in the territory. Surely one of them will suit her."

CHAPTER NINETEEN

ADA WOKE DETERMINED to fight. She was a little surprised *how* determined. Always before, she'd been content to settle—for an ounce of compassion from her parents, for any notice against Melinda's engaging charm, to survive after being left destitute. This time she would not settle until she knew Thomas was happy. Even if he decided he could not marry her, she would not allow Melinda to ruin his life.

She was up and dressed before her sister lifted her tousled head from the feather pillow. Honestly, what woman had the right to look so lovely before she'd even gotten out of bed!

"Is it morning already?" Melinda asked, blinking.

"Yes," Ada said, tucking the last bit of hair behind her head. "Thomas will be downstairs in a quarter hour."

"A quarter hour!" Melinda sank back onto the pillow. "I can't possibly be ready by then. Tell him to wait."

"No," Ada said, starting for the door. "I won't."

"Ada!" The frantic wail hinted of tears. "Please, Ada. You know how long it takes me to be ready. You could have woken me."

She could have. She'd woken her sister any number of times, for school, for church services, for their parents' funeral. Perhaps Melinda had assumed Ada would do so today. But Melinda was no longer her responsibility.

"I'll let him know you'll be down shortly," she promised.

"Just hurry."

Melinda waved a hand—in acknowledgment, in thanks? Leaving her sister to her fate, Ada headed for the stairs.

She'd spent much of the night considering what she would say to Thomas. She owed him an apology and an explanation. He'd said he wanted her trust. She was ready to give it, even if it cost her everything.

The lobby was strangely quiet as she stepped down into it. Some of the out-of-town visitors had already left for home, it seemed. Others, like her sister, must be sleeping late. From the door to the dining room, Roy sent her a smile as he stood in his apron, drying a glass. She managed to send a smile back before turning and watching the main door. Her fingers met before her gray poplin gown and tightened around each other. Her breath felt trapped in her chest.

Then Thomas walked in, and her breath left in a rush as if fleeing before she made a mull of things.

She lifted her head as he approached. He was dressed in his green coat today, his dark hair brushed back. But lines bracketed his eyes, and even his cheeks seemed to have hollowed, as if someone had taken a piece out of him. She was very afraid that person was her.

"Good morning, Ada," he said. His voice was calm, measured.

Her throat was parched, her lips dry, but her voice came out equally calm. "Good morning, Thomas. Melinda will be down shortly. I was hoping we could talk first."

She nearly collapsed in relief when he nodded and motioned her to two of the crimson velvet chairs on one side of the lobby. She started talking before her skirts hit the upholstered seat. It was either that, or run.

"I must apologize," she said, hands clasping in her lap.

"I should not have kept the truth to myself for so long. At first, I couldn't seem to find a good time to tell you, but I realize now I was only making excuses. The truth is that I didn't want to tell you. I wanted to be Melinda Williamson just once."

His frown looked more confused than condemning. She took comfort in that.

"Why?" he asked. "Your name didn't matter to me. And you asked me to call you Ada in any event."

"But you still thought I was Melinda," she pointed out. "Beautiful, charming, talented Melinda. I wanted to pretend I was that beautiful, charming, and talented."

He shook his head. "You're pretty as a picture, everyone likes you, and you have an amazing talent."

Despite her best efforts, tears were gathering. "Oh, Thomas, if only that were so."

"It is so," he insisted, leaning forward. "I see the fellows glancing our way when we walk or drive. I'm not the only man attracted to you. And you quickly won over the Wallins, Haggerties, and Freemans. Besides, you can write. That's a real gift in these parts."

Ada stared at him. "After meeting my sister, can you honestly say any man would pick me over her?"

He reached out, gently untangled her fingers, and took one hand in his. "I can't speak for every man. But I would."

Every part of her trembled. "But I lied to you, or, at the very least, I let you believe a falsehood."

He cocked his head. "And I'm still not sure why."

He truly didn't. What an extraordinary man!

And that meant she truly must share her heart. He deserved as much. And maybe, maybe, he really could care for her as she did for him.

But she couldn't look at him, waiting to see the light fade from his eyes.

"I don't think my parents ever wanted another child

after Melinda," she told their joined hands. "They had her late in life, you see, and she was their perfect little miracle: healthy, happy, and lovely. Three years later, I arrived: sickly, grumpy, and wrinkled as a prune, my mother used to confess to other mothers. I was an inconvenience. They would have been happier without the burden of me, but duty required them to take care of me. They did so reluctantly. Everything was always about Melinda."

His grip tightened, as if he meant to protect her from the hurt even now. "I am so sorry you had to live that way, Ada. I don't know why your parents didn't see the beautiful person that you are, but the fault lies with them, not with you. As you reminded me, parents can be cruel."

His words knit together pieces of her heart. "My thoughts could be equally as cruel. When they died and Melinda and I learned they had run through all the money my father had inherited, I knew I had only my sister to rely on for a future. After all, I had no skills, and no man had ever looked my way. But if Melinda married, she might give me a home. I was the one who convinced her to place an advertisement as a mail-order bride."

He shook his head. "If your sister is as talented and charming as you say, why couldn't she find a husband in Boston?"

Ada pulled away from him to throw up her hands. "Because she refuses to say yes! I thought perhaps she wanted a wealthier husband or one with more prestige, but the sons of some of the richest, most prominent families in Boston courted her. Then I thought maybe she was waiting for a particular sort of fellow, but it didn't seem to matter their temperament, faith, or dreams. I even thought she might have a vision of the man, but dark-haired, blond, or redhead, mustache or no, burly or slender—it didn't seem to matter. Honestly, Thomas, I was at my wit's end."

"She gave you no reason?" he asked.

"Every reason! He was too talkative, not talkative enough. He had sweaty palms." When his brows rose, she nodded. "Yes, that trivial a reason. Finally, I managed to convince her that we needed her to marry or we'd no longer be able to support ourselves. The bank was threatening to foreclose on the house. That's when she agreed to place the advertisement."

"And you responded to the answers," he said.

Ada nodded. "Most I merely thanked for their trouble. But Thomas, yours was so heart-felt. You made me see Seattle; you made me hope for the future! You even affected Melinda, because she agreed to your proposal. And then, in San Francisco, she was so well feted she decided she'd rather stay. She was going to write to you, but I insisted on coming to tell you. I think I just wanted to see if the man and the pictures he'd painted in my mind were real. And everything was so wonderful, just as I'd dreamed. Melinda sees it too, but I can't believe she truly wants to marry."

Now came the most difficult part. "And I found I'm not content to stand in her shadow any longer. I love you, Thomas. I don't want you to marry Melinda. I don't think she would make you happy." She met his gaze. "I want to make you happy. I wish *I* was your mail-order bride."

There, she'd said it. The choice was his. If he really saw her worth next to Melinda, now was his chance to tell her.

His face softened, and he opened his mouth to respond.

Melinda's heels clicked against the hardwood as she stepped down from the stairs and hurried to their sides.

"Late again," she sang out, as if it were an endearing quality. "Do forgive me, dear Thomas. Shall we get something to eat? I'm famished."

There must be a whole lot of fools in the world.

That was the only conclusion Thomas could reach when he considered that any man might prefer Melinda Williamson to Ada. Oh, Melinda was a beauty. That was even more apparent in the light of day. Golden curls tumbled around a flawless face with long-lashed blue eyes and pouty pink lips. That figure in the lavender gown would have set any number of fellows to gawking. According to Ada and those letters, Melinda was talented too—she sang, she played the piano, she cooked.

But charm? No, he didn't think that so true. Thanks to Ada and Beth, he could see beneath the thin veneer. Melinda believed the attentions paid her, thought she deserved them, and no longer made any effort to earn them. Ada hadn't said as much, but Thomas felt certain her sister had refused to marry because some of those attentions might fade. Good men didn't chase a married lady.

He'd have just as soon told her to take herself off. But he'd brought her here, and he owed her breakfast at least.

"Let's see if we can convince the dining room to serve breakfast this late," he said, rising. But he offered his arm only to Ada.

She took it, wide-eyed. There was so much he wanted to say to her, but not in front of her sister. To reassure her, he gave her a wink. Color bloomed in her cheeks.

Melinda remained oblivious. She linked her other arm with his and offered him a look that was no doubt meant to make him hear wedding bells ringing. All he heard was the rumble of someone's stomach.

He escorted them to the door of the dining room, but no one came to meet them. Indeed, now that he wasn't solely focused on Ada, he noticed the emptiness of the lobby. Even Carter was away from his station at the tall desk. From outside came shouts, cries.

Ada must have noticed the commotion too, for she frowned and glanced toward the door of the hotel. "Were there more celebrations planned for today?"

Thomas shook his head, but he released them both. "Stay here. I'll find out what's going on." He strode to the door.

He'd walked from the house, leaving Bobby sleeping, so at least the carriage and horses weren't standing. That was a good thing, because Commercial Street was in turmoil. Wagons veered past, horses plunging through the mud as if escaping a coming peril. Workers in flannel and denim and businessmen in fine wool coats stood on the boardwalk, pointing and waving. Ladies came out of shops, skirts billowing, to cluster with bonnets bumping brims.

Hart rode past on Arno, face grim.

"Stay back," he called. "Keep calm."

Stay back from what? Thomas glanced toward the water but saw nothing except the usual ships at anchor. Then he looked up toward Second Avenue. Down the street, thick clouds of black smoke billowed out of a store.

TP Freeman's store.

He didn't stop to think. He dashed back into the hotel and crossed to Ada's side. "There's a fire, at the Pioneer Variety Store. I'm going to help."

Melinda pressed a hand to her beribboned chest. "A fire! How frightful! Are we in danger?"

Ada grabbed his arm. "I'm coming with you!"

He put his hand over hers. "No, Ada. It could be dangerous. I don't want anything to happen to you."

"I don't want anything to happen to you either," she assured him, "but we must think about the Freemans. TP needs our help."

"I don't understand," Melinda put in, glancing from

one to the other. "Are the Freemans important people?"

"Yes," Ada snapped. "They're our friends. Stay here, Melinda. We'll be back as soon as we can. Now, hurry, Thomas!"

CHAPTER TWENTY

THOMAS HESITATED ONLY a moment, then nodded, and together, he and Ada left her sputtering sister to hurry out onto Commercial.

The crowd wasn't nearly as big as at the Centennial Celebration, but men and women filled the boardwalk opposite the Pioneer Variety Store, from which black smoke billowed. Voices were raised in concern, excitement. Ada's gaze darted from face to face, recognizing a few from church and others who had helped decorate the town for the celebration. Mr. Clancy had his back against another shop wall and was watching the inferno with a grin.

She shuddered, looking away. And then she sighted TP at the edge of the muddy street.

"There," she told Thomas, pointing, and he pushed his way through the crowd to bring them out beside their friend.

TP didn't acknowledge their presence at first. His dark eyes were fixed on his shop. Through the window, flames danced over his treasures. Ada wanted to run across and rescue them, but she knew she wouldn't have made it a few steps into the shop before her skirts caught fire.

"Rosanna, Harriett, and Alfred?" she asked him, touching his arm.

He spared her a look at last. "Home, thank the Lord." He returned his look to the store. "At least, home for now. Not sure how we'll make do after this."

Ada glanced around again. Deputy McCormick was the only one in the street. He must have warned other traffic away. "Where's the fire department?" she asked. "I don't hear the bell. Why aren't they bringing the pump?"

"Seattle doesn't have a fire department," Thomas explained, face tight. "No hoses or cisterns either."

"No water stored up anywhere," TP agreed, voice deepening with his frown. "Even rain wouldn't help much right now."

"No water?" Ada spun to point toward the harbor. "You have acres and acres of water right there. All we need is buckets and barrels."

"Bucket brigade," TP said, brow clearing. "It might work."

Thomas bracketed his mouth with his hands and raised his voice. "Bucket brigade! Fetch anything that will hold water—ask Kellogg's to donate. And call for Michael Haggerty and his men."

Around them, men went running and ladies ducked back into other shops to request help. The few remaining fellows shook their heads.

"Not spending my money to save him," one muttered with a look to TP.

Thomas rounded on him. "If you won't do it to save a respected Seattle businessman, do it to save the other businesses on the block. This thing will only spread. And I'll pay for the buckets!"

That got the rest of them moving. The last to leave was Mr. Clancy, hands in his pockets and smile eerily satisfied.

Others returned quickly, armed with everything from wash tubs and mixing bowls to casks and barrels. With them came Rosanna, Albert, and Harriett, faces tight.

"Someone brought word," Rosanna told Ada, glancing

around. "Where's TP?"

"Safe," Ada assured her, pointing to where the businessman was organizing his makeshift volunteer fire department into two lines. His family hurried to join him.

Ada took up her place next to Beth and Ciara, who had been alerted to the fire as well, on the far side of the street from the store. Other women lined up with them. On the other side, men and youths ranged from the store down to the wharves. Soon containers of salt water were being passed up one side to be tossed into the blaze. Empty vessels went back down the other for refills. Rosanna and her daughter moved in next to Ada, mouths set in grim lines, for they knew they fought for their future.

Michael Haggerty, Roy from the hotel, and others worked across from them, water jostling as they passed it from hand to hand. Thomas stood between TP and Hart McCormick. His face shone with sweat, his arms where he'd removed his coat strained against the heavy buckets. Voices called encouragement, only to pause to cough against the acrid smoke that flowed down the street like molasses from a broken cask.

Between containers, Ada kept glancing at the fire. Were the flames a little less red, the smoke lighter?

Harriett must have thought so too, for she cried, "Look, Ma! It's working!"

Her call was like slapping the reins on a team of horses. Faster the buckets came. Their precious contents sizzled and popped as they hit the target. The mud turned into a black river, running down toward the Sound. More people joined in, coming from all parts of the city to spell those who had tired. One of the ladies from Trinity Church came up to Ada and Rosanna as if to take their places. Ada stepped aside to let her in, but she didn't stop.

Slowly, the angry red color inside the store faded, and

the smoke turned white.

"It's out," Hart shouted. "Haggerty, help me check for embers."

Michael dropped his bucket and went to lend a hand. Ada and Rosanna hurried to meet TP and Thomas.

"Can anything be saved?" Ada asked her friends.

"We'll know soon enough," TP said. "Thank you for helping today, Ada and Thomas." He wrapped his arm around his wife. "We're not done for yet."

"Praise the Lord," Rosanna murmured. "But how did it start? Did you leave a lamp burning last night?"

"Not me," her husband promised. "I'd like a word with my upstairs tenant."

Ada glanced at the building, a chill going through her. The glass on the two upstairs windows had warped with the heat and smoke had escaped to darken the paint, leaving them looking like eyes blackened by a fight.

"Someone lived upstairs?" she asked.

"As of a week ago," TP told her. "I let the space to a traveling salesman, name of Clancy. He got out. When I saw flames eating at the back of the shop and ran, I spotted him on the street. Didn't see him among the workers, but he might have been closer to the harbor."

"He wasn't," Thomas said. "Come with me, TP. We need to talk with Deputy McCormick."

Ada wasn't sure what he was about, but just then another woman hurried up. "Mrs. Freeman, I'm so glad you and your family are all right. You can count on all your church brothers and sisters for any help you need."

"Thank you, Mrs. Horton," Rosanna said, reaching out to squeeze the woman's hand.

Ada could only nod. She'd make sure to set aside some of the money from her correspondence work to donate where needed. Whatever happened between her and Thomas, she intended to make Seattle her home.

Mrs. Horton and Rosanna were still discussing next

steps when Thomas and TP returned a short time later.

"Seems this Mr. Clancy and Mr. Rankin are connected," TP told Rosanna and Ada.

"He tried to interest me in partnering with him," Thomas added, "and I refused. I couldn't vouch for his character, and what little I knew troubled me."

Ada drew herself up, knowing she was about to fuel rumors. She no longer cared. "Mr. Clancy came up on the steamer from San Francisco with me. He knew something I was ashamed to admit until today, and he tried to blackmail me into convincing Thomas to partner with him. I didn't, but if it hadn't been for me, he might not have approached either of you."

TP glanced at his store. "You think he set the place on fire, because he knew we were becoming friends?"

"We can't be certain," Thomas said. "It's not easy to tell how a fire started, but Hart's going to look into the matter as much as he can. At the very least, Clancy will be told there are no further business opportunities for him in Seattle. I'll make sure there's a berth waiting for him on the outgoing steamer for San Francisco, and Deputy McCormick can get word to the sheriff he's coming." His voice hardened. "We stick by our neighbors in Seattle. It's time we sent a message to folks like Clancy that *they're* the ones who aren't welcome here."

"Well said, Mr. Rankin," Mrs. Horton cheered. "Have you ever considered running for office? Gideon Weed and Henry Yesler could use the competition for mayor."

Ada beamed even as Thomas stood taller. "Thank you, Mrs. Horton. For now, I have my sights on something else. There's already talk of organizing a volunteer fire department, so this kind of tragedy never happens again. We'll be holding a meeting tomorrow."

"I'll be there," TP promised.

Thomas clapped him on the shoulder, then turned to Ada. "We should go see to your sister."

She would rather have stayed with Rosanna, but she knew he was right.

"You have a sister?" TP asked, his former smile hinting. "Soon as I rebuild, you know where to bring her shopping."

"Absolutely," Ada said with a grin.

Her smile faded as they started back for the hotel.

Thomas's hand, as damp and dirty as her own, curled around her fingers as he led her down the block. "I'm sorry I couldn't answer you sooner."

Ada managed a laugh. "First my sister, then the fire. You didn't have much of a chance."

"I'd like to answer you now."

She wasn't sure she was ready, but she nodded.

He gave her hand a squeeze as if in understanding. "You talked about being in the shadows, Ada. I know that feeling. I stepped out from under my father's shadow. You stepped out from your sister's. When she refused to honor her word to me, you insisted on coming to tell me. When you saw the truth might shame me, you held your tongue. Whatever I needed, you were there to provide. When there was danger to people you cared about, you ran to meet it. That's the woman I fell in love with. That's the woman I want to marry."

She stopped in the street, pulling him up short, every other sound shutting off. "Did you just ask me to marry you?"

"Not properly." Despite the mud, despite the wagons that were once more trundling through the area, the riders on horseback, and the retreating volunteers, he went down on one knee in front of her and turned his smoke-streaked face to hers.

"Ada Williamson, I fell in love with you before I ever met you, reading the heart that spoke through your letters. Being with you these last couple of weeks has only confirmed my feelings. Will you do me the honor of marrying me?"

"Yes, oh yes!" Tears warmed her cheeks as she helped him rise. He drew her close, lips brushing hers in a promise of devotion. He tasted like smoke, but also of home and everything good. She cuddled against him, love and joy dancing inside her, until she thought her feet might join in.

"Mr. Rankin."

Thomas pulled back, and they both eyed Hart McCormick, once more on horseback and frowning down at them, hat dented from his work, hard gray eyes narrowed.

"Is there a problem, Deputy?" Thomas asked.

"Impeding commerce, obstructing traffic, inciting riotous behavior," the lawman rattled off. He bent closer. "Congratulations. Now, get off the street. I was hoping to never have to jail you."

Thomas grinned. "Unless there's a law against being too happy, you won't."

Hart straightened with a nod and rode on.

Heart full, Ada walked with Thomas to the door of the hotel. Even after all they'd been through, a part of her quailed at the thought of confronting her sister. Thomas must have noticed her hesitation, for he glanced her way.

"What will we tell Melinda?" she asked, throat beginning to tighten again.

"You leave that to me," he said, and he pushed through the door.

Melinda cried when Thomas told her he would not be marrying her after all. He would have bet on that. She kept sniffing and dabbing at her blue eyes, which only grew more luminous with her tears.

"But I came all this way," she protested, as if Ada hadn't traveled just as far. "Endured so much. How can you cast me aside?"

"I'm not casting you aside," he told her. "It's simply clear to me that Ada and I are better suited."

She blinked. "You're choosing Ada over me?"

The incredulous tone, the shock on her lovely face, only reinforced what Ada had told him about their relationship. Thomas put an arm around Ada's waist.

"Today and always."

Ada offered him a watery smile, dimple pointing him to where he intended to kiss her next.

Melinda sniffed again. "But where will I go? What will I do?"

Ada squeezed his arm. "You have a large house, Thomas…"

Which would never be large enough to share with the overbearing Melinda. He was not about to see Ada taken advantage of again.

"There's a fine lodging house on Fourth," he said. "I'd be happy to pay for a room for you, Melinda, while you look for employment."

Her eyes widened. "Employment!"

Ada reached out her other hand and patted her sister's arm. "Don't worry, Melinda. There are many things a woman can do in Seattle. You can be anything you want, anyone you want." She gazed up at him, heart in her eyes. "You might even find a man you can love."

He had to kiss her then, even though he heard a gasp from her sister. There was only one perfect mail-order bride for him, and he would always be thankful God had led her here, into his city, into his life, into his heart.

Out of the shadows and into the light.

CHAPTER TWENTY-ONE

THREE WEEKS LATER, Seattle saw the largest, fanciest wedding ever held in the town. Beth assured Ada that was true, and Ada believed her. She couldn't muster one ounce of guilt. Thomas just looked so happy.

It didn't hurt that Hart McCormick had been able to find enough evidence to link Mr. Clancy to the fire. The villain was lodged in the jail, awaiting trial for arson. TP and Rosanna were already working on rebuilding the store, bigger and better than before.

That didn't stop them from taking part in the wedding. Once again, everyone had come together to make it happen. Nora and Dottie Wallin had sewn Ada's wedding dress, a sunny blue, with daisies along the neckline and hem, embroidered by Catherine and Rina. Beth made the wedding veil, a long drape of lace that ran down Ada's back to her hips and was held in place by a silver circlet Michael Haggerty had fashioned.

Melinda went so far as to help Ada dress and fix her hair.

"You look like a princess from one of the stories Father read us," she said with a sigh that sounded only a little bit envious.

Ada felt like a princess. Everyone had been so generous! Drew and John had made her a beautiful wooden chest, and TP, Rosanna, Bobby, Harry, and the other members of the logging crew had chipped in to fill it with housewares and linens, so she could bring something besides herself to the marriage. Simon had made arrangements with a fine hotel in Victoria for the honeymoon, and James would be driving them to the steamer tomorrow in style with his famous steel dusts, Lance and Percy, horses that just might have been finer than Jack and Skip.

They held the ceremony at Trinity Church, and Rosanna Freeman was Ada's matron of honor, with Beth and Melinda as bridesmaids. Hannah Wallin walked down the center aisle, sprinkling petals of daisies Sutter and Frisco had picked, and Callie played the piano at the church.

Levi, Bobby, and Clay stood up with Thomas. Every nook and cranny of the church was filled with vases of orchids Thomas had had shipped from San Francisco, their perfume scenting the air. And afterward, the entire city was invited to treats from the Pastry Emporium, courtesy of Maddie, Ciara, Aiden, and the Howards, and a dance at Yesler's Hall, with the Seattle Brass and String Band playing and Hart and the Irish Brigade patrolling to keep the crowd orderly.

"Look at them," Ciara said as she, Beth, and Ada took a break from the dancing. She nodded to the knot of men surrounding Melinda, who was in her element flirting and being flattered. "You'd think they'd never seen a woman before."

"Well, not that many women," Beth allowed with a giggle. "But don't worry about Miss Williamson. I have plans for her." She wiggled her brows.

"She can have all the men in Seattle for all I care," Ada said, gaze seeking Thomas, who had gone for refreshments. "I have the only man I ever wanted."

Ciara sighed. "Just my luck. Surrounded by men, and I can't find one to suit me."

Beth tapped her chin with one finger. "Hm. I may have to do something about that too."

Ciara took a step back. "No you don't, Beth McCormick. I don't need a matchmaker."

Beth turned this way and that, pink silk skirts swishing across the planks. "*Everyone* needs a matchmaker. Some just haven't realized it yet. I've already begun working on Harry and Jesse. And once I figure out Kit's secret, I'll see to him as well."

Ciara's shoulders relaxed a little in her emerald gown. "Oh, good. It will be weeks before you get around to matchmaking for me."

Beth smiled. "Oh, I wouldn't say that. Once you start your restaurant at Wallin Landing, you'll have plenty of opportunities."

There he was! Ada's smile broadened as her husband moved to her side to offer her a glass of lemonade.

"Did I hear something about matchmaking?" he asked.

"Beth has her sights on my sister, Ciara, and Drew's logging crew," Ada told him.

Thomas toasted Ciara. "Of the lot of them, I'd say we'll be dancing at your wedding next."

"I don't need help making a match," she insisted, face reddening.

Thomas slipped his free hand about Ada's waist. "I didn't think I needed help either, but I wouldn't have met Ada if Beth hadn't pointed me to her ad."

"I never asked," Ada realized, glancing to her friend. "What made you pick the ad I wrote, Beth?"

Beth beamed. "Because it was obvious you were a woman of character and grace, the perfect mail-order bride." She dusted her hands together. "Another couple happily wed."

The music started up again then, and Thomas set aside his glass and Ada's to sweep her back onto the dancefloor. Perhaps she never would know why her letters had touched his heart the way his had touched hers, but she had no doubt that at his side and in his arms was where she was meant to be.

Thank you for choosing Thomas and Ada's story. Thomas first appeared in *Would-Be Wilderness Wife*, which also introduced the Wallin family. You can find the full list of Frontier Matches stories on my website at http://www.reginascott.com. Readers have been begging me to write a story just for Thomas. I hope you enjoyed it. Note, too, that TP and Rosanna Freeman and their family were real Seattle pioneers. TP's store did burn down around Independence Day in 1876, resulting in the creation of the first fire department in the city. His advertisement in the local paper of his new store, titled "Not dead yet!", inspired me to include him in the story.

But the Wallins aren't riding into the sunset! As the local matchmaker, Beth will have her hands full. And what about Bobby and Gillian? Make sure you sign up for my newsletter on my website to hear when their stories will be out.

Turn the page for a sneak peek of Ciara's story. Beth may have plans for her friend, but when the talented cook opens her own restaurant at Wallin Landing, she'll find there's more simmering than venison stew.

SNEAK PEEK:

Her Frontier Sweethearts

Book 2 in the Frontier Matches Series by Regina Scott

Seattle, Washington Territory, August 1876

SHE WAS ABOUT to enter a whole new world.

Ciara O'Rourke hugged her carpetbag close, watching as the rough skyline of Seattle disappeared behind a wall of trees. The late July sun speared through the limbs and warmed the shadows of the forest bracketing her. Still, she couldn't help her shiver.

"Everything all right back there?" Harry Yeager called from the bench of the wagon, as if he'd heard the thoughts piling up inside her head like storm clouds on the horizon.

Ciara shifted to set the carpetbag among the other belongings crowding the bed of the wagon. "Fine, Harry. Thanks for asking. And thanks again for driving me out to Wallin Landing."

"I was coming for the mail anyway," the big logger said. She glanced over her shoulder at him in time to see his broad shoulders move in a shrug of muscle inside his red flannel shirt. "Besides, I can't wait until you're the one doing the cooking."

She drew in a breath. The briny scent of salt water and

the dust of mill shavings were fading, to be replaced by the moist tang of cedar and fir. Above the tall tops, clouds scudded across a blue sky. Somewhere in the wood, a bird called.

Her whole life, she'd seldom stepped outside the borders of a city—first in the warren of tenements that was Five Points in New York, where she'd been born, then Seattle. Oh, sailing through Patagonia and the Straits of Magellan to reach Seattle had been a grand adventure, but that had been ten years ago, when she'd been only eleven. Then, she and her brother, Aiden, had been mostly confined to the ship. Now she was going into the wilderness to start her own business.

The first restaurant in the settlement of Wallin Landing.

Another shiver went through her, and she raised her chin. Already, the breeze was tugging strands of her dark hair out of her coronet braid to flick past her eyes. She should have worn a bonnet or a hat, but she'd been in too much of a hurry, as if Harry would have left her, and the mail, behind.

"Sure you don't want to ride up on the bench?" he asked over the creak of the wagon.

"I'm fine," Ciara repeated. Harry had made no secret of the fact that he was seeking a wife. She didn't plan to give him the least encouragement. She'd heard him enlisting the help of her friend, Ada Williamson, now Rankin, in writing for a mail-order bride. He was handsome enough, with his wavy brown hair and confident swagger, and he'd proved up his claim, so some lady might leap at the chance to marry him.

Not her. If she had been looking to marry, she would have had her pick as one of the few unmarried ladies in a sea of bachelors. Since it had become known she was leaving town, she'd had to refuse six proposals. She hadn't shed a tear over any of them. From what she'd seen, a husband was more hindrance than help, especially when it came to a lady with dreams for her future.

"Looks like trouble up ahead," Harry said, and she felt the wagon slowing as he must have reined in Lance and Percy, the team of sturdy steel dusts pulling it.

She gathered her blue chambray skirts so she could rise to her knees and peer up over the wagon's rough plank side. A black horse stood at the edge of the rutted dirt track that led out to the settlement, an older man squatting next to it. As Harry drew the team to a stop, Ciara could see a baby sitting among the wildflowers, rubbing fists into eyes red from crying. The pitiful sobs pierced the air.

"Need any help, friend?" Harry asked.

The older man rose. He wore pin-striped black trousers and a jacket that looked far too fine for Seattle, much less the forest, even covered as they were in dust. His long face sagged. There was a hint of desperation in his voice as well.

"How much farther to Wallin Landing?" he asked as if he'd already traveled a great distance.

"At gentle pace for your horse, about an hour and a half due north," Harry supplied with a nod in that direction. "You're welcome to ride along with us. We're heading to the landing."

The man's face cleared, and he bent and picked up the baby. Closer now, Ciara could see the little girl had eyes as deep a brown as hers, and black wisps of hair stuck out from the edges of the white ruffled cap on her head. Aiden had been between one and two years when he'd reached that size.

The fellow thrust the baby at Harry. "Take her with you. Please."

Ciara started, but Harry recoiled, setting Lance and Percy to fretting in their traces.

"There's room in the wagon for you both," Harry told him. "I have no call to take her."

"I can't keep this up," the man said, turning his tortured gaze now on Ciara. "I'm a manservant, not a nursemaid. She needs her family, Christopher Weatherly. All you have to do is deliver her."

"Kit?" Harry asked. "Why? Where's the mother?"

The man lifted the baby over the wagon's side and dropped her into Ciara's lap. Ciara's arms came around her to steady her, even as the baby hiccoughed her surprise at the sudden movement. Before Ciara could protest, the man slung a carpetbag and an envelope into the wagon bed as well.

"Everything is explained in the note," he said, backing away from the wagon. "Please. I must go. They'll be following me. If I disappear, Grace has a chance."

"Now, wait a minute," Harry said, but the man flung himself up into the saddle and urged his horse back toward Seattle.

"What'd he mean, grace has a chance?" Harry demanded, as if Ciara could know any more than he did.

She glanced to the baby, who was studying her, one fist lodged in her mouth. At least she'd stopped crying for the moment.

"Grace might be her name," Ciara mused. "Is that right, Grace?"

Grace dropped her hand and beamed, as if Ciara had done something particularly clever.

Harry shifted on the bench to glance back at them. Grace's beam turned into a scowl.

"What are we supposed to do with her?" he asked, and now the desperation in the stranger's voice had infected his as well.

"I suppose we better take her to Mr. Weatherly," Ciara said. "Isn't he a member of Drew's logging crew?"

Harry nodded. "Me, Jesse Willets, and Kit."

She knew Harry, and she'd met the stoic giant that was Jesse. She couldn't recall meeting Mr. Weatherly.

"Does his wife live in town?" she asked. She wrinkled her nose at the baby, and Grace's happy smile returned. She leaned her head against Ciara's shoulder with a sigh. Ciara's arms tightened even as something fluttered inside her, a need to comfort, to protect.

Harry snorted. "Kit doesn't have a wife. Never had a sweetheart, either, that I can tell. Keeps to himself mostly. That manservant fellow had to be touched in the head to send a baby to him."

"Still, we don't have any other choice," Ciara pointed out, rocking Grace gently in her arms. Already the baby's dark lashes were sweeping down over her reddened cheeks. "We'll deliver Grace as requested. Let's go, Harry."

Shaking his head, Harry faced front and clucked to the horses. Lance and Percy picked up their paces as they headed for home.

Ciara gazed down at the baby in her arms. What sort of man abandoned his child? Her sister, Maddie, had had to leave her and Aiden behind when she'd come West with the Mercer Expedition ten years ago, but neither sibling had been this little. And Maddie had sent for them as soon as she could raise the fare for passage. Kit Weatherly had been only a couple of hours away, less on a fast horse.

Why had he left Grace behind? Had he no feelings? No sense of responsibility?

Either way, she'd have a few choice words for him once she delivered this precious bundle into his care. And then she would get on with building her dream.

Kit Weatherly stretched sore muscles as he lowered his ax onto the porch of the cabin. A good day's work, Drew Wallin, their leader, had said, and more logs ready to be shipped down the cut to the Sound. A satisfaction he'd been searching for most of his life curled around him like smoke from a campfire. Good work, good friends, good weather. A man couldn't ask for more.

Well, maybe an edible dinner.

He grimaced as he glanced in the window, sighting Jesse staring at the stove in the rear section of the building as if he could cook the food from sheer force of will. He, Jesse, and Harry managed to take care of themselves, but, since Beth Wallin had married and moved into town, Drew had had a difficult time finding a cook for his logging crew, and the last few weeks, the three of them had been taking turns at the task. His stomach growled as if protesting another night of it.

But all that was going to change soon. Miss O'Rourke had made a proposal to Drew Wallin. She'd cook for the crew, and he'd allow her to turn the bottom floor of the big cabin into a restaurant that would cater to travelers and those around the area who wanted a good meal.

A good meal.

His smile tilted up. Though he'd eaten a treat or two at the Pastry Emporium in town since moving to Seattle two years ago, he'd never crossed paths with the sister of the famous owner. But if she could take over the cooking, he liked her already.

A lad with straw-colored hair came pelting around the cabin, untucked cotton shirt flapping about the trousers he perpetually outgrew. "Wagon coming in. Frisco spotted it through the trees. Do you think it's the baker?"

Kit smiled at Sutter Murphy, kin to their local minister, Levi Wallin. "Harry went to fetch her today, so it stands to reason."

Sutter vibrated faster than the wings of a hummingbird. "I hope she brought cinnamon rolls with her. Her sister, Mrs. Haggerty, makes the best cinnamon rolls." He heaved a sigh, as if he could see the creamy icing dripping down the sides even now.

"She might not have had time today," Kit warned him as the wagon rolled into the clearing and pulled up next to the barn.

Sutter took off running anyway. His twin brother came out of the woods to join him.

Their own baker and cook. What a blessing! Wallin Landing was small as settlements went—the main cabin that housed him, Jesse, and Harry in the loft sat on a bench overlooking Lake Union. Along the shores next to the lake sat the mercantile and post office. Across the clearing, beyond the massive barn, Drew and his family had a cabin, with his brother Simon up on the hill. Brothers James and John had spreads just beyond, and Levi had a log parsonage next to the church. At the back of the clearing stood the schoolhouse.

Beth's old cabin was through the trees to the north. He'd heard Drew intended to allow Miss O'Rourke to use it.

He could just spot a dark head peeking up above the side of the wagon. She didn't seem to be in a hurry to leave its shelter. Was she already reconsidering her decision to move out so far? His stomach rumbled again. Maybe he should welcome her, assure her they were all eager for her help.

Harry was seeing to the horses, so Kit ambled closer. The wagon was full of crates, boxes, and sacks. Some would be supplies for the settlement. Others, he hoped, would be supplies for the kitchen. She'd already sent ahead one wagon load, and he and Jesse had stood over the boxes studying their contents.

"Why would she need a bowl with holes in it?" Jesse had asked, poking a thick finger at the perforated mass of tin.

"I think it's a colander," Kit had told him. "For straining things. My sister's cook had one."

Jesse had eyed him. People often did that when he

mentioned his family, so he mentioned them rarely. It was easier if no one questioned why the brother of one of Tacoma's wealthier matrons was slinging an ax instead of directing the wheels of industry.

Frisco and Sutter had beat him to the wagon bed and were holding out hands to Miss O'Rourke. She managed to stand, and he stopped in his tracks.

Somehow, he's expected someone older, more seasoned. Mrs. Haggerty was in her thirties. Her sister was quite a few years younger, with hair as warm and rich as hot chocolate and cheeks as rosy as an apple. Combined with a slender figure and her ability to cook, she was guaranteed to draw the attention of every bachelor within miles.

Likely they wouldn't have a cook for long.

"Would you hold her a moment, Frisco?" she was saying, bending toward one of the twins.

Her?

Frisco opened his arms, and Miss O'Rourke surrendered a chubby-faced baby into them.

A baby?

Funny. He didn't recall hearing she'd married.

"That's Kit," Sutter volunteered, pointing at him as if Miss O'Rourke had asked his direction.

She jumped down from the wagon, arranged her blue skirts, took back the baby, and marched up to him. Her eyes were as dark as hot chocolate too, but at the moment they were more fire than warmth.

She held out the baby to him. "Mr. Weatherly. Your daughter."

Kit blinked. "Daughter? I don't have a daughter."

"Told you," Harry said, striding past with a crate in his arms.

Her pretty face set into surprisingly firm lines. "We were told to deliver this sweet child to you. Do you deny your responsibility, sir?"

The baby kicked its feet as if none too pleased to be

left dangling between them. Kit reached for her to steady her.

Eyes as dark as his peered into his face. Curls as dark as his escaped her little cap. A smile that reminded him of what he saw in the mirror on a good morning turned up her lips.

Small wonder they thought she was his. She looked just like him!

"She can't be mine," he said aloud. "I've never had a sweetheart."

"Told you," Harry repeated, passing them for the wagon.

Miss O'Rourke's face melted into confusion. "Are you certain, Mr. Weatherly?"

Kit peered closer at the baby, a frown of his own gathering.

The baby met his gaze, opened her mouth…

And shrieked at the top of her lungs.

He nearly dropped her, but he managed to hang on as the sound rent the air. Crows launched themselves off their perches in the cedars. Frisco and Sutter clapped their hands over their ears. Chickens in the coop nearby ran in agitated circles. The goats in the nearest pasture huddled together for safety.

"Is she all right?" Miss O'Rourke asked, moving closer.

The baby grinned at them both, showing a few pearly white teeth.

"I think she's rather pleased with herself," Kit marveled.

Miss O'Rourke lay a hand on his arm. "Perhaps we should bring her into the house. The man who gave Grace to us left a note. You should read it."

He should at that. Tucking Grace a little closer, he joined Miss O'Rourke as she retrieved a carpetbag and envelope and headed for the cabin.

They had barely set foot inside before Jesse ducked his massive frame to poke his russet head through the kitchen archway.

"You cooking?" he asked Miss O'Rourke, holding up a wooden spoon as if ready to coronate her with it.

"I wasn't planning to start until tomorrow morning, Mr. Willets," she told him, dropping the carpetbag to the planks. "I have much to do to settle in first."

Kit could feel Jesse's sigh from across the room. The big man shambled back to the stove.

Miss O'Rourke handed Kit the envelope and held out her arms. He gave her Grace, and she began walking the baby around the room, murmuring words no doubt meant to calm. Over her shoulder, Grace watched him.

Kit broke open the envelope. The first words took his breath, and the next few took the heart right out of him. He sank onto the bench at the table near the door and devoured the rest. How? When?

Why?

He lowered the note to find Miss O'Rourke standing in front of him, waiting. As if she saw the blow he'd been given, she perched on the bench beside him, jostling Grace on her knee.

"What's happened?" she asked, gaze searching his.

"Grace is my sister's child," he told her, amazed he could still form words. "I didn't know she had one. She always wanted children, but none came. We haven't spoken in years, though I write her to let her know where I am and what I'm doing. It seems she and her husband have died, and I'm all Grace has left."

"Take a moment," she murmured. "I'll put the kettle on."

He shook himself as she rose with the baby and turned for the kitchen. "But you're just getting settled," he protested.

"That doesn't mean I can't help," she countered

before disappearing into the kitchen with his newfound responsibility.

Help, she'd said. He had a feeling he was going to need it.

Learn more at
www.reginascott.com/herfrontiersweethearts.html

OTHER BOOKS BY REGINA SCOTT

Grace-by-the-Sea Series
The Matchmaker's Rogue
The Heiress's Convenient Husband
The Artist's Healer
The Governess's Earl
The Lady's Second-Chance Suitor

Fortune's Brides Series
Never Doubt a Duke
Never Borrow a Baronet
Never Envy an Earl
Never Vie for a Viscount
Never Kneel to a Knight
Never Marry a Marquess
Always Kiss at Christmas

Uncommon Courtships Series
The Unflappable Miss Fairchild
The Incomparable Miss Compton
The Irredeemable Miss Renfield
The Unwilling Miss Watkin
An Uncommon Christmas

Lady Emily Capers
Secrets and Sensibilities
Art and Artifice
Ballrooms and Blackmail
Eloquence and Espionage
Love and Larceny

Marvelous Munroes Series
My True Love Gave to Me
The Rogue Next Door
The Marquis' Kiss
A Match for Mother

Spy Matchmaker Series
The Husband Mission
The June Bride Conspiracy
The Heiress Objective

And other books for Revell,
Love Inspired Historical, and Timeless
Regency collections.

About the Author

REGINA SCOTT STARTED writing novels in the third grade. Thankfully for literature as we know it, she didn't sell her first novel until she learned a bit more about writing. Since her first book was published, her stories have traveled the globe, with translations in many languages, including Dutch, German, Italian, and Portuguese. She now has had published more than fifty works of warm, witty historical romance.

She loves everything about England, so it was only a matter of time before she started her own village. Where more perfect than the gorgeous Dorset Coast? She can imagine herself sailing along the chalk cliffs, racing her horse across the Downs, dancing at the assembly, and even drinking the spa waters. She drank the waters in Bath, after all!

Regina Scott and her husband of more than 30 years reside in the Puget Sound area of Washington State on the way to Mt. Rainier. She has dressed as a Regency dandy, learned to fence, driven four-in-hand, and sailed on a tall ship, all in the name of research, of course. Learn more about her at her website at *www.reginascott.com*.

Printed in Great Britain
by Amazon

45647443R10126